LAW AND THE RURAL ECONOMY
IN THE ROMAN EMPIRE

LAW AND RURAL ECONOMY IN THE ROMAN EMPIRE

Dennis P. Kehoe

THE UNIVERSITY OF MICHIGAN PRESS
ANN ARBOR

Published in the United States of America by
The University of Michigan Press
Manufactured in the United States of America
♾ Printed on acid-free paper

2010 2009 2008 2007 4 3 2 1

A CIP catalog record for this book is available from the British Library.

Library of Congress Cataloging-in-Publication Data

Kehoe, Dennis P.
Law and the rural economy in the Roman Empire / Dennis P. Kehoe.
p. cm.
Includes bibliographical references and index.
ISBN-13: 978-0-472-11582-2 (cloth : alk. paper)
ISBN-10: 0-472-11582-0 (cloth : alk. paper)
1. Land tenure—Rome. 2. Farm tenancy (Roman law). 3. Law—Economic aspects—Rome. 4. Agriculture—Economic aspects—Rome. 5. Law and economics. I. Title.
HD137.K44 2006
333.3'230937—dc22 2006025451

ISBN13 978-0-472-02535-0 (electronic)

For my friends Carl and Nancy,
and for all of my family.

Preface and Acknowledgments

In this book, I apply some of the lessons of the contemporary debate about the relationship between law and the economy to provide a better understanding of the role that law played in the Roman economy. This book offers a new perspective on the debate whether the Roman economy experienced substantial growth and whether its fruits benefited an elite class alone or were more broadly shared by the empire's population. My project has developed out of previous studies that I have undertaken of various aspects of the Roman agrarian economy, in particular my recent book, *Investment, Profit, and Tenancy: The Jurists and the Roman Agrarian Economy* (University of Michigan Press, 1997). In that book, I investigated the classical Roman jurists' treatment of crucial areas of the law affecting private property to explain upper-class Roman conceptions of *investment* and *profit* in agriculture. I then traced how these conceptions in turn affected the strategies of landowners in adapting the institution of farm tenancy to their economic interests. I now build on this research by pursuing the broader question: what role did the legal policies of the Roman government play in the Roman economy? At issue is a basic understanding of the relationship between the Roman imperial government and the empire's subjects, whether the legal institutions of the state served primarily to foster the interests of the elite or, rather, the law and legal institutions played a more complex role and helped to offer the vast majority of the empire's subjects some protection against exploitation by the powerful and well connected. If the law served this latter purpose, it was much more likely to have promoted long-term economic growth.

I have many people and institutions to thank for supporting my work on this project. A grant from the Committee on Research from Tulane University in the summer of 1998 and a Summer Stipend from the National Institute for the Humanities in 2002 have facilitated my research. I have made many trips to the University of Michigan to use both the law library and the papyrology collection, where Traianos Gagos has always welcomed me. My work on this project has been informed by the research that I did when I held a Humboldt Fellowship at the Institut für Papyrologie of the University of Heidelberg in 1989–90, and again in the summers of 1991 and 1992. I am very grateful to Professor Dieter Hagedorn, Professor Bärbel Kramer, James Cowey, and Wolfgang Habermann for their friendship and hospitality at the Institut, and to Professors Géza Alföldy and Fritz Gschnitzer for welcoming me to the Seminar für Alte Geschichte in Heidelberg.

I am also grateful to the many scholars who have provided me with copies of their own work, read parts of my work, or otherwise provided much-needed support, including Elio Lo Cascio, Luigi Capogrossi Colognesi, Domenico Vera, Pasquale Rosafio, Walter Scheidel, Richard Saller, Michael Peachin, Roger Bagnall, Brent Shaw, Carl Anderson, Cynthia Bannon, Susan Martin, Joseph Manning, Willem Jongman, Gabor Hamza André Tchernia, Wolfgang Habermann, Kai Ruffing, H.-J. Drexhage, Jesper Carlsen, Luuk de Ligt, Andrea Jördens, Amphilochios Papathomas, and Bärbel Kramer. Tulane University has been very supportive in my research. In addition to the summer research grant, I have also enjoyed the friendship and support of colleagues, especially Kenneth Harl, Joe Poe, Thomas Frazel, Susann Lusnia, Michael Kuczynski, and, earlier, David Stone, who always have been willing to discuss ideas. Suzanne Faris painstakingly read several chapters and greatly improved my presentation. I have really enjoyed discussing economic history with Herman Freudenberger, who has given me a lot of guidance with the economic history and, in particular, with the New Institutional Economics.

I completed much of the research at the School of Historical Studies at the Institute for Advanced Study in Princeton, where I spent a wonderful term during the winter and spring, 2005. I would like to thank Glen Bowersock and Heinrich von Staden and the School's administrative officer, Marian Zelazny, for their warm hospitality at the Institute and for fostering an ideal atmosphere for conducting research and exchanging ideas. I am especially grateful to Christian Habicht for his friendship and for all his help with Greek epigraphy and Greek law. I greatly benefited from discussing my work with the economists at the Institute, including Eric Maskin, professor in the School of Social Science, and Konstantin Sonin, a member there. Agnès Rouveret and Boris Dreyer, fellow members in the School of Historical Studies, have read some of my work and provided lots of encouragement. While in Princeton, I very much enjoyed the warm hospitality of Michael Peachin and Beate Witzler.

Above all, I wish to acknowledge my teacher Bruce Frier, who introduced me to the debate in the fields of law and economics and the New Institutional Economics. I have continued to learn from Bruce long after completing my Ph.D. and value my conversations with him about law and economics during my frequent visits to Ann Arbor.

I have had the opportunity to make oral presentations on subjects connected with this book at various settings, including meetings of the American Philological Association and the Classical Association of the Middle West and South, the American Society of Legal Historians, the European Social Science History Conference, and the Société Internationale "Fernand de Visscher" pour l'Histoire des Droits de l'Antiquité, as well as during visits to Stanford University and Indiana University and during my stay at the Institute for Advanced Study. Chris Hebert, Christine Byks, Mary Hashman, the copy editor, and the other staff of the University of Michigan Press have been very helpful in expediting the publication of this book, and the readers for the press have provided very helpful suggestions.

Finally, in between the time that I submitted my manuscript to the University of Michigan Press and its acceptance, Hurricane Katrina struck. I do not want to say anything about the hurricane, except to acknowledge that in this difficult time we have experienced the wonderful generosity of colleagues, friends, and family. I was fortunate to spend the fall semester of 2005 in the Department of Classical Studies at the University of Michigan. I am grateful to Richard Janko and Bruce Frier for providing me with a place to work and involving me in the intellectual life of the department, to the graduate students in Greek 501 for their kindness, and to all the faculty and staff in the Classics Department for being so welcoming and gracious. Netta Berlin and Arnold Juster, Philip Gorman, and Thomas McGinn have been real friends during this difficult period. I will never be able to repay all the generosity that my friends Carl and Nancy Anderson have shown toward me during my extended visit with them. I will never forget my stay in Ann Arbor. My wife, Constance Mui, has edited lots of my work, helping me to focus my arguments, and beyond that I treasure her love and support, as I do the love and support of my niece Candace Mui, who also, when a student at the University of Michigan, provided me with many reasons to visit Ann Arbor.

I dedicate this book to my friends Carl and Nancy and to my immediate and extended family on both sides, including my in-laws, cousins, and aunts, whose love and generosity have been overwhelming.

Contents

Abbreviations

CIL	*Corpus Inscriptionum Latinarum*.
CJ	*Corpus Iuris Civilis*. Vol. II, *Codex Justinianus*. Ed. and rev. P. Krueger. Berlin, 1954. Reprint, Hildesheim, 1989.
CTh	*Codex Theodosianus*.
D.	*Corpus Iuris Civilis*. Vol. I, *Digesta*. Ed. T. Mommsen. Rev. P. Krueger. Berlin, 1963. Reprint, Hildesheim, 1988.
FIRA I	*Fontes Iuris Romani Antejustiniani*. Part 1, "Leges." 2d ed. Ed. S. Riccobono. Florence, 1941.
IG	*Inscriptiones Graecae*.
IGLSyr.	*Inscriptions grecques et latines de la Syrie*.
ILTun.	*Inscriptions latines de la Tunisie*. Ed. A. Merlin. Paris, 1944.
SEG	*Supplementum Epigraphicum Graecum*. Leiden, 1923–.

References to papyri follow the conventions of J. F. Oates, R. S. Bagnall, S. J. Clackson, A. A. O'Brien, J. D. Sosin, T. G. Wilfong, and K. A. Worp, *Checklist of Editions of Greek, Latin, Demotic and Coptic Papyri, Ostraca and Tablets*, Web edition (December 2005), http://scriptorium.lib.duke.edu/papyrus/texts/clist.html. Abbreviations of journals in classical studies are as in *L'Année philologique*. Other common abbreviations are also used. Translations of quoted passages are my own unless otherwise noted.

INTRODUCTION

Legal Institutions and the Roman Economy

In this book, I explore the relationship between Roman private law and the development of the Roman rural economy at the height of the Roman Empire, during the first three centuries CE, as well as in the fourth century, when the institutions of the later empire began to develop. In recent years economic historians have used many different methodological approaches to assess the performance of the Roman economy, with particular emphasis on whether, and to what extent, the Roman Empire experienced any significant degree of economic growth. This debate has focused on population and technology as major factors determining the possibilities for economic development in the ancient world.[1] I approach the Roman economy from a quite different perspective, from that of the law and legal institutions surrounding the economy. The current scholarly debate among economists and legal theorists over the relationship between contemporary law and the economy suggests that the Roman laws and legal institutions likewise had important but complex effects on the agrarian economy of the Roman Empire. I hope to apply some of the lessons from this debate as I use the laws regulating land tenure, and the Roman government's enforcement of those laws, as a window through which to develop a more comprehensive view of the Roman economy.

In a predominantly agrarian economy, the financial well-being of Roman landowners was inextricably linked to the fortunes of agricultural laborers and small farmers.[2] Agriculture employed the vast majority of the empire's population, and it played a crucial role in the Roman government's efforts to govern the empire. Agriculture constituted the basis for the wealth of the Roman upper classes, who dominated the government both in Rome and in the cities of the empire, and whose social and political privileges it was the imperial government's policy to foster. Many upper-class Romans derived their fortunes from estates cultivated by small-scale tenants. More generally, the economic situation of large landowners was affected by their relationships with small-scale farmers, who worked as laborers on large estates, received credit from larger landowners, and, in some circumstances, competed with them for land, resources such as water, and even access to markets. In addition, the ability of the Roman Empire to tax the provinces, to provide for the maintenance of the city of Rome, and to finance the defense of the empire was, to a large extent, a function of the economic prosperity of the small farmers who made up the bulk of the empire's population. It stands to reason that much can be learned about the Roman economy by examining the property rights established by the Roman state, especially as they affected the contractual relationships between the wealthy landowners and smaller farmers.

I focus my discussion on farm tenancy, which was an economic institution of fundamental importance to both the private agrarian economy and to the state. This is not to overlook the fact that other forms of land tenure characterized the Roman economy. Small-scale private landowners, operating probably at a near-subsistence level, occupied a great deal of land. In addition, estates were often cultivated with slave labor, especially in Italy but also in other parts of the empire, while the important role of wage labor in agriculture has been the subject of recent scholarly focus.[3] However, farm tenancy was a legal institution for which the Roman imperial government showed continuing concern, so studying the state's policies in this area of the law provides a way to understand the role that the state played in the economy more generally.

In this book, my aim is not simply to consider whether the Roman government was impartial in adjudicating competing claims but, more important, to draw some conclusions about the nature of the Roman agrarian economy itself. To put the question succinctly, did the Roman government develop laws with an eye toward strengthening the agrarian economy, and if so, did these laws work in the way they were intended? To be sure, self-interest would dictate that large landowners would only have invested their wealth in ways that would help to increase agricultural productivity and therefore expand the economy if they were confident that the state offered adequate protection of their property rights.[4] If so, the Roman government would have established clear-cut rules on the basis of which landowners and tenants could form contractual relationships that resulted in an efficient use of the factors of production in the economy, including land, labor, livestock, and other equipment.[5] If the law did serve such a purpose, we might hypothesize that the Roman government was neither unconscious of, nor indifferent to, the economic effects of its policy of striving to define property rights and contractual relationships in a more or less uniform fashion. But at the same time, any incentives to invest would have been affected by the degree to which the imperial administration intervened on the small farmers' behalf in agrarian disputes to maintain the rights that they had exercised by formal law or even by custom.

Another possibility is that the law served chiefly as an instrument for the state to protect the social and economic interests of the empire's landowning elite against those of the small farmers who cultivated the bulk of the land. Under this scenario, the law might have sacrificed economic efficiency to preserve the privileges of large landowners. They, in turn, could have used the legal institutions of the Roman state to support their efforts to exact as great a share as possible of the surplus produced by their tenants or other people serving as laborers on their estates. The empire's farming population, meanwhile, would remain vulnerable, always subject to the power of larger landowners, on the one hand, and to the power of the state, in the form of taxes and liturgies, on the other. In this circumstance, most tenants would have produced chiefly to meet their subsistence needs, whereas the landowner could exact a share, or even the lion's share, of the tenants' surplus production as rent.[6]

If landowners simply usurped most of the surplus from their farm tenants, this would certainly have impoverished the vast countryside and led to economic stagnation. Roman laws and legal institutions would have largely served to promote the ability of well-placed people to exact "monopoly-rents"; that is, landowners could monopolize the surplus produced by their tenants without making any corresponding financial investment in improving the estate on their own part.[7] Moreover, the expenditures that the elite made to secure these transfers of wealth would ultimately have been costly to society in general. The costs to society of such expenditures, termed *rent seeking*, can be considerable, though difficult to measure, and a whole field of inquiry is devoted to this subject.[8]

In the Roman Empire, landowners could use their elevated social position and connections to manipulate officials in the imperial administration to exact additional rents and services from their tenants. In addition, landowners would have to spend some of their own resources to secure the cooperation of governmental authorities, whether by gifts or even by bribes. The relationship between landowners and tenants would be based not on market forces but on the social hierarchy of landowner and tenant.[9] Indeed, in his analysis of the role of friendship in the economy of the late republic, Koenraad Verboven argues that the influence gained through personal connections filled a gap created by inadequate legal institutions and provided Roman businesspeople with a way of approaching governmental authorities to use the legal institutions of the state to defend their interests.[10] The influence exercised by the well connected would have left tenants or other small farmers little chance when they came into conflict with landowners of higher social status.

At issue is the intersection of three components of fundamental importance for understanding the Roman Empire, namely, the agrarian economy, law, and the social concerns of the Roman government. To assess the relationship between Roman law and the agrarian economy of the Roman Empire in light of these considerations, I think we can learn a great deal from the innovative theoretical models developed in the current scholarly debate about the complex relationship between law and the economy. This debate has generated a rich body of literature that provides ancient historians with new and innovative theoretical constructs to analyze the available evidence for Roman legal institutions. Among legal scholars, the law and economics approach provides a method of analyzing the likely economic effects of legal arrangements and court decisions.[11] In addition, we can put various legal and social institutions in the Roman economy in a broader perspective by learning from the ongoing debate in the field of the New Institutional Economics (or Neoinstitutional Economics, NIE). The term New Institutional Economics refers to an interdisciplinary field involving scholars primarily in economics and law, but in other fields as well, who are concerned with the role of institutions in economics.[12] The goal of NIE, in Peter Klein's description, "is to explain what institutions are, how they arise, what purposes they serve, how they change and how—if at all—they should be reformed."[13] Of particular importance for a historian of the ancient world is a subfield of the NIE, called Historical New Institutional Economics (HNIE), represented by the work of such economic historians as Douglass North and Barry Weingast, among others.[14] Scholarship in NIE provides ancient historians with new, helpful methodologies to analyze the likely effects on the economy of the Roman government's legal policies. This is not to claim that applying the methodologies of law and economics and the NIE will tell the whole story about the Roman economy. Indeed, NIE makes certain assumptions about how economic actors make decisions in the face of uncertainty, whereas our understanding of how people make decisions in economic matters is far from complete and there are many controversies.[15] Still, the debate in these two fields provides a way of asking new questions about Roman law and legal institutions, and so of coming to a better understanding of the role that law played in the Roman economy.

THE ECONOMIC BACKGROUND

The Roman imperial peace fostered conditions for increased commerce, and one of the hallmarks of Roman rule was the development of a flourishing urban culture, even in areas where cities had scarcely existed before. But it is still debated to what extent the development of Rome's urban culture engendered growth in the economy beyond what can be accounted for by population increase alone. Such growth would have involved the increasing productivity of labor, resulting from the development and dissemination of new technologies. These developments, in turn, would have made possible the creation of substantial manufacturing and commercial sectors, particularly in cities.[16] But above all, growth in the Roman economy as a whole would have depended on expanding agriculture, which remained the dominant sector of the Roman economy throughout antiquity. In investigating the possibilities for growth in the Roman economy, it is crucial to consider how Roman law and the legal institutions affected the interests of crucial actors in the agrarian economy, including the state, large landowners, and smaller farmers.

There can be no doubt that the development of a flourishing urban culture in the Roman Empire had profound consequences for the welfare of the empire's rural population. In fact, the Roman Empire in the early imperial period experienced substantial population growth, from a population of about 45 million at the time of Augustus to a peak of 55–65 million in the Antonine period. It is likely that much of this growth took place in the many cities of the empire.[17] The growing urban culture of the Roman Empire was characterized by consumer cities; that is, cities whose wealth was not primarily derived from their own production, say, of manufactured goods. Instead, consumer cities in the Roman Empire depended on a transfer of wealth from the countryside. Much of this transfer of wealth came in the form of the rents and other income, both in cash and in kind, that large landowners acquired from their estates, a large portion of which they spent in the cities.[18] Roman landowners depended for their wealth on their ability to capture a portion of the surplus produced by the peasants in the countryside, whether they were working on their land as hired laborers or as tenants.[19] So the development of the urban economy in the Roman Empire was a function, to a large extent, of the degree to which the urban elite controlled the surplus produced in the countryside. The net balance of payments between cities and the countryside in the Roman Empire almost certainly favored urban culture and expanding urban economies. This observation does not mean that the relationship between cities and the countryside was entirely parasitical, however. As Walter Scheidel points out, cities could relieve population pressure in the countryside by offering opportunities for people unable to find adequate employment in agriculture. Indeed, since the dreadful living conditions in premodern cities produced higher mortality rates than in rural areas, such cities depended for their survival on a continuing influx of people from the countryside.[20]

But whatever positive conditions the Roman imperial peace may have created for investment and trade, the economic development of the Roman Empire, like all premodern societies, was subject to severe constraints. Two key factors determining the possibilities for economic development in ancient societies were population and technology, as the recent debate on the Roman economy has emphasized.[21] To deal with technology first, a number of technological improvements helped to increase productivity in agriculture. The most important of these new technologies for agriculture was probably the lever olive press, which made it possible for landowners investing in this heavy and expensive piece of equipment to process much more olive oil than possible with smaller presses. As David Mattingly argues, landowners in North Africa (and probably in other areas of the empire as well) invested considerable resources in developing large pressing installations. These installations were especially suited to handle the occasional bumper crops characteristic of olive oil production. This type of investment, then, provided large landowners with a means to process large volumes of oil produced by numerous tenants. Landowners gained from this type of investment not by increasing the productivity of olive culture but rather by enhancing their control over large marketable surpluses of olive oil.[22] The Roman economy benefited from other significant advances in technology as well, such as in water mills and irrigation for agriculture.[23]

As impressive as certain technological developments in the Roman Empire were, it seems likely that the most important overall constraint on the Roman economy was its population. In the Roman economy, a relatively constant rate of population growth was a necessary (albeit not sufficient) condition for economic growth. Indeed, in his analysis of the relationship between population and economic development in the ancient world, Scheidel demonstrates the connection between population increase and economic development.[24] As Scheidel argues, the Roman Empire, like other ancient societies, was characterized by high mortality balanced by high fertility. Such a regime imposed severe constraints on the possibilities for economic development. Because of high mortality, there was only a low return on investment in human capital, for example, the type of investment represented by education. Under this circumstance, population growth, rather than investment that would increase the productivity of labor, was the principal factor affecting economic growth. Population increase would lead to changes in technology that would permit more intensive methods of agriculture and the development of other industries to provide employment outside of agriculture. Such intensification of agriculture would not necessarily be a blessing for the rural labor force, however, since it would require a greater expenditure of effort for each unit of land cultivated.[25]

Nevertheless, intensification of agriculture would allow the production of a surplus necessary to support an urban society in which a substantial portion of the population was employed in nonagricultural pursuits. But as Scheidel points out, there are limits to the type of growth possible in an ancient society subject to a high-pressure demographic regime. If population increase led to greater productivity, the increase in productivity of labor would still not be so large as to make possible sustained, long-term growth in the economy. Instead, an ancient society would be subject to periodic cycles of growth and contraction, as an expanding population, unable to develop new technologies that would make labor more productive as the population increased, would place pressure on available resources. Thus the Roman economy was subject to a "'low equilibrium trap,' in which in the long term, limited increases in output will raise surpluses less than population size and the latter will eventually offset intermittent productivity gains."[26]

Even if population established a basic constraint limiting the overall development of the Roman economy, however, historical preindustrial economies have experienced periods of what E. L. Jones characterizes as *intensive* growth, when the economy expands beyond what could be accounted for by population alone (termed *extensive* growth) and overall per capita incomes rise. Under intensive growth, a combination of factors would promote increasing returns to investment so that the economy would grow by developing more intensive methods of agriculture that could support an increasingly large population employed outside of agriculture. This nonagricultural population might be employed in industries or trade. In preindustrial economies, formal legal institutions and informal cultural institutions may either promote or inhibit the possibilities for such specialization and investment.[27] For the Roman Empire, it seems to be a likely hypothesis that the substantial legal and administrative changes Roman rule brought to the empire had important consequences for the empire's economy. Scholarship ascribing economic development to changes in population and technology tends to view institutions as largely epiphenomenal, in the sense that they are by-products of economic conditions determined by the larger forces of population and technological development.[28]

In recent years, however, economic historians, especially those writing from the perspective of NIE, have increasingly focused on the role played by institutions in the economic performance of historical societies. This type of analysis sees institutions as crucial factors in shaping economic performance. Coming under the rubric of institutions as defined by NIE scholars are the "institutional environment" and "institutional arrangements." The institutional environment includes laws and property rights, court systems, and the like, as well as informal institutions, such as social norms and customs, that establish the rules of the game under which individuals engage in economic activity.[29]

Institutional arrangements examined by economic historians also include specific types of contracts that represent the "'governance structures'—designed by trading partners to mediate particular economic relationships."[30] Formal institutions seem to be differentiated by their ability to promote efficient allocations of resources, in the sense of maintaining property rights and other incentives for investment that are conducive to generating wealth, as opposed to establishing conditions under which well-placed individuals can simply take advantage of the rules of the game to enrich themselves without increasing the social product, that is, the aggregate wealth of society. The informal institutions of a society can also play a crucial role in creating conditions conducive to economic growth.[31] In Peter Klein's formulation, the study of institutions is important to economic history because "[economic] development is seen as a response to institutions that support social and commercial relationships. Economic growth thus depends on the degree to which the potential hazards of trade (shirking, opportunism and the like) can be controlled by institutions, which reduce information costs, encourage capital formation and capital mobility, allow risks to be priced and shared and otherwise facilitate cooperation."[32]

To apply this approach to the economic history of the Roman Empire, it seems reasonable to posit that, overall, constraints imposed by population in a low-equilibrium trap limited the possibilities for economic growth and therefore explain why the Roman Empire never experienced an economic transformation that would lead to substantial economic growth and dramatic changes in the standards of living for the empire's population. At the same time, the formal and informal institutions of the Roman Empire established the conditions affecting such growth as did occur, and more important, these institutions helped to shape the distribution of wealth among the state, the elite landowners who dominated Roman society, and the large numbers of smaller farmers on whose production elite landowners depended for their incomes and the state relied for its tax revenues. In the formulation of Alexander Field, "if we take the fundamental task of economic history to be understanding and explaining economic performance over time, then an interest in institutions . . . is ultimately relevant only to the degree that it can shed light on such performance."[33]

Again, I want to emphasize that this approach does not tell the whole story about law in the Roman economy. Indeed, one of the weaknesses of NIE is that it does not really address how institutions come into existence in the first place—it is more concerned with their performance and evolution. From the perspective of Institutional Law and Economics (an intellectual movement distinct from but overlapping with NIE), economic institutions evolve as the result of a complex relationship among law and legal institutions, economic forces, and social values. Economic activity, then, "is determined by the structure of rights that exists in society, with the levels of and changes in each of these variables being in part a function of the legal structure and legal change over time."[34] The function of law and legal institutions is to resolve conflicts that arise from economic actors making choices that are affected by and impinge upon the choices made by other actors. But the rights among which the state mediates do not exist in and of themselves but are created and maintained by the state.[35]

My focus in this book is not on the origins of Roman legal institutions but on their likely implications for the interests of crucial actors in the Roman economy. I contend that this approach, even if it cannot provide a comprehensive account of the Roman economy, is important because institutional arrangements created incentives and disincentives for economic activity that affected the welfare of the empire's population. Indeed, as Field also argues, the various approaches to defining property rights in different legal systems in some cases may have significant effects on the distribution of wealth within a society. This conclusion suggests that the precise rules according to which land-tenure arrangements were structured in the Roman Empire were significant not only for the possibilities of economic growth but also for the welfare of landowners and the tenants cultivating their land.[36]

Given the overall limitations imposed by the ancient demographic regime, it must be conceded that no amount of institutional change could have altered the fundamental conditions surrounding the Roman economy. Nevertheless, even if a study of the role of law and legal institutions in the Roman economy cannot be used to generate predictions about the size of the Roman gross domestic product or the rate of economic growth over time, such a study remains crucial for understanding the particular structure of the Roman economy and the relationships among its principal actors. At the very least, an analysis of the legal institutions surrounding the Roman economy will help us to understand better the factors that tended to foster or suppress economic growth in the Roman Empire. In E. L. Jones' formulation, the legal regimes surrounding land tenure played a significant role in determining whether investment in more productive forms of agriculture was economically attractive to aristocratic landowners, which would have been an important component of intensive growth. The alternative is that if such investment produced inadequate returns, the interests of upper-class landowners would have been better served if they simply took advantage of their enviable social and economic position by squeezing revenues out of the production of their tenants and other farmers, without regard for adopting long-term investment strategies conducive to growth.[37]

My purpose in this book, then, is not to use an analysis of the legal institutions surrounding the Roman agrarian economy as a means to predict the extent of economic growth in the Roman economy. Verification of such a hypothesis would be difficult enough, and it would be even more difficult to isolate the role that legal institutions might have played from other factors that fostered economic growth. From a theoretical standpoint, it seems likely that if the Roman government defined and enforced property rights in a consistent manner, this legal policy would be a positive factor in promoting increased trade and economic growth. This is, at least, the prediction of Yoram Barzel, who, in his analysis of the economic function of the state, considers the Roman Empire to have been a "rule-of-law state," whose strict and impartial enforcement of clearly defined property rights resulted in greater economic activity than would have been the case in a "tyrannical state." In a such a state, the tyrant and a group of supporters use the power of the state to increase their own wealth even at the expense of the common social product and, in so doing, tend to diminish the types of exchange that generate wealth.[38]

My goal is more modest: to examine how law and legal institutions affected the economic interests and relative bargaining power of Roman landowners and tenants. The empire's institutional arrangements ultimately played a significant role in shaping the distribution of wealth between larger landowners and smaller farmers in the Roman economy. Specifically, did the law help Roman landowners to exhaust the countryside of its wealth and leave the rural labor force impoverished, able only to produce the revenues that elite landowners required? Alternatively, did the law promote a more equitable distribution of wealth between landowners and the rural labor force? In either scenario, the policy of the Roman state is likely to have played a significant role in influencing this transfer of wealth. Wealth taken from the countryside as rents and taxes might foster the growth of urban economies, but wealth left in the hands of rural producers would promote economic growth in the countryside. The greater the portion of their own surplus that peasant producers controlled, the more they would be able to sell to urban markets, and the more they could invest their gains in greater productivity either on their farms or in rural industries that would allow them to supplement the incomes that they derived from agriculture. The point is to trace the overarching considerations—legal and economic—that guided the Roman legal authorities in dealing with issues involving land tenure and then to determine the likely effects of Roman policy on economic performance.

INTERPRETING THE EVIDENCE OF ROMAN LEGAL LITERATURE

Analyzing the rather complex relationship between landowners and small farmers is crucial for understanding the Roman economy, but the challenge is to find evidence that can inform us about the place of legal institutions in it. We can gain some understanding of the policies of the Roman government in defining and protecting property rights by considering the evidence provided by Roman legal literature. Here, the principal sources of evidence include the two essential law codes, those of Justinian and Theodosius.

The first source, the sixth-century Code of Justinian, preserves numerous rescripts issued by emperors in the early empire in response to petitions concerning agrarian disputes, as well as more general laws promulgated by emperors beginning in the fourth century. These petitions concern areas of the law central to the rural economy such as farm tenancy, debt, and the resolution of ownership disputes. Since these petitions came from people of varying social and economic classes, they provide a valuable resource for analyzing the complex role that the Roman government played in mediating the interests of the state, landowners, and small farmers. The second source, the fifth-century Theodosian Code, preserves, among many decrees issued by emperors in the fourth and early fifth centuries, a number concerning legal issues affecting the rural economy.[39] But as important as rescripts and other imperial decrees are for understanding the law surrounding land tenure, they do not paint the whole picture. In my book I read them in light of the writings of the classical Roman jurists on private law as preserved in the Digest of Justinian. These afford us a more complete understanding of the principles by which the Roman government regulated a whole range of legal relationships crucial to defining the Roman economy. To define how the law would apply, jurists generally examine individual cases, often hypothetical ones, that reveal specific legal problems. Except when they cite rescripts by the emperors, the writings of the jurists do not preserve legal decisions taken in actual courts of law but rather prescriptions as to how the law should be applied. So the classical Roman legal literature does not always inform us directly as to how the law was applied in everyday situations.

Another difficulty in interpreting Roman legal literature is that it is not immediately clear what the law preserved in the Digest and in the Code of Justinian represented or, more precisely, which groups in the Roman Empire were actually affected by the rules formulated by the jurists either for farm tenancy or for other areas of the law connected with the agrarian economy and the rescripts written by the emperors on these issues. Scholars of Roman law have vigorously debated whether the jurists, when developing rules for Roman private law, were concerned with responding to what they perceived to be contemporary social concerns. The alternative view is that the jurists operated within a closed intellectual tradition, one divorced from social concerns and largely subject to its own internal logic.[40]

But it now has been demonstrated in several areas of the law that the jurists were concerned with responding to what they perceived as contemporary social concerns, especially ones that impinged directly on the interests of the upper classes. This can be seen in such areas of the law as urban leasing, the building industry, overland transportation, and even the regulation of adultery and prostitution.[41] In my previous work on the Roman economy, I argue that the Roman jurists, when developing rules affecting private property, did in fact respond to what they perceived as the economic interests of their own class, that of upper-class landowners, and the realities of the Roman economy. In addressing farm tenancy, the jurists did this by developing rules that were aimed at preserving what was most advantageous in farm tenancy to landowners, namely the tenant's long-term and productive cultivation of the land.[42]

This legal evidence is complemented by a corpus of inscriptions recording petitions by farming communities, especially those in Africa and Asia, to the imperial government. These petitions, and the accompanying responses from the imperial government, allow us to trace the capacity of rural communities to avail themselves of the legal institutions of the empire to protect their interests. In addition, they also allow us to trace what principles the imperial government followed in defining rights to land. Finally, documentary papyri from Roman Egypt preserve numerous petitions and responses from governmental officials on legal questions impinging on the agrarian economy and so offer an additional source of evidence for the economic role of Roman legal institutions.

THE ECONOMIC SIGNIFICANCE OF ROMAN LEGAL INSTITUTIONS

One issue to be addressed at the outset is whether legal institutions played any significant role in the Roman economy. The alternative is that economic relationships were established on the basis of factors not subject to the control of law. By law, I am referring to Roman private law and other systems of law in the provinces governing farm tenancy, as well as the legal policy of the emperor and other officials in the imperial administration in responding to disputes involving the rural economy, and even tenure regulations established by the Roman government for imperial estates. Certainly there are reasons to question the adequacy of legal institutions to defend the rights of small farmers.[43] One issue that must be addressed concerns the degree to which the conventional rules of Roman law defined relationships in the countryside. A skeptical view would hold that the juristic sources, at best, allow us to form a very imperfect picture of the historical conditions surrounding the agrarian economy in the Roman Empire. For example, the Roman legal authorities have been viewed as concerned primarily with responding to the needs of those classes most likely to avail themselves of the courts and the other legal protections offered by the state. In the case of farm tenancy, the major concern of the jurists and the Roman state would therefore have been to define the legal rights and obligations of only the very wealthiest tenants, that is, those most able to press their claims in a court of law on an equal basis with landowners. As a result, the legal sources concerned with farm tenancy would tell us very little about the conditions under which the vast majority of tenants across the Roman Empire occupied their land.[44]

At the same time, it is possible that many tenure relationships were established largely by social rather than by legal relationships, with dependent populations compelled by the social convention to cultivate the land belonging to large landowners.[45] We might expect such land-tenure systems to be survivals of pre-Roman social and political structures.[46] To be sure, the economic independence of small farmers was constrained by their ability to defend their interests against larger landowners through courts of law and other legal institutions. In his study of Apuleius' *Golden Ass*, Fergus Millar suggests that small farmers in the Roman Empire enjoyed few protections from the state. In a novel whose action takes place against the background of what seems to be a realistically depicted picture of provincial life in the Roman Empire, the state and legal institutions, in Millar's view, are portrayed as being quite remote from the everyday lives of farmers.[47] Under this hypothesis, the legal rules preserved in the Digest of Justinian and the law codes were largely irrelevant to the affairs of the bulk of the farmers in the Roman Empire. The work of the Roman jurists, then, could have had but little impact on the situation of the vast majority of the Roman Empire's farmers.

From another perspective, in a wide-ranging study of the administration of justice in the Roman Empire, Michael Peachin emphasizes that a substantial disparity could exist between the written law and the practice of the courts.[48] The principal reason for this is the inability of the Roman courts to handle the volume of business that the imperial peace fostered. One factor exacerbating the situation was the shortage of professional judges: most judges in the Roman Empire were aristocrats, very few of whom had specialized training in the law. The administration of justice thus tended to be haphazard, with judges lacking any specialized knowledge of the law issuing rulings on complex legal issues. Concerned about the ineffectiveness of the local courts, litigants often turned to the emperor as the ultimate source of law and justice, assailing him with an ever-increasing tide of appeals. This suggests that when the professional jurists, often serving in the emperor's council in an official or unofficial capacity, were developing the elaborate and sophisticated system of Roman private law preserved in the law codes and the Digest of Justinian, they were engaged in a largely academic exercise and had all too little effect on the actual decisions rendered in Roman courts. The disparity that might have existed between the written law and the practice of the courts would make it seem unlikely that small farmers enjoyed much protection at all from legal institutions. The result was hardly favorable for the small farmer in the Roman Empire. Indeed, in a recent study of law in the village life of Roman Egypt, Deborah Hobson has argued that the legal institutions of that province were inadequate to offer villagers any sort of relief in legal disputes.[49]

Finally, another possibility is that the law, when it did in fact play a major role in rural relationships, served chiefly as an instrument for the state to enforce the social and economic privileges of the empire's land-owning elite against the small farmers who cultivated the bulk of their land. Under this hypothesis, the courts of law were dominated by the elite, who, by virtue of their social position, could effectively bar the access of potential litigants to protection that was theoretically due them.[50] Indeed, the main purpose of the laws would have been to provide landowners with the support of the state in enforcing contractual obligations against tenants and small farmers. The likelihood that many contractual arrangements in the Roman Empire involved parties of widely divergent social status would have restricted the access of the weaker party to the courts and surely allowed socially superior creditors to exercise unilateral power over debtors, as Alfons Bürge argues.[51] The law would not have served as an impartial arbiter in this scenario but rather would instead have tilted the balance of bargaining power between landowner and tenant decisively in favor of the former party. Such a function of the law would have served the economic interests of upper-class landowners, but it would not necessarily have contributed at all positively to the general development of the Roman agrarian economy. Indeed, such a function of the law could well have impeded productivity in the rural economy.

For example, the administration of the law in the Roman Empire could have had a similar effect in the Roman Empire as in the rural hinterland of early-modern Madrid, where legal institutions helped to keep the peasantry economically and socially dependent on the land-owning elite. The result of this was that the land-owning elite remained socially and politically dominant, but the rural economy performed poorly in comparison with other areas of early-modern Europe, such as the Netherlands, where the law did not serve to suppress the peasantry.[52] Similarly, in the Roman Empire, the privileges of the land-owning elite would have been enhanced as the imperial government legislated general rules affecting the rural economy in response to requests or petitions from individual landowners.[53] Thus legal institutions, according to this model, would have essentially helped to preserve a status quo in which the land-owning elite remained dominant, and so it would have represented a considerable obstacle to any economic growth that might result from the economic freedom of small farmers and other actors in the Roman economy.

The apparent weakness of legal institutions in the Roman countryside helps to explain the widespread conception of Roman farmers as vulnerable agents who were economically and socially dependent on larger landowners. For example, C. R. Whittaker has viewed farming populations in the Roman Empire as bound to larger landowners in a relationship of social dependence.[54] Similarly, in their analyses of tenancy in the Roman Empire, both L. Capogrossi Colognesi and E. Lo Cascio have seen economic dependence as an inherent aspect of lease relationships in the Roman world.[55] Indeed, Willem Jongman has argued that landowners at Pompeii derived much of their income from land leased out to tenants who had few resources of their own and who eked out a marginal existence, always living close to starvation.[56] Perhaps the most dismal assessment of the situation of peasant farmers in the Roman Empire is that of G. E. M. de Ste. Croix, who sees a continuing deterioration and even "enserfment" of farm tenants and other peasant cultivators throughout the period of Roman rule.[57]

We can gain a broader historical perspective on how legal institutions could affect incentives to invest by considering Robert Brenner's analysis of the medieval European agrarian economy. As the population of Europe grew in the early medieval period, land became more scarce, and competition for land increased among tenants. This increased competition for land had various consequences for the development of the agrarian economy, and one key factor was the interplay between peasant and noble social institutions and the development of class structures in the rural workforce. In some parts of Europe, notably France, peasant tenants, with the backing of the monarchy, were able to establish strong rights of tenure over their land, but the result was not completely favorable to their welfare. Instead, peasant holdings tended to become fragmented as the rural population grew. The increased competition for land did not lead to the adoption of new technologies to increase production. Rather, because feudal lords in France could only exact a fixed cash rent (*cens*) that could not be raised and consequently had less value over time, they had neither the incentive nor the capacity to plow any profits back into the land to increase production. At the same time, the peasants themselves could not reap the profits of higher prices for agricultural products because the state exacted most of their surplus in the form of taxation. Stagnation in the agrarian sector also inhibited industrial growth, since the peasantry, unable to keep much if any of the surplus that it produced, did not have adequate wealth to purchase manufactured products to any significant degree.

England, by contrast, had a quite different experience. There, the institutions of the peasantry were not strong enough to resist the efforts of landlords to consolidate holdings and adopt more efficient, that is, more cost-effective, methods of managing their land. English landlords were able to replace peasant tenants cultivating their land under feudal bonds with either wage laborers or larger-scale tenants. There were greater incentives for investment in agriculture on the part of both landowners and tenants in England than in France. Unlike their counterparts in France, English landlords could reap the profits of their investments by exacting higher rents. English tenants could also enjoy the benefits of their own investments. They could keep some of their surplus rather than see it confiscated either by the state or by a feudal lord with the support of the state.[58] Whether or not Brenner has precisely captured the essential issues surrounding the economies of medieval and early-modern France and England, his arguments suggest how legal rights to the land might affect the incentives for investment and the possibilities for economic growth in a preindustrial society.[59]

To be sure, the prosperity of the Roman upper classes derived from their ability to exact a share of the surplus from their tenants or the other farmers cultivating their land. But Brenner's formulation of the terms of the debate about the agrarian economy of medieval Europe suggests a range of questions that need to be addressed if we are to arrive at a more complete understanding of the Roman agrarian economy. For example, did small farmers in the Roman Empire exercise any independence at all, or were they completely subject to the economic and social domination of larger landowners? To answer this question, we need to consider not only the legal definition of their tenure of the land but also the degree to which such farmers could defend their rights to the land. This means examining the access of small farmers to the legal institutions of the Roman state and also the more local communal structures that existed in many agrarian communities. The potential strength of legal and social institutions in the countryside raises another set of questions. If small farmers did exercise such independence, say, by virtue of having secure rights of tenure over their land, was this independence conducive to economic growth or did it lead to fragmentation of holdings, stagnation of agricultural techniques, and poverty? Finally, what role did the state play in the Roman agrarian economy? Was the Roman state more concerned with supporting landowners or smaller farmers, and did its interventions in the Roman economy promote stagnation or growth?

As I argue in this book, scholars have generally been too pessimistic in their assessment both of the access of smaller farmers to the protection of the courts and of the strength of Roman legal institutions in regulating the rural economy. First, the numerous petitions preserved in the Code of Justinian suggest that people representing a wide range of social and economic status and living in different areas of the empire regarded petitioning the emperor as a reasonably effective way to protect their interests in legal disputes. Indeed, as Peachin has argued, the office of the emperor in the course of the early empire had to handle an increasing volume of cases, as the emperor became more and more identified as the ultimate source of legal protection for the empire's subjects.[60] The fundamental importance of the emperor's role as judge led to the creation of a bureaucracy designed to deal with the petitions that came to the emperor. In some cases, either to take the place of an unavailable emperor or to reduce the volume of business that the emperor had to handle, high-ranking officials were given special powers to judge cases in the name of the emperor; the decisions of *iudices vice Caesaris* carried the same legal authority as decisions by the emperor himself. Thus subjects from around the empire, often in anticipation of litigation, appealed to the emperor for an authoritative legal position on their cases. If the emperor gave support to the petitioner's legal position, he or she might use the resulting rescript as authoritative support at trial at home.[61] Such petitions stand behind many, if not most, of the rescripts issued to private individuals from the time of Hadrian to Diocletian preserved in the Code of Justinian. Indeed, the importance of the rescript process to the emperor's subjects is suggested by repeated efforts to collect them. Two important collections date to the reign of Diocletian. The first of these collections, called the *Codex Gregorianus*, was compiled around 292 and includes rescripts dating back to the reign of Hadrian. The second collection, compiled by the jurist Hermoginianus, includes mainly rescripts from the years 293–94.[62]

The rescript process might have enhanced the effectiveness of Roman legal institutions in responding to the needs of the empire's subjects. As J.-P. Coriat argues, the Roman emperors, especially from the time of the Severans in the early third century, used the rescript process as a way of creating new remedies that judges, including provincial governors, would be required to grant litigants. In other words, in responding to petitions that often had provincial origins, emperors could use rescripts as a way to issue instructions to judges that, in effect, would modify law as established in the Praetor's Edict, which had received its final redaction under Hadrian. The emperors could use rescripts, then, to extend the scope of remedies in established law to new situations. The rescript process, accordingly, played a profound role in the process of developing and adapting Roman law, particularly to serve the needs of the people in the provinces.[63]

The rescripts and the imperial offices created to handle them suggest the overall viability of legal institutions in the daily economic life of the empire. The existence of numerous rescripts and also the efforts of later legal authorities to collect them indicate that the empire's subjects viewed petitioning the emperor as a reasonably effective means of defending their rights. This is not to say that the system worked impartially or that the wealthy did not enjoy distinct advantages but rather that the legal institutions were accessible to a broad range of the empire's population. To be sure, the Roman legal authorities recognized that the theoretical equality before the law that Roman citizens enjoyed might not always be realized. Accordingly, they took some efforts to overcome some of the difficulties that poorer people would encounter in using the courts.[64] Thus Ulpian, in his discussion of the duties of a proconsul, urges the proconsul to make sure that people of modest station be able to bring cases. In particular, the proconsul was to watch out for the interests of people who might experience difficulties in finding advocates to plead their cases, such as women, pupils, and the mentally incompetent, and also those who might be prevented from gaining the services of an appropriate advocate because of the power of their adversary (Ulp. *D.* 1.16.9.4–5, *de offic. proconsulis*). In more general terms, as Bürge argues, the jurists were concerned with establishing rules for civil procedure that made the process of bringing a lawsuit understandable and predictable for laypeople.[65]

The Roman government on occasion enacted specific measures to ensure a level playing field in its courts. Thus Diocletian approved of an effort on the part of the emperor Claudius II Gothicus to maintain the integrity of Roman courts by outlawing the practice of patronage in the courts (*patrocinium*) (*CJ* 2.13.1, 293). Provincial governors were to take action against powerful people (*potentes*), including senators, who presented under their own names law cases originally pressed by litigants of modest standing (*tenues*). The point was to prevent the courts from being completely dominated by the powerful, so the government sanctioned litigants who looked for powerful patrons with the automatic forfeiture of their cases.[66] In the third and especially in the fourth centuries, the office of the *defensor civitatis* (community advocate) developed, at least in part, to provide greater access on the part of the humble to the protection of the state's legal institutions. In the formulation of Valentinian I, this office was to help country people, "innocens et quieta rusticitas," to defend their rights in court, particularly, in all likelihood, in connection with tax issues (*CTh* 1.29.5; *CJ* 1.55.3, 370).[67] Finally, beginning in the fourth century, the development of bishops' courts, whose decisions Constantine recognized as legally binding, may have helped to enhance the availability of legal institutions to common people.[68]

In the later empire, the imperial government imposed the costs of the judiciary on litigants by establishing fees to be paid to imperial officials for various legal services. To judge by a fee schedule published in Thamugadi in Africa in 361–63, called the *Ordo salutationis*, these fees might be considerable, and they could have effectively barred access to the governor's and emperor's court for many average citizens, as Christopher Kelly has recently argued.[69] But this may be too pessimistic an assessment of access to courts in late antiquity. Many court cases, including presumably ones involving disputes between landowners and tenants, would have been handled at the municipal level, where these prohibitive fees did not apply.[70] In the early empire, this was the case. For example, at Irni, a small town in Spain, the local magistrates would appoint judges to hear a wide range of cases involving judgments of less than 1,000 sesterces. In addition, suits could be heard locally if both parties agreed.[71]

The papyrological evidence from Roman Egypt also suggests that legal institutions played an important role in the lives of everyday Romans. In this connection, it is worth emphasizing that scholars now recognize the relevance of papyrological evidence for broader issues in the Roman economy. The economy of Egypt was subject to the same basic constraints that affected the Roman economy generally, even if the unique geographical and historical conditions of Egypt affected the ways in which agriculture and other industries developed there. In addition, the imperial administration fostered civic institutions in Egypt similar to those in other areas of the eastern Roman Empire.[72] To return to the papyri, they preserve numerous petitions to various officials, from the local *strategoi* (the officials in charge of the administration of Egypt's thirty-nine administrative divisions, or nomes) to the governor, or prefect. It is clear that these petitions come from many people besides the wealthy elite of the province. Adjudicating legal disputes was such a basic aspect of the prefect's duties that he spent much of each year touring the province, holding assizes at various central locations.[73] The volume of business that the governor had to contend with might be overwhelming. Thus the prefect Subatianus Aquila reportedly received 1,804 petitions in fewer than three days during his *conventus* (court session) in the Arsinoite nome (*P.Yale* I 61, ca. 208–10).[74]

When we consider the access that farm tenants and other small farmers may have had to the protection of legal institutions, the issue becomes somewhat more complicated because of the potential influence that a landlord might exercise by virtue of his or her superior economic status, not to mention possible ties to the governor or other judges, and the resulting economic dependence of the small farmer. Even so, the papyrological evidence indicates that even tenants of humble status, at least on occasion, could call upon the protection of the state in disputes with landowners, even with landowners belonging to the provincial elite. The corpus of papyri documenting legal disputes between landowners and tenants is limited in size, but a small number of petitions concerning legal disputes between seemingly humble farm tenants and much wealthier landowners suggests the central role that legal institutions played in resolving disputes arising from the rural economy.[75] The lease relationship created for the tenant in Egypt certain legal rights, which the tenant could enforce in courts of law. Even small-scale tenants had written leases, and such potentially contentious issues as arrears in rent and rent abatements were negotiated in terms of legal norms. In addition, both landowners and tenants had some degree of confidence that the terms of the contract could be enforceable in courts of law; otherwise the observance of legal norms in the drawing up of leases would have been an empty exercise.[76]

As Clifford Ando argues in his wide-ranging analysis of the factors that promoted loyalty in the Roman Empire, the confidence displayed by the empire's subjects in Roman legal institutions was to a large extent the result of carefully managed communications by the Roman state. The state's concern for the publication of official documents made its rulings more authoritative and certainly buttressed the idea that people could effectively seek redress for grievances by petitioning the emperor.[77]

In more general terms, the presence of numerous petitions suggests that the imperial authorities were compelled to respond to the needs of petitioners representing a broad spectrum of economic and social status. The reason for their involvement stems, as Peachin argues, from the expectations of the empire's subjects that the emperor would be the arbiter of justice and the source of legal recourse to the oppressed.[78] That the government's insistence on its legal authority was actually observed in the provinces is strongly suggested by the Albertini Tablets, deeds of sale from the Vandal period (493–96) in Africa. These sales involved parcels of land on an estate located in the predesert region, on the Algero-Tunisian border (discussed in chaps. 2 and 4). These documents are associated with what can fairly be described as a remote corner of the Roman Empire. Even so, the documents demonstrate the importance of Roman legal norms for the way in which residents of this area defined property rights and conducted their business.[79] If Roman law shaped the way in which small cultivators organized important financial transactions on a remote estate in the late fifth century, indeed in an area no longer under Roman authority, it seems all the more likely that Roman law played a significant role in the lives of people across the empire under the Principate. Corroborating evidence for this supposition comes from the archive of legal documents connected with a family's financial affairs that were hidden in a cave during the Bar Kochba War. The Babatha archive indicates that a second-century Jewish woman used Roman legal institutions, particularly those involving tutorship, to protect the interests of her family. This archive indicates that Babatha and other Jewish people had settled in the Nabataean kingdom in the late first century CE. Under Nabataean rule Babatha had conducted her affairs in accordance with Nabataean law, but after the Roman annexation of the kingdom in 106, the legal relations among members of Babatha's family were framed in accordance with Roman law.[80] So when, as I argue in subsequent chapters in connection with issues involving land tenure, the Roman government insisted on the ultimate authority of its courts to settle disputes, this was, in all likelihood, not simply an academic claim but one that had some bearing on the lives of the empire's residents.

Thus we might expect that the imperial government's involvement in settling disputes involving land tenure would offer a check on the unfettered power of larger landowners in their local communities. Indeed, the rescripts in the Code of Justinian enjoining landowners from altering the traditional terms of land tenure (to be discussed in chap. 4) were presumably preserved, like other such rescripts, because they addressed basic issues affecting land tenure. A key to the ability of small farmers to maintain their rights, then, was the availability of Roman legal institutions to which they could turn for protection.

We can appreciate the type of protection available to rural communities by considering a petition, preserved on papyrus, from the middle Euphrates region in 245 CE. This petition came from a group of villagers at a site called Beth Phouraia, and they addressed their petition to the brother of the emperor Philip the Arab, Iulius Priscus, who at that time was serving both as prefect of Mesopotamia and as governor of Coele Syria. It is in this latter capacity that the petitioners approached him (*P.Euphrates* 1).[81]

These four petitioners, Archodes son of Phalaios, Philotes son of Nisraiabos, Vorodes son of Sumisbarachcs, and Abedsautas son of Aberdiardas, describe themselves as being from an "imperial village" near the town of Appadana.[82] The petitioners in all likelihood cultivated land designated as imperial property. They were involved in a dispute of some duration with fellow villagers over the rights to land that they had been occupying, and they had sent a representative to Antioch, to the seat of Priscus, to present their case. After eight months of their waiting for an answer, Priscus finally responded that he would decide the case during his assize tour. In the meantime, the petitioners alleged that their rivals had forcefully evicted them from the land in question. The petitioners were requesting that Priscus order the imperial procurator at Appadana, Claudius Aristo, to issue an edict protecting them against forceful eviction from the land under dispute until the final adjudication of the case. Priscus' response was that the aforesaid procurator would rule on their petition. This procedure of referring the decision to the lower authority on the scene is often seen in petitions from Egypt, and we can imagine that the local authority would be expected to sort out the facts of the case after hearing both sides.

What is remarkable about this document is not only that, as Fergus Millar points out, peasants could have access to so high an authority in the Roman hierarchy.[83] Rather, the farmers from the imperial village seem well acquainted with the possible legal remedies open to them, including ones that were based on Roman private law.[84] Like their counterparts from Asia Minor (discussed in chap. 2), moreover, the petitioners referred to the imperial constitutions that protected people possessing lawfully from eviction from their property. We cannot be sure about the outcome of this petition. But the fact that the residents of the imperial village were able to go to such trouble to present their case to the Roman governor suggests they were not without resources of their own. The bottom line, however, was that the dispute over property rights would be judged by the appropriate authorities in the Roman government. Even cultivators in a seemingly remote location had access to the protection of imperial legal institutions, and they thought it worth their while to use them.

The efforts of the farmers from the imperial property at Appadana to gain protection from the Roman legal institutions suggest that residents of the empire had confidence that these institutions would work in the way they were intended.[85] This impression draws some confirmation from John Crook's study of the role of legal advocacy in the Roman world.[86] Crook's basic thesis is that legal advocacy, in which a professional advocate represented litigants in trials before Roman authorities, remained a fundamental aspect of the administration of justice throughout antiquity. Crook presents an array of evidence to show both that advocacy continued to function under the Principate and also that it played a major role in trials in the provinces. One important source of evidence for the role of advocacy is provided by documentary papyri from Roman Egypt. These papyri, often fragmentary, record proceedings before various types of judges in the province and preserve the speeches of advocates on behalf of their clients. The documents from Egypt suggest that there were professional advocates who followed the governor as he visited locations throughout the province to hear cases, and these advocates could be hired by people bringing a lawsuit, even by people of relatively humble status.

Some of the cases record the role advocates bore on issues concerning the rural economy. Thus a document of Domitianic date shows villagers using an advocate to defend themselves against a lawsuit by tax collectors for nonpayment of taxes (*P.Vindop.Worp* 1).[87] Another document records a case heard before the prefect Appius Sabinus about the obligations of certain villagers to perform liturgies in the metropolis of the Arsinoite nome (*SB* V 7696, ca. 250).[88] The villagers, represented by two advocates, were paired against representatives of the council of the metropolis, who had four advocates speaking on their behalf. One advocate representing three individual villagers cited a constitution of Septimius Severus, issued some fifty years previously, that exempted villagers from metropolitan liturgies; the metropolis' answer to this point was that the constitution had been issued under very different circumstances than obtained in the present day, when the finances of the cities in the empire were strained (lines 82–103). The point is that the villagers were in a position to gain knowledge of the relevant law to protect their interests, whatever the merits of their case might have been.

We can also see the role that the legal institutions of the state played in resolving agrarian disputes in a record of proceedings before the provincial governor (of the province of Aegyptius Herculea, after the early imperial province was divided into smaller administrative units; *P.Ryl.* IV 653, 321). The dispute in question pitted residents of two villages in the Arsinoite nome against one another over access to an irrigation canal. Both sides were apparently represented by advocates.[89] In another dispute from the same period, the adversaries were two sisters and certain residents of the village of Karanis, in the Fayum (the Arsinoite nome). At issue were tax obligations; the sisters were seeking to avoid tax liability for land that they had abandoned and that the villagers were compelled to cultivate

(*P.Col.* VII 175, 339). It is noteworthy in this case that the advocate for the villagers made an elaborate argument in applying the *praescriptio longissimi temporis* (the rule that set a forty-year limitation on suits for restitution of property).[90] An inscription from third-century Phrygia also discussed by Crook records a series of disputes, before imperial procurators, over the obligations of villages to provide draft animals for the imperial post (*SEG* XIII 625). In these hearings, the cases were argued by representatives from the villages, rather than professional advocates.[91]

Finally, an inscription from Syria records a hearing before the emperor Caracalla over a dispute about the priesthood of a temple dedicated to Zeus Hypsistos and located in the village of Goharia in Syria (*SEG* XVII 759, 216). The residents of the village had petitioned the emperor about the actions of an individual who had usurped the priesthood, and they were promoting their own candidate. Both sides were represented by advocates. In fact, the representative (*defensor*) of the petitioning villagers, Aurelius Carzeus, made use of the services of an advocate of high standing, Egnatius Lollianus, a senator famous for being an orator. The defendant was also represented by someone who was probably a senator and orator, Iulianus Aristaenetus. In view of the lofty status of the advocates, this case has been interpreted as a rhetorical exercise staged for the emperor's entertainment, but the fact that the villagers—described by their advocate as "your farmers," that is, imperial tenants—set up the inscription recording the trial suggests that the dispute was quite serious to them. Thus they used the inscription to commemorate the rights that they were able to preserve.[92]

If the legal institutions of the state played a greater role in establishing the conditions surrounding land tenure in the Roman Empire than has previously been acknowledged, it is also clear that understanding these legal institutions can only tell us part of the story of how the Roman rural economy functioned. Also important are the informal institutions (see the preceding), which played a profound role in determining how the individual actors in the economy, including state officials, large landowners, and tenants, used the state's legal institutions to advance their interests. Thus it is crucially important to ascertain to what extent the actors in the Roman rural economy respected the formal legal institutions of the state and abided by their norms, or by the decisions of Roman authorities. But in broader terms, the informal institutions of the state are a function of the expectations that these actors had about the Roman economy and, of particular interest for our purposes, the landowner-tenant relationship.

TOPICS OF INDIVIDUAL CHAPTERS

I divide my book into five major chapters, all of which are concerned with the implications that the Roman government's legal policies had for property rights. I begin by sketching the theoretical basis on which I examine the role of legal institutions in the Roman agrarian economy. In this connection, I believe that the concepts developed by scholars researching in the tradition of the New Institutional Economics provide useful theoretical tools for analyzing the Roman economy. Accordingly, in the first chapter, I explain in greater detail what I understand to be the principal contribution of the NIE approach for understanding the Roman economy, and then I illustrate in broad terms how the NIE approach can be applied to the Roman Empire.

In the second chapter, I explore the legal and economic principles that the Roman government followed in defining rights to land by examining the cultivation rights that it established on state-owned land. The focal point of this chapter is on the Roman government's response to petitions involving land-tenure rights on imperial estates in North Africa and Asia Minor. As I argue, the Roman government consistently protected the tenure rights of tenants on imperial estates, and this policy had important implications for tenure arrangements on private land.

In the third chapter, I examine farm tenancy on private estates, focusing on the degree to which Roman legal policy helped to overcome impediments to investment in agriculture, particularly those involving the tenant's security of tenure and the risk posed by weather. The legal policies of the Roman government tended to support the efforts of landowners and tenants to maintain mutually beneficial long-term tenure arrangements. The importance of long-term tenancy relationships in the Roman Empire created legal complications for the imperial government, however, as it sought to sort out competing rights and claims of landowners and tenants arising from local, customary tenure arrangements.

In the fourth chapter, then, I assess how the Roman legal authorities accommodated within the conventions of Roman law long-term tenure regimes that in all likelihood derived from local custom. The de facto tenure that the imperial government recognized for some classes of tenants created ambiguities in the competing rights of landowners and tenants. Beginning in the third century and continuing into late antiquity, we can trace how the Roman government sought to resolve these conflicting claims through its effort to create a legal order in the countryside. At the heart of this policy on the part of the Roman government was its insistence on the sole authority of Roman courts to resolve disputes involving the Roman economy. Accordingly, the Roman government actively discouraged the use of self-help by parties involved in legal disputes.

Finally, in the last chapter, I investigate how the binding of certain farmers to their land that began in the fourth century affected the efforts of the Roman government to define and enforce the property rights in agriculture explored in previous chapters. Of particular concern are the likely effects that imperial fiscal policy had on the incentives for investment in agriculture. Since *coloni* (tenants) were bound to the land and had rents that could not be raised, they had some incentive to invest in the productivity of the land. However, this positive incentive was countered by the disincentives for landowners, who had little capacity to realize any return. So the role of the government in the fourth century and afterward was to mediate between landowners and tenants, countering the increased bargaining power that tenants enjoyed and protecting tenants from exploitation on the part of powerful landowners.

I come to a more complete understanding of the Roman agrarian economy by analyzing how the various economic, fiscal, and legal policies of the Roman government impinging on agriculture affected this sector of the economy. Admittedly, it is not possible to quantify the economic benefit or loss that various groups in the Roman economy derived from the Roman state's legal policies. Even so, I believe that one can reasonably predict what economic relationships are likely to have arisen from the property rights as defined and supported by the Roman state. These economic relationships had important implications for the welfare of the various groups participating in the Roman economy, including the Roman state, large landowners, small landowners, tenants on private land, and tenants on imperial estates. The state's ability to protect property rights, in turn, depended on the strength of its legal institutions in regulating the rural economy, specifically on the degree to which Roman law and legal institutions governed relationships between Roman landowners and the bulk of the empire's farming population. Analyzing the role that the state played in the Roman economy allows us not only to evaluate more closely the strength of the Roman economy and even of the Roman state but also to situate the Roman economy in its proper historical place in relationship to other preindustrial economies.

CHAPTER I

The New Institutional Economics and Roman Legal Policy

In this chapter, I explore in greater detail the methodology that I use to analyze the role of law and legal institutions in the Roman agrarian economy. My purpose is to apply this methodology to understand better how the legal policies of the Roman state affected incentives for productive investment in the rural economy. Accordingly, I am concerned with tracing whether the Roman state's policies in creating and enforcing property rights facilitated productive contractual arrangements between landowners and tenants. The alternative is that the law simply protected the interests of well-placed groups, in particular landowners, at the expense of the economy in general.

In this analysis, I am primarily concerned with the *institutional arrangements*, especially contracts, that individuals made in conducting their business. But these arrangements should be considered in terms of the *institutional environment* surrounding the rural economy. This latter category includes both *formal* and *informal institutions*. The formal institutions include the rules that the Roman state established to define property rights, legal rules relating to farm tenancy and other aspects of land tenure, as well as the courts and other institutions through which individuals could defend their rights. The formal institutions also include policies of the Roman government, such as how it defined and defended property rights, how it mediated between competing claims by various classes of landowners and tenants, and, ultimately, whose property rights it tended to foster. But institutional environment also embraces the informal institutions that helped to determine how formal institutions worked, that is, the social values and practices that helped to establish the "rules of the game" for the rural economy in the Roman Empire.[1] Thus I investigate the institutional arrangements that private individuals and the state made in response to the legal environment maintained by the Roman state, as well as in response to the overall constraints limiting the possibilities for economic planning in the Roman world.

This type of analysis raises a major question at the outset, namely, whether and to what extent actors in the Roman economy, including the Roman state and private individuals, were capable of formulating consistent long-term plans that reflected a concern with pursuing wealth or otherwise maximizing their utility in accordance with the basic assumptions of neoclassical economic theory. The alternative to the basic assumption of neoclassical economic theory is that economic planning in the Roman Empire would be subsumed under the informal institutions of Roman society. In other words, the Roman economy would be "embedded," in the sense that social considerations would play the decisive role in determining the economic choices made by individuals. Moreover, these social values would also have played the decisive role shaping the legal institutions surrounding the Roman economy.[2]

It is difficult enough to analyze the role played by legal and social institutions in any economy, but for the Roman economy this task is especially difficult because of the incomplete nature of the documentation. But I believe we can overcome this problem to some degree by applying to the existing evidence some of the lessons from a rich body of literature on the relationship between law and the economy, especially the literature in the broad field of the New Institutional Economics. This literature offers a useful way of analyzing the issues raised in this study, both as they pertain to the policies of the Roman state and the institutional arrangements made by private individuals.[3] In making this assertion, I am not claiming that social factors had little influence on the economy. To the contrary, while recognizing the crucial role that social factors played, I also believe that we can learn a great deal about the economy by using the methodology of NIE to examine the economic incentives that legal arrangements created. This means that I seek to apply the basic approach of NIE, that is, to analyze the likely responses of economic actors to incentives created by various property rights and contractual arrangements as they seek to increase their wealth or utility in the face of uncertainty and the obstacles to making decisions posed by existing institutional arrangements. Admittedly, as Douglass North has recently argued, economists have not succeeded in developing a comprehensive theory to explain decision making in economic matters.[4] But at the same time, the methodology of NIE provides an approach to analyzing the incentives for investment created by Roman legal policies surrounding land tenure, even if we cannot hope to provide a comprehensive account of economic mentalities in the Roman Empire.

NIE builds upon neoclassical economics by taking into account the constraints affecting economic activity and decision making. Neoclassical economics analyzes the relationships among economic actors who are assumed to seek to maximize their wealth or utility. This utility that neoclassical economics posits as the basic concern of economic actors is usually understood as referring to maximizing wealth, but the term *utility* could also be understood more broadly to cover other types of concerns, such as economic security or even promoting social values. For the sake of analytical purposes, neoclassical economics posits that these actors pursue their utility with complete information about their welfare and the effects that changes in contractual arrangements will have on it. Consequently, neoclassical economics views economic actors as making rational decisions in pursuit of clearly defined and well-understood goals. At the same time, neoclassical economics posits that there are no costs (transaction costs) involved in enforcing the type of contractual arrangements that will promote utility or wealth maximization. As discussed in the following, the term *transaction costs* refers to the costs that an economic actor must bear when engaging in any form of economic activity. In NIE, transactions involve many costly activities, such as acquiring information about potential business partners, products, and alternative business arrangements; negotiating contracts; and enforcing contracts, whether through courts of law or through informal means. All of these activities involve costs, even if they are only measured in terms of time rather than money spent.

As critics of neoclassical economics have observed, its way of evaluating economic relationships seems too idealized to be useful for analyzing the economy of the contemporary world, since economic decision makers obviously do not have perfect information and transactions (i.e., moving from one allocation of property rights to another) are not costless by any means. Still less can neoclassical economics alone account for the economic relationships of the Roman Empire. Even so, neoclassical economics still provides an analytic basis to evaluate the relative efficiency of contractual arrangements and the likely economic implications of various distributions of property rights. The contribution of NIE, however, is to provide a theoretical basis on which to analyze economic relationships starting from more realistic assumptions about the real world. In the view of NIE, economic activity is subject to all sorts of constraints, or transaction costs.

Recognizing the same basic incentives that represent the premise of neoclassical economics, scholars working in the neoinstitutional tradition seek to analyze how the various ways in which property rights might be allocated affect the incentives to engage in the type of bargaining that would promote economic growth. In other words, neoinstitutional economics seeks to analyze the constraints that real-world conditions impose on economic behavior and, on the basis of analyzing these constraints, to explain the development of institutions and institutional arrangements.[5] "What is new is that we are now able to explain why the observed institutional arrangements are as they are," as Steven Cheung asserts.[6] One basic question raised by this approach is whether institutions evolve to achieve greater economic efficiency by reducing transaction costs, as Cheung argues, or, in the formulation of Gary Becker, "institutions evolve to increase the well-being of powerful groups that 'exploit' others, even when efficiency suffers."[7]

This new approach to analyzing economic relationships draws much of its inspiration from the work of Ronald Coase. Of particular significance is the analytical approach that Coase developed, which is now commonly referred to as the Coase Theorem. According to the Coase Theorem, the distribution of property rights and the precise form under which legal relationships are defined do not matter if transaction costs are zero, because the economic actors involved will find ways to bargain in such a way that rights and resources always find their highest-valued use.[8] This is the case as long as the property rights are defined fully. According to this principle, then, it does not matter what kind of legal structure surrounds the allocation of property rights, since, out of self-interest, people will bargain to promote their own utility. In other words, since transaction costs are zero, people will encounter no difficulty in bargaining to circumvent what might be at first sight inconvenient or inefficient legal rules, and they will have every incentive to seek a mutually agreeable bargain. In so doing, they will make arrangements according to which the people who value a given resource the most will be able to use it.[9] As Coase formulates the principle: "But it is to be remembered that the immediate question faced by the courts is *not* what shall be done by whom *but* who has the legal right to do what. It is always possible to modify by transactions on the market the initial legal delimitation of rights. And, of course, if such market transactions are costless, such a rearrangement of rights will always take place if it would lead to an increase in the value of production."[10] This is not to say, of course, that in the real world transaction costs are ever actually zero. Rather, the Coase Theorem expresses a basic relationship that provides a starting point for analyzing economic institutions.

It should be noted that defining transaction costs has been a subject of controversy in economic literature.[11] The approach to analyzing the role of transaction costs in economic activity that derives from Coase may be termed the *property rights* approach, and this is the one that has informed NIE. The property rights approach focuses on the economic rights a person might exercise over a piece of property. These economic rights would include the legal rights as defined by the state, but they would also include much more, in fact any use or enjoyment that a person might derive from a piece of property, such as what might arise from the use of a commodity, say water to irrigate land, that formally belongs to another person. As Yoram Barzel defines them, economic rights represent "an individual's ability, in expected terms, to directly consume the services of an asset, or consume it indirectly through exchange."[12] In the property rights approach, according to D. W. Allen, transaction costs may be viewed essentially as "the costs [of] establishing and maintaining property rights."[13] Such costs include ascertaining information, negotiating and enforcing contracts, and indeed any costs that "hint at the protection of property rights and implicitly recognize the threat of appropriation or theft."[14] In this approach, "every distribution of property rights" is viewed as carrying certain costs. The "grand hypothesis" of the property rights approach to transaction cost economics is that "the distribution of property rights that maximizes the gains from trade net of all costs is the optimal distribution."[15] This conception of transaction costs is to be contrasted to that of neoclassical economics, which takes a narrower definition, viewing transaction costs as the costs directly associated with "the transfer of property rights."[16] They do not include the costs of supervision (e.g., within a firm) but only "those costs that occur between firms or individuals from the process of market exchange."[17]

The Coase Theorem has often been interpreted as having a normative aspect, in that it is taken to provide a theoretical basis for the view that the free market allocates resources in the most efficient manner, assuming that property rights have been defined specifically. According to this view, the free market accomplishes this purpose much more efficiently than the government, for instance, since any government intervention (i.e., through regulation or tax policies) is likely to "make matters worse rather than better."[18] But as S. G. Medema and R. O. Zerbe, Jr., point out, the Coase Theorem is not a prescription for economic or legal policy but rather a statement of underlying relations. Its assumptions of clearly delineated property rights and costless exchange are admittedly unrealistic, but they provide a starting point for analyzing the efficiency of particular forms of economic organization.

The most significant analytical tool that the Coase Theorem provides is to assess forms of economic organization in terms of the transaction costs that they create, since these transaction costs represent an impediment to the gains that parties might achieve from exchange. So one task of economists is to assess what forms of economic organization carry higher transaction costs. Medema and Zerbe define the overall contribution of the Coase Theorem to economic analysis as follows:

> The Theorem is not, in the end, about markets or about costless bargaining; rather, it is about the costs of coordination. If coordination is costless, markets function perfectly; but so does government. If coordination is costly, markets function imperfectly; but so does government. The task for legal-economic policy thus becomes that of ascertaining the magnitude and influence of these costs and the resulting implications for alternative institutional-policy arrangements. The true and valuable legacy of the Theorem is all of the subsequent work on transaction costs that explore the costs of coordination under different regimes and in different situations.[19]

This transaction cost approach can be usefully applied to analyzing the economic relationships arising from the various forms of land tenure documented in the Roman Empire and the Roman government's legal policies in regulating land tenure. The issue, then, is to analyze how and to what extent the Roman government's legal policies specified property rights and facilitated exchange. As I argue, a transaction costs approach helps to explain the persistence of forms of land tenure that, from the point of view of neoclassical economics, might appear to be quite inefficient. But such tenure arrangements can be viewed as well suited to economic conditions in the Roman Empire if the costs of shifting to another arrangement, including those of negotiation and enforcement, were prohibitive or introduced side effects that imposed costs that Roman society was unwilling to bear. Indeed, what appears to have been the consistent policy of the Roman government to protect the tenure rights of small cultivators (as discussed in chap. 2) can be explained in this way. To be sure, one can imagine that the consolidation of small properties in many instances could lead to economies of scale and thus more productive forms of agriculture. But such consolidation might pose significant costs of enforcement on landowners or even the state, which would not be balanced by the additional revenues achievable through economies of scale.

The crucial role that law can play in promoting productive bargaining can be seen in analyses of this issue from the perspective of game theory. Of particular significance is the work of Robert Cooter, who seeks to nuance the application of the Coase Theorem by examining how bargains will be struck among parties bargaining with imperfect information.[20] In this situation, bargainers will engage in what is termed *strategic behavior*, that is, adjusting their own offers in accordance with their expectations of the preferences of the other party. According to Cooter's analysis, bargaining will not always result in cooperative outcomes because the strategy of the bargainer "is best against opponents on average, but not best against every individual opponent."[21] In the example that Cooter uses, the bargaining over the price of a car, if the buyer and seller cannot come to an agreement about the price, then the bargain will not take place, and as a result, the *surplus*, defined as "the joint benefits from cooperation" will be lost.[22] In other words, the buyer and seller will both be worse off having failed to reach an agreement over the price of a car that the former wanted to purchase and the latter wanted to sell.

In Cooter's perspective, then, the role of the law is not simply to remove obstacles to bargaining, as the Coase Theorem posits, since even with low transaction costs (i.e., low costs of obtaining information) a cooperative outcome may not occur. Cooter thus formulates a "Hobbes Theorem," based on the notion of a powerful sovereign establishing a legal order that protects humans from their baser nature. In Cooter's Hobbes Theorem, law should function to reduce the likelihood of "noncooperative outcomes" to bargaining.[23]

The concern of NIE for the effects of institutional arrangements on the economy suggests some important questions about the relationship between law and the rural economy in the Roman Empire, or, put another way, about the balance the state struck between fostering the interests of elite landowners (including the state itself) and promoting greater productivity in agriculture. Did the structure of property rights that defined land tenure on imperial estates and on privately owned land promote the kinds of bargains (e.g., between landowners and tenants) that would result in the sharing of resources for investment and greater productivity, or did this structure present obstacles to such bargaining? And if there were structural impediments to achieving more efficient forms of land tenure, did the Roman government intervene in any way to facilitate bargaining?

As I show in my analysis of the institutions surrounding the agrarian economy in the Roman Empire, there are no simple answers to these questions: if institutions such as farm tenancy did achieve a certain degree of efficiency, in view of the overall constraints imposed by conditions in the Roman world, they also tended to preserve the privileges of powerful landowners, who were not necessarily chiefly interested in achieving economic efficiency. At the same time, however, these institutions also helped to protect the interests of small farmers by protecting their property rights and so promoting a more egalitarian distribution of wealth. In the following pages, I sketch out how the problem can be approached.

To illustrate how the property rights approach based on transaction costs helps us to understand the economic consequences of land-tenure arrangements, let us consider the subject addressed in the next chapter, namely, the policy of the Roman government of maintaining ownership of large amounts of farmland in the Roman Empire. The Roman government maintained control of this land and assigned it to *coloni* to cultivate under perpetual leaseholds. This policy might be viewed as a hindrance to investment in agriculture by large-scale landowners, since much of the land would be in the hands of small farmers who themselves would want to cultivate this land to secure their livelihoods. But, according to the Coase Theorem, if the costs of transacting new contractual or ownership arrangements are zero, then the *coloni* will bargain with the large landowners to make the most efficient use of the resources in question. If this means that the most economically efficient outcome would involve all land winding up in the hands of large landowners, the original distribution of property rights would not inhibit this result. Furthermore, all parties would have used the bargaining process to maximize their utility, and the final result would be "Pareto efficient," in the sense that no further change in the distribution of property rights could be made to increase someone's utility without diminishing the utility of another person.[24]

In the real world, however, bargaining to exchange legal rights often imposes substantial costs, and in some circumstances it can be prohibitively expensive to bargain away property rights. The degree to which transacting is costly can vary considerably from one society to another, and a state may devise legal rules that make transacting more or less difficult. In some circumstances, the state can establish insurmountable legal barriers to the types of transactions that would result in the most economically efficient allocation of resources. In the case of the imperial estates, if the state protected the perpetual rights granted to the *coloni*, this policy could have effectively ruled out other potentially more productive land-tenure arrangements. In late antiquity, the laws binding *coloni* to the land made it very difficult for landowners and *coloni* to contract to find alternative ways to cultivate the land. Other constraints can be socially rather than legally imposed. Thus we might hypothesize that social considerations inhibited Pliny the Younger, a senatorial landowner who experienced continuing problems with his tenants, from kicking all of his tenants off of his estate and cultivating all of the land with slaves (as discussed in chap. 3).

UNCERTAINTY AND ECONOMIC CHOICE

The uncertainty that arises from the difficulty of acquiring information had an important effect on the persistence of particular forms of land tenure in the Roman Empire. The costs of information undoubtedly affected the strategies that ancient landowners and tenants followed, as well as the policies that the Roman government established as it sought to mediate between the interests of these two groups. When neoclassical economics assumes that economic actors make rational choices in pursuing their utility, it posits that economic actors have full information at their fingertips, both of what their utility is and of the steps that can be taken to maximize it. One of the contributions of the NIE approach to economic analysis is to account for the role that uncertainty plays in economic decision making.

The uncertainty model of NIE traces some of its roots back to the work of Armen A. Alchian, in particular, to his very influential 1950 article about the role of uncertainty in economic analysis.[25] In Alchian's view, people find their economic way in a world fraught with uncertainty, and it is for all practical purposes impossible for an economic actor to know fully the consequences of any economic decision. Again, the amount of information that an economic actor will have at his or her disposal will vary from one circumstance to another, but no one ever has complete information. Consequently, we cannot analyze economic decision making simply in terms of the rational pursuit of wealth or utility maximization, since it will be impossible for any individual to know fully how to attain this or even to recognize when he or she has achieved this goal.

Particularly useful for understanding economic decision making in the face of limited and costly information are the concepts of *bounded rationality* and *satisficing* decisions developed by Herbert Simon. According to Simon, our ability to make rational decisions in the sense of neoclassical economics is limited because we never have perfect information. This does not mean that we make irrational decisions, but that our rationality is bounded by our limited understanding of the world in which we live. Simon distinguishes between *substantive* and *procedural* rationality, with the latter concept adapted from cognitive psychology. Substantive rationality posits that the decision maker's knowledge of the world is unlimited, whereas procedural rationality views this knowledge as subject to constraints. In Simon's view, "the rational person of neoclassical economics always reaches the decision that is objectively, or substantively, best in terms of the given utility function."[26] All we would need to predict with certainty the decision of a given person, then, would be knowledge of his or her utility function. But in Simon's view, it is more useful to see people making decisions in accordance with procedural rationality (i.e., decisions that make sense in terms of the person's knowledge). Satisficing decisions solve problems on the basis of this type of rationality. These are decisions that do not necessarily result in the optimal allocation of resources. Rather, they enable a person to achieve a desired goal in terms of the means available, which ultimately depend on the knowledge at his or her disposal.[27] It should be noted, however, that empirical studies indicate that the bases on which people make decisions in contracts and other economic matters are often more complicated than assumed in standard economic analysis, which is based on "rational choice theory."[28]

To return to the theory of Alchian, given the lack of information surrounding any economic decision, and the impossibility for any economic actor to know fully the consequences of any particular action, we cannot analyze economic decisions in terms of wealth or utility maximization. Instead, we need to recognize that people or institutions will find various strategies to pursue what they perceive to be their utility in a changing world that they understand imperfectly. There will be winners and losers. Some people will react to changing economic circumstances by undertaking risky innovations that make them (or their institutions) successful and wealthy, while others will adopt innovative but risky strategies that will prove disastrous. Still others will react more cautiously. But the point is that even if some actors display greater wisdom and understanding than others, none of them act on the basis of complete knowledge. So it is possible that someone who otherwise might be considered reckless will wind up being wildly successful, but often such success should be more attributed to good fortune rather than to any special virtue. Others who are just as smart will fail. But most people will fall back on time-honored arrangements that, in the past, have proven beneficial.[29] The success of such decisions is measured in the extent to which they leave the person in question in an incrementally better position than before, but this cannot be understood as the same thing as maximizing wealth or utility, because the person in question could never measure whether his or her wealth or utility is in fact maximized—there is no way to test alternatives.

Instead of applying neoclassical techniques to the analysis of decision making, Alchian proposes to view the development of contractual forms and economic organization more along the lines of evolutionary biology, with certain forms surviving because of chance selection rather than because of the rational choices of economic decision makers. But as critics of this evolutionary approach have pointed out, the institutions that survive are not always the most efficient (assuming that the efficiency of institutions can be measured). Indeed, institutions often find ways to perpetuate themselves even at the expense of economic growth.[30] The traditional techniques of neoclassical economics, however, do make it possible to analyze the likely effects of certain contractual forms and economic decisions, given a hypothetical set of economic conditions. The point is that economic actors will rarely have enough information to understand fully the conditions under which they are forced to make economic decisions, and so they will pursue strategies that they think will enhance their welfare. Whether such strategies are the best possible ones is a question that no one can answer.

RATIONALITY IN ROMAN ECONOMIC PLANNING AND LEGAL POLICY

The concepts of bounded rationality and transaction costs that underlie the approach of NIE provide a useful starting point for analyzing Roman legal and economic institutions. The concept of bounded rationality allows us to trace overall economic goals informing the legal policy of the Roman state and the economic planning of individual actors without having to posit that the state and private individuals had sufficient knowledge of the economy to pursue economic goals rigorously and systematically by finding suitable forms of investment and measuring one form of investment against another. In the agrarian economy, such rationality on the part of landowners or the state would involve measuring the relative returns of one form of production against another and choosing among alternative strategies to manage agricultural properties in such a way as to realize revenues or profits commensurate with the risks involved in cultivating various crops.

So if we reject as a starting point for analyzing the Roman agrarian economy the view that actors in the Roman economy pursued wealth with complete knowledge of the alternative strategies available to them and the ability to switch costlessly from one form of investment to another, we must also reject the view that neither the Roman government nor Roman landowners were capable of systematic, long-term economic planning. What can usefully be characterized as rationality in the Roman economy lay somewhere between these two extremes. The high level of rigor attainable in ancient economic planning is suggested by the Heroninos archive, which documents the management of portions of an estate in the Fayum in Egypt (ancient Arsinoite nome) belonging to Aurelius Appianus, a member of the provincial aristocracy in Egypt in the third century.

This archive, consisting of some 650 documents, including accounts and letters exchanged among administrators, indicates that the managers of the estate implemented a complex system of management that involved minimizing costs through the sharing of resources among the various divisions of the estate. At the same time, the detailed accounts made possible a great deal of planning and monitoring of the costs of production.[31] In his groundbreaking analysis of the Heroninos archive, Dominic Rathbone argues that the management of the estate of Appianus was conducted on economically rational lines, oriented toward the production of crops to make the maximum profit possible for the owner, given the overall constraints limiting an estate owner's capacity to manage his or her land. Rathbone's analysis of the estate is based on a hypothesis that there was a free market for both the crops produced on the estate and for the labor that the estate employed. This interpretation, however, has recently been challenged by Jean Andreau and Jérôme Maucourant, who, skeptical of the possibility of the free markets Rathbone hypothesizes, interpret the organization of the estate as resulting more from power relations in the Egyptian countryside rather than from an economically rational pursuit of profit.[32]

The cautions of Andreau and Maucourant about the imperfection of the markets for labor and agricultural commodities are well taken, and as they argue, social relations surely played a significant role in influencing the organization of the estate of Appianus and presumably of other estates in the Roman Empire. At the same time, the recognition of these factors does not seem to be incompatible with the principle that the owner of an estate in the Roman Empire was motivated by a desire to increase profits and so organized an estate in such a way as to achieve this goal. From the perspective of NIE, what Andreau and Maucourant describe could be viewed as the formal and informal institutional constraints limiting a Roman estate owner's scope for action. The existence of such constraints would not diminish the landowner's motivation to improve his or her financial situation but would rather affect the ways in which a landowner would go about this task—and the willingness of a landowner to invest in an overall economy with limited growth and uncertain returns. Admittedly, Andreau and Maucourant would question even this premise, seeing the Roman economy as embedded in social values that trumped economic motivations.[33]

To turn to the Roman state, the assumptions of bounded rationality and transaction costs help to explain the policies of the Roman legal authorities when they implemented policies with significant economic consequences. On a broad level, the Roman government viewed the cultivation of the land as the most basic duty of the empire's population, since it was only through this that tax revenues vital for the defense of the empire could be raised. This ideology finds expression in a decree issued in 215 CE by the emperor Caracalla, who expelled native Egyptians from the city of Alexandria to prevent them from fleeing their villages of origin and avoiding their duty to cultivate the land (*Sel.Pap*. II 215).[34] Finally, agriculture provided the basis of the most important social programs of the empire, including the distributions of grain and other foodstuffs in Rome, as well as the state-sponsored and private alimentary foundations in various cities in Italy and the provinces.[35]

In various areas of private law, a similar conception about the importance of agriculture informed the Roman government's policies. One example would be the law of tutorship. One of the principal aims of tutorship was to safeguard the financial interests of fatherless children, especially those of the elite. Roman law defined very carefully the obligations of tutors in administering the property of pupils or wards and imposed severe sanctions on tutors who were deemed to have failed in their obligations.[36] Accordingly, to make sure that pupils had the financial resources necessary to maintain a standard of living befitting their family's status, the Roman government required tutors administering their property to invest their wealth in land. At the same time, the government restricted the capacity of the tutor to sell or otherwise alienate land belonging to a pupil, since doing so might threaten the pupil's financial security. In the legal policy of the Roman government, agriculture represented the preeminent form of investment providing economic security, so any action that a tutor took in managing the property of a pupil was, if possible, to preserve the pupil's access to an income from his or her lands.[37] This is not to imply that there were not other methods for upper-class Romans to achieve safe incomes, but from the point of view of establishing a legal policy to be applied broadly across the Roman Empire, the Roman government simplified matters by ignoring other possible ways of investing and imposed severe restrictions on the tutor's discretion in managing the pupil's property.

The legal rules surrounding the duties of the tutor derived from a belief that the Roman government shared with elite Romans about the preeminent value of land as a form of economic security. At the same time, the restrictions on the tutor's scope for action also helped to create a set of workable and predictable rules that tutors could apply when managing their pupils' property and avoid liability for mismanagement. A set of rules that recognized all the possibilities for investing property and judged the actions of tutors on the basis of individual circumstances rather than broad principles might have promoted a more optimal investment of resources, but such rules would probably have been overly complex and resulted in numerous difficult legal disputes. In view of the difficulty of developing more-nuanced rules, the Roman state sought to achieve a social goal by privileging agriculture as a form of investment. It allowed the tutor to make other types of investments of the pupil's funds, particularly in loans, only when sufficient funds were not available for the purchase of land. This simplification of economic reality helped to create a set of rules that could be enforced by the state at reasonable cost. One of the costs imposed on society was constraining the market for agricultural land, as Richard Saller has suggested. If as many as one-third of all children lost their fathers before the age of puberty, then the rules that the government and the jurists developed for the administration of a pupil's property surely affected the availability of agricultural property for purchase as well as the way in which a great deal of agricultural property was managed.[38] The law of tutorship was designed to achieve a social goal, and it was rooted in general upper-class conceptions of the value of land as a form of economic security.

The methodologies of the NIE, I would argue, help us to analyze the capacity of the Roman government to formulate and implement long-term legal policies involving land tenure. Rather than simply rejecting the possibility that it could pursue any long-term legal policy with economic consequences, we should rather analyze the Roman government's policies in terms of its efforts to achieve certain basic goals in the face of the constraints posed by bounded rationality and transaction costs. Fergus Millar, in his synthetic study of the governmental activities of the Roman emperor, outlines the basic constraints limiting the government's scope for action. Millar concludes that the imperial government lacked the institutional capability of formulating long-term policies in many areas of administration.[39] Specifically, according to Millar, there was little systematic maintenance of information, and the Roman emperor, who spent much of his time answering petitions from subjects on a wide range of issues, tended to formulate administrative policy on an ad hoc basis, in reaction to problems that petitions from individuals or communities presented. Adding to the institutional problems connected with the difficulties of gathering information was the questionable competence of many of the individuals involved in administering Roman legal policy. The Roman government had no real civil service, and appointments to governmental posts were regularly made on the basis of patronage rather than merit.[40] The judges in the provinces responsible for applying policies formulated by the central government might be ill informed about the law itself, or worse, they might tend to judge cases not on the merits of the law but on the basis of social considerations so that a litigant of humble status would stand little chance of prevailing over a better-connected opponent.[41] Indeed, as John Lendon argues, honor was a basic value, even an ideology, that defined status and reinforced the hierarchical structure of Roman society by fostering obedience to imperial authority by the empire's subjects. Thus the sense of honor at the core of Roman aristocratic values might trump other considerations when Roman officials implemented Roman legal policy, including the legitimate basis of a legal claim made by a litigant of humble status.[42]

LEGAL INSTITUTIONS AND THE ENFORCEMENT OF POLICY

If the law was to play a role in the economy, it was crucial for the Roman state to maintain the authority of its legal institutions in spite of a range of factors that made this task difficult. Roman policymakers (i.e., the jurists and the Roman chancery) strove to assert the centrality of the law in resolving legal disputes, even if they could not always count on their agents, the local officials often deciding cases, to carry out their intentions.[43] These efforts helped to provide some protection for smaller farmers when they were in conflict over property rights with larger landowners. The central role played by law does not mean that all disputes were decided in courts of law, but the possibility of going to court influenced how disputes surrounding land tenure might be resolved. Indeed, the influence of the wealthy and well connected notwithstanding, the Roman government itself professed as one of its guiding principles the protection of the humble from oppression by the stronger party. This principle remained a central theme to Roman legislation both in the Principate and in the later Roman Empire.[44] To be sure, as Jill Harries argues, the efficacy of the laws in protecting individuals depended on the individuals' knowledge of the law, and in this respect, the imperial government provided its subjects some help.

Under the Principate, the access to the emperor's justice afforded by the *libellus* (petition) procedure put the central Roman government in a position of resolving local disputes. When litigants appealed to the emperor seeking legal support, the state would intervene in the rural economy and impose legal solutions to disputes based on conventional Roman norms. In the later empire, the major contribution that the imperial government could make in this respect occurred when it undertook to codify imperial constitutions and legal literature, first under Theodosius II (in 439) and then later, and to a more comprehensive degree, under Justinian. These efforts at codification represented part of a great effort to standardize the laws.[45] The fact that the laws could not be standardized completely does not diminish the significance of the effort.

The state's method of responding to legal disputes in the *libellus* procedure helped to foster a legal order in the countryside. Such a legal order did not in and of itself define land-tenure arrangements, but rather it delineated the distribution of property rights that would be decisive when negotiations between landowners and tenants broke down and the parties turned to the legal institutions of the Roman state to resolve disputes.[46] The possibility of going to court is likely to have influenced how landowners and tenants negotiated terms of land tenure. In addition, the creation of normative methods to resolve disputes and the availability of the petitioning process surely created incentives for people to become familiar with Roman laws and procedures to gain access to the protection afforded by the state's legal institutions.

Admittedly, the efficacy of Roman legal policy was continually countered by the sheer difficulty of enforcing laws in a consistent manner across a diverse empire. This situation certainly compromised the authority of Roman institutions and no doubt led economic actors to pursue solutions that did not involve the intervention of Roman legal authorities. As I discuss in greater detail in chapter 3, the difficulty of enforcement tended to lead to land-tenure systems that were in some respects outside the control of the law. In this situation, we might expect landowners and tenants to have based their relationships on norms based largely on social values or custom that were not necessarily consistent with state-sanctioned law.[47]

Still, the Roman state constantly struggled to assert the authority of its courts and other legal institutions to settle disputes involving the agrarian economy. This effort to establish the authority of Roman legal institutions may well have led to a degree of institutional *path dependence*. Path dependence is a concept usually applied in analyzing the choice of technologies. In path dependence, the increasing returns resulting from an initial choice, whether of a technology or an institutional arrangement, make the costs of shifting to other arrangements too high. There is a great deal of controversy about the extent to which initial choices in technology make the future adoption of more efficient technologies cost prohibitive.[48] But institutional path dependence is a theme that Douglass North emphasizes in his analysis of the relationship between institutions and the economy. North's application of this concept can help to explain why legal systems can be slow to adapt in the face of inefficiency.[49]

To apply this concept to land tenure in the Roman Empire, the initial choices that the Roman government made in defining property rights in the rural economy tended to reinforce themselves, whether or not they resulted in the most efficient allocation of resources. The Roman state would tend to adjudicate disputes in terms of established law rather than by creating new law, and this established law would set the conditions in accordance with which landowners and tenants likewise would arrange their own relationships as they adapted themselves to the institutional and economic environment of the Roman Empire. This is the evolutionary model that Geoffrey Hodgson has developed to explain the development of firms in their manifold forms.[50] However, any success on the part of the Roman government in asserting the authority of its legal institutions would have tended to favor the interests of smaller farmers. It would be to the advantage of smaller farmers if their relationships with their landowners were conducted in accordance with state-sanctioned legal norms rather than social conventions outside the purview of the law. Such conventions would surely have favored the interests of economically and socially powerful landowners.

ECONOMIC INSTITUTIONS IN THE ROMAN EMPIRE

Two fundamental factors shaped the role that legal institutions played in the countryside in the Roman Empire: the development of large private estates and the growing role of the state as a landowner. In the sphere of private landownership, Roman rule fostered the creation of large estates in the provinces, as the elite of the Roman Empire, including the senatorial and equestrian orders as well as the members of town councils, came to be made up of wealthy landowners throughout the more urbanized provinces.

Over the course of the early empire, landownership became increasingly stratified, and it seems clear a greater portion of wealth was concentrated in fewer hands.[51] Elite landowners took advantage of the commercial opportunities offered by the Roman Empire by producing cash crops, including wine and olive oil, for urban markets, and they used the wealth that they derived from agriculture to increase the extent of the land that they controlled.

Where urbanization was a product of Roman rule, in the western provinces, especially, an emerging elite derived its social privileges from the ownership of large estates. The pace of estate development varied from province to province, but in general, the western provinces saw the development of a municipal elite class that was socially and politically dominant and derived its wealth from agriculture. In Gaul, for example, Greg Woolf has traced the development of Italian-style *villae* in the first two centuries CE. These *villae* were in all likelihood on the order of one hundred to two hundred *iugera* (twenty to forty hectares) in size.[52] In Africa, one of the major transformations of the landscape under Roman rule was the creation of large estates producing olive oil; these estates had central installations with numerous oil presses. They were to be found in many locations, such as the Kasserine plain and in Tripolitania in the region surrounding Lepcis Magna.[53] Beginning especially in the Flavian period, the province of Baetica in Spain underwent a similar transformation, with the development of numerous substantial villa sites, particularly in the Guadalquivir valley. Baetican estates produced grain, wine, and olive oil for export, primarily to Rome. The Baetican agrarian economy provided an important source of wealth not just for senators and equestrians but for a much larger group of independent landowners.[54] The elite classes in the urbanized eastern provinces, which had existing municipal structures when Roman rule began, also benefited from the economic opportunities offered by Roman rule.[55]

The eastern empire also experienced increasing stratification of landownership, although the pace of development of large estates was connected with the presence of municipal structures when Roman rule began. In Asia Minor, a provincial elite that included wealthy people from Italy began creating large estates from the time of Augustus.[56] Large estates also developed in Egypt, beginning in the second century but especially in the third, possibly as the result of the establishment by Septimius Severus of a municipal structure similar to that found in other urbanized areas of the empire. In the third century, Egypt saw the rise of a provincewide landowning elite. The most famous example is Aurelius Appianus, the owner of the large estate in the Fayum region described in the Heroninos archive (on which, see the preceding). Aurelius Appianus, a councilor in Alexandria, was also a member of the equestrian order, and other large landowners in this period occupied a similar status.[57] In other regions of the eastern empire, such as Palestine, the development of large estates came later, beginning in the fourth century.[58]

These large estates were organized in a variety of ways, including with slaves, with free labor hired on a short-term basis, and with tenants, themselves occupying their land under a wide variety of arrangements. For much of the Roman Empire, we have little direct evidence for how labor was organized on the estates belonging to the landowning elite, and so we must determine what seems to have been the most likely organization of labor based on the evidence that we do have from some parts of the empire. In general, it seems likely that large estates were organized much like the *latifundia* that came to characterize much of agriculture in Italy during the early and later empire, with sprawling estates that consisted of numerous individual farms. These estates are likely to have been economic units only in a limited sense, with some sharing of centrally maintained resources, such as olive installations, whereas the individual farms would have been cultivated independently from one another, sometimes occupied by tenants.[59] This may also have been the pattern on privately owned estates in North Africa, where in certain locations centrally located olive-oil factories, with numerous olive presses, may have served extensive estates producing olive oil and other crops, such as wheat, which was often cultivated between the olive trees. How such estates were organized is uncertain, but one likely scenario is that they were divided into numerous individual farms under the supervision of tenants, who pressed their olives at the central facility and paid their landowner their rent out of the proceeds.[60] In the eastern part of the empire, estates often subsumed villages (see chap. 2).

My concern is to analyze the role that law and legal institutions played in the diverse tenure arrangements of the Roman agrarian economy. In all likelihood, many important aspects of the agrarian economy, such as the organization of estates, the decision whether or not to lease, the choice of contractual forms, and the crops to be cultivated, developed on the basis of factors outside the law, including geography and the customs of the regions involved, not to mention the social and economic power of the elite landowners, as emphasized by Andreau and Maucourant.[61] Even under these circumstances, the law and legal institutions could play a decisive role in shaping the relationships between landowners and tenants. Legal rules could modify traditional arrangements in such a way as to enhance economic exchange.[62] Another possibility is that the state would enforce certain property rights at the expense of efficiency. Thus the Roman state might have been motivated by "distributional" considerations, for example, by protecting the rights to land of small-scale cultivators, even if larger landowners might be in a position to put the land to a more profitable use. In addition, the state might raise barriers to bargaining for political purposes as well.

THE ROMAN STATE AS A PROPERTY OWNER

The tendency for large estates to develop in various regions of the empire over time suggests that the Roman government generally established and protected the property rights of elite landowners. However, the growth and influence of private estates were to some extent mitigated by the considerable role that the state played as a landowner. Since the state was by far the largest landowner in the Roman Empire, the administrative policies that it followed affected the terms of land tenure on a significant portion of the empire's most productive farmland. As I argue, the Roman state's policies in administering its estates were likely to have had enormous consequences for the Roman agrarian economy as a whole. To some extent, the state's fiscal interests may have worked to impede the growth of the large estates of the empire's elite. The policy of the state to maintain direct control over vast tracts of land throughout the provinces surely inhibited the accumulation of land in private hands and fostered the continuing existence of a class of cultivators independent from the domination by private landowners.

In administering its own properties, the Roman government faced a complex set of interests and conflicts. During the early empire, the Roman government maintained control over a vast complex of properties, including mines and agricultural lands.[63] This property was under the general administration of the imperial treasury, or Fiscus, which was headed by an official of equestrian rank, the *procurator a rationibus*.[64] State-owned property consisted of the land and other property belonging to the emperor, and this category included both the emperor's own personal property as well as the patrimony passed on from one emperor to the next. In addition, imperial property included land that might be more conventionally defined as state land, such as the land once owned by the monarchies in states that became Roman provinces. The best example of this is the various categories of lands in Egypt under the control of the Ptolemies that became imperial properties when Egypt came under Roman rule. Imperial estates also included the property of condemned criminals, people who had defaulted on fiscal obligations, and intestate landowners. Once such properties passed into imperial control through bequest or confiscation, they were administered as state land. In many parts of the Roman Empire, the imperial government not only was the largest landowner but also controlled a quite considerable portion of the productive land. This was certainly the case in Egypt, where public land (*ge demosie*) represented a large portion of the arable land in virtually every nome.[65] The portion of land in imperial hands was also quite substantial in Africa and probably in many other provinces of the empire.

Imperial properties furnished substantial revenues, supplying wheat and olive oil, for example, for the *annona* at Rome (the state-sponsored programs of food distribution). In addition, revenues from imperial estates helped to support the army as well as the imperial bureaucracy. The Roman government maintained control over its properties as a means to safeguard its access to much needed foodstuffs. In this way, it avoided having to depend on what was apparently an insufficiently stable private market for such products.[66] In the early empire, the properties over which the central government exercised control almost certainly grew considerably in their extent. Although the state would sell or donate some of its property to private owners, on balance, the state's acquisition of agricultural properties through confiscation or bequest seems to have far outstripped any transfer back to private ownership. Even the immense estate of Aurelius Appianus in Egypt passed to the control of the state by the year 276, not long after Appianus' death.[67] Imperial estates clearly represented crucially important assets to the Roman government. The government would normally only sell or give imperial property away when it was derelict. The state rarely if ever resorted to selling off productive agricultural properties to meet fiscal emergencies, although it might auction off imperial treasures.[68]

The consequences for the private rural economy of extensive state landownership are apparent in several provinces. In Egypt, as can be seen in Michael Sharp's study of landowning patterns in the village of Theadelphia in the Fayum during the second century, access to public land fostered a more egalitarian distribution of wealth, with a class of public tenants side by side, and possibly overlapping with small-scale landowners resident in the village. All of this tended to work against the domination of the village economy by outside landowners, who did, however, seem to be interested primarily in developing vineyards in the village territory.[69] To be sure, there were some large estates in Egypt in the Ptolemaic period, but extensive private estates especially became a prominent feature of Egypt's agricultural economy in the third century CE.[70] There are of course many reasons why Egypt was slower than other provinces to develop large estates. Indeed, the growth of large privately owned estates in the third century may have been spurred by the development of a municipal elite at that time similar in economic status and political outlook to the political elites of other urbanized parts of the Roman Empire.[71] In Africa, the government worked to create private, taxable property alongside its imperial estates. This effort can be seen in the development of *castella* (walled towns) in Mauretania Caesariensis into quasi-municipal entities in the early third century. This land was not simply turned over to large estate owners, if there were indeed any, but was rather in the hands of what appear to have been more modest landowners.[72]

If the state kept a great deal of productive land out of the hands of private landowners, this is not to say that the state's policy of confiscating land for various reasons seriously undermined the security of private property rights. For the most part, property passed into the ownership of the Fiscus only under clearly defined circumstances, such as the absence of lawful heirs or tax arrears. The occasional substantial confiscation of estates of high-ranking Romans convicted of treason or for other political offenses, as happened on the largest scale under Septimius Severus (193–211) in the aftermath of civil war, certainly affected the fortunes of many wealthy Romans and must have, at least on occasion, created an atmosphere of uncertainty that diminished incentives for investment. But such confiscations did not lead to the economic collapse of the landowning elite in the Roman Empire and so did not seem to have undermined the Roman state's strong commitment to the maintenance of private property rights.[73]

It is not possible to say whether the state's policy in maintaining control over imperial estates represented the most economically efficient allocation of resources, in the sense of maximizing production, and it is doubtful that the people in charge of the empire's finances could have made such a calculation.[74] The imperial administration sought to achieve particular goals, such as making sure that the state had adequate revenues and also access to supplies of basic foodstuffs that were distributed in Rome or used to support the armies in the field. In this sense, the development of the system of imperial estates represented a satisficing solution to the problem of securing vital resources. This is not to say that the fiscal administration in the Roman government did not recognize any of the costs of its policies, but it adopted the system of exploiting the imperial estates that is documented in the sources because this seemed to be a reasonable way of ensuring the Roman state its access to revenues and food supplies. So even if this might not have been the best system in all possible worlds of exploiting the resources represented by the imperial estates, it nonetheless accomplished a particular set of goals.

The Roman administration did not have the luxury of experimenting with many different ways of managing these estates, and it could not have tested the outcomes of these experiments until it was long too late. Instead, we should imagine that the state developed its strategy of managing the imperial estates based on its previous experience with managing agricultural property and its general albeit imperfect understanding of the changing economic conditions of the Roman Empire. In addition, its policies may have been influenced by ideological considerations, such as protecting the tenure of the small farmer against inroads by large and powerful landowners. At the same time, the initial endowment of property rights by the Roman administration, such as the perpetual leaseholds granted to imperial *coloni* in North Africa in the early imperial period, created its own institutional path dependence, since this endowment of rights would dictate how the estates would be exploited and so would also set the parameters for the continuing administrative policy of the Roman government. So the imperial estates as economic institutions would develop on the pathway established by initial policy decisions made for whatever reason by the Roman government.

In view of the large share of the rural economy they represented, analyzing land tenure on imperial lands helps us to gauge the range of possible solutions available to private landowners seeking to exact wealth from their estates. In this connection, it is not sufficient simply to examine the contractual arrangements that existed among the imperial tenants, the imperial administration, and, when applicable, the large-scale lessees who collected the rent from the tenants. Rather, we must also examine how the state enforced property rights on the imperial estates and resolved conflicts that arose in connection with these rights. As Barzel suggests, a state will only define and enforce those property rights whose enforcement is advantageous to the state, since such enforcement is costly.[75] In doing so, the state will seek to achieve "economies of scale" (i.e., in enforcing property rights by adjudicating disputes in such a way that will have clear applicability to other parties in similar situations). However, the state will tend not to bother with adjudicating disputes that are idiosyncratic in nature and have no wider applicability.[76]

The terms of land tenure that the state established on imperial estates are also significant because they must have affected the contractual arrangements between private landowners and their tenants. Since the state owned substantial properties in many regions of the empire, the terms of tenure that it offered its tenants necessarily affected the tenure arrangements on purely private land. In the most general terms, then, the emergence of the Roman state as the largest landowner in the empire by far must have mitigated, to some degree at least, the power that large private landowners could exercise over the farmers cultivating their estates. Imperial estates offered favorable terms of land tenure for tenants. If these terms did not draw tenants away from private landowners, they at least created competition with private landowners for the services of tenants. Such competition surely affected the terms of tenure of private farm tenants, even if the growing power of large landowners and the concomitant subjection of much of the rural population must be acknowledged.

To conclude, the debate from the New Institutional Economics suggests that the law and legal institutions played a quite complex role in the Roman agrarian economy. This role went beyond simply supporting the social and economic privileges of the landowning elite or, alternatively, defending the empire's smaller farmers against the power of this elite. Rather, an approach to understanding land tenure in the Roman Empire based on NIE suggests both some of the general constraints that affected the choices of economic actors and the policies of the Roman government, as well as the likely implications that various institutional arrangements had for the interests of the actors involved in the Roman agrarian economy, including the state, larger landowners, and smaller farmers.

These arrangements can be analyzed in terms of the likely economic goals of the parties involved, and they affected the incentives for investment on the part of landowners and tenants. In the following chapters, I examine in greater detail the institutional arrangements that shaped land tenure in the Roman Empire. I begin by examining imperial estates to understand better the basic economic goals of the Roman government and the most important impediments to reaching these goals. Afterward, I turn to the question of how the state mediated between the interests of private landowners and tenants, as well as how these groups adapted to the institutional arrangements fostered by the state.

CHAPTER 2

The Creation of Rights in the Countryside

We can appreciate the capacity of the Roman government to develop legal policies for land tenure by considering its efforts to manage the well-documented imperial estates in North Africa and Asia Minor. These estates are known to us from a series of inscriptions from the second and third centuries CE. The inscriptions include regulations defining land tenure as well as petitions to the imperial government from tenants seeking to defend their rights. These important documents, then, allow us to discern, at least to some degree, the principles that the Roman government followed in establishing property rights on imperial estates and in resolving conflicts arising from the competing claims among the groups involved in cultivating this land. The policies that the government pursued in managing imperial estates, moreover, inform us more broadly about the rural economy, since these policies were a product of the general overall constraints limiting the scope for economic development in the Roman world and also influenced the conditions surrounding land tenure on private land. Consequently, an analysis of the Roman government's approach to defining property rights on imperial estates will help to clarify how it dealt with these same constraints as it sought to resolve legal issues connected with private farm tenancy. In discussing property rights, I am referring not simply to rights of ownership, as formally defined by law, but instead to any rights that individuals or groups might exercise over a piece of property, no matter who the ultimate owner of the property might be. It might be more appropriate to use the term *economic rights*.[1]

The system of land tenure that the Roman government maintained on imperial estates was a product of its efforts to achieve specific long-term economic goals. It is a likely hypothesis that the government maintained direct control over imperial estates, especially in important food-producing provinces, to ensure its access to crucial agricultural products, particularly grain and olive oil.[2] Imperial estates in the provinces supplied revenues in kind that helped to provide food for the politically sensitive distribution programs in Rome, and the revenues from imperial estates, both in foodstuffs and in cash, also supplemented the revenues achieved by the taxation of private land to support the infrastructure of the government. In maintaining a vast system of estates, the government could assure itself of direct access to important foodstuffs and avoid having to compete for them on the open market. Given the frequency of drought in the Mediterranean world and the possibility of localized but serious food shortages, the risks of depending on the private market alone to supply food for Rome were too high for the Roman government to bear.[3] The decision to lease imperial property out to small-scale tenants, then, can be seen as a solution to the problem of achieving stable revenues in the face of the uncertainty surrounding other methods of exploitation and the highly imperfect markets that characterized trade in the Roman world. This policy was grounded in long-term considerations for stable revenues, rather than from an effort to extract immediate short-term revenues from imperial properties.[4]

Leaving the land in the hands of small-scale cultivators, however, carried significant costs. One of the requirements under the Coase Theorem for the type of bargaining that will lead to the most efficient allocation of resources is that property rights be fully specified. As we will see, this was far from the case on imperial estates in North Africa and Asia, and the state was forced time and again to intervene in disputes over property rights between imperial tenants and either the middlemen who collected their rent or officials from neighboring towns responsible for collecting taxes. Moreover, the Roman government's interventions were typically not proactive but in response to crises. The government's consistent policy of protecting the tenure rights of small-scale cultivators on imperial estates, from the point of view of Institutional Law and Economics, was a "normative activity" that had important consequences for the economy. It achieved a distributional goal, in that it helped to maintain an economically important class of people whose prosperity was easily threatened by tax authorities.[5]

At the same time, it should be recognized that once the Roman government implemented such a policy, it committed itself to maintaining a whole complex of property rights and so established a basic institutional framework for a significant portion of the Roman economy. This is so because it would have been exceedingly difficult for the Roman state to reverse its policy and develop an alternative method of exploiting its imperial estates, such as selling portions of them back to large landowners who themselves would take on the responsibility of furnishing the state with revenues. The Roman state's creation and maintenance of various property rights in the rural economy produced a degree of path dependence: the revenues of the Roman state depended on the continued cultivation of imperial properties by small-scale tenants, and so the policy of the state was designed to make sure that the small-scale tenants would remain as undisturbed in their occupation of their land as possible and continue to fulfill their primary duty to cultivate it.[6] Thus the original disposition of property rights that the state created in some sense dictated the response of the government when disputes arose concerning the tenure rights of cultivators on imperial estates. The Roman government had no choice but to uphold the tenure arrangements that it had established, even when doing so created unforeseen conflicts over the costs of liturgies, as can be seen in the inscriptions from Asia Minor.

The results of the Roman government's policy on its imperial estates, then, can be contrasted with the developments that Jairus Banaji has seen as characterizing the rural economy of Byzantine Egypt.[7] There, the province's largest landowners exploited the opportunities afforded them by their role in collecting taxes assessed on agriculture by storing up wealth and reinvesting at least a part of this in commercially oriented agriculture, especially viticulture. This process enriched the largest landowners in Egypt and led to the growth of impressive estates that rewarded their owners with immense profits and social and political privileges. But the prosperity of these large landowners also depleted the peasantry of much of the wealth that it might otherwise have controlled.

It is likely that the policy that the Roman government followed on imperial estates in North Africa, Asia Minor, Egypt, and other regions of the empire involved tradeoffs between enriching the wealthiest class of landowners and maintaining the viability of a larger class of cultivators. Giving the former group access to the land and labor of the imperial estates might have promoted further investment in the urban infrastructure that was the hallmark of early imperial rule. Africa, to be sure, experienced substantial development of urban life and commercialized agriculture in the early imperial period. Its principal city, Carthage, had a population measured in the hundreds of thousands, but Roman rule saw the growth and development of numerous other cities with Roman institutions. Africa became a center of Roman society and culture as well. By the second century, numerous Roman senators and equestrians were recruited from the elite classes of African cities, culminating with the elevation of the emperor Septimius Severus (193–211), who came from Lepcis Magna, in what is now Libya.[8] But the Roman government's intervention in the rural economy also protected those farmers on whose continued cultivation of the land both the state and large landowners ultimately depended. The Roman Empire was arguably better off because its government followed a policy that, within the overall constraints of a social order benefiting a wealthy elite, resulted in a more equitable distribution of wealth. Indeed, David Mattingly and Bruce Hitchner argue that Roman North Africa under the Principate experienced intensive growth, that is, economic growth that involved increasing per capita GDP. At the root of this economic growth was the ability of landowners to organize the production of agricultural products, especially olive oil, for commercial markets. Mattingly and Hitchner suggest that a "dynamic form of share tenancy," in all likelihood similar to or based on the *lex Manciana* (the lease regulation on North African imperial estates), provided the security of tenure that made it possible to develop olive culture on a large scale on private estates.[9]

PROPERTY RIGHTS ON NORTH AFRICAN IMPERIAL ESTATES

The principles that the imperial administration followed in seeking stable, long-term revenues can be traced in its regulations for the North African imperial estates. A series of inscriptions provides detailed information about the terms of land tenure established by the imperial government. These inscriptions document conditions on estates in the fertile Medjerda (ancient Bagradas) River valley in the northern part of Tunisia, in the Roman province of Africa.[10]

The efforts of the imperial treasury, or Fiscus, to exploit its North African estates centered around harnessing the efforts of the *coloni*, who were the permanent farmers. The rights that the *coloni* exercised were created by two laws, a first-century regulation called the *lex Manciana* and a more general enactment issued by the emperor Hadrian (117–38) in the second century. *Coloni* occupying their land in accordance with the *lex Manciana* were sharecroppers, paying generally one-third of their crops as rent, and they held their land under perpetual leaseholds. The *lex Manciana* is first recorded in an inscription from a site called Henchir-Mettich (*CIL*

VIII 25902, HM). This inscription, dated to the reign of Trajan (98–117), preserves regulations enacted by imperial procurators in charge of the administration of an imperial estate, the *fundus Villae Magnae Varianae sive Mappalia Siga*. These regulations spelled out in substantial detail the conditions under which *coloni* on the estate in question were allowed to cultivate certain unoccupied lands associated with the estate, termed *subseciva*. This term is associated with land surveying, and it often refers to parcels left out of the centuriation scheme because they were located on hills or in other locations inconvenient for assignment to individual owners. In the context of the inscriptions from the North African imperial estates, the term seems to refer to lands unoccupied for a variety of reasons.

The precise origin and scope of the *lex Manciana* remain a scholarly controversy. One possibility is that it simply regulated the occupation of unused lands, the subject with which the inscriptions referring to the *lex Manciana* are concerned. Another, more likely possibility is that it established terms of land tenure on a broader basis. In any case, the *lex Manciana* is likely to have originated as a private lease regulation. The Roman administration later adapted this lease arrangement for imperial estates as property to which it was applied passed into imperial control. Although it is difficult to be certain on this point, the law would have served to establish terms of land tenure on a newly formed private estate.[11] Under this scenario, when the *lex Manciana* was first applied on a private estate, much if not most of the land concerned could have been viewed as unused, in the sense that it was not already being occupied under conditions that either the private owner of the estate or the imperial government recognized.[12] The inscriptions in which the *lex Manciana* is mentioned as a lease arrangement document a later stage of its implementation, as *coloni* were encouraged to bring previously unused lands under cultivation.

When the Roman government adopted the *lex Manciana* as a regulation for imperial estates, it could effectively enforce the perpetual rights of the cultivators to their land, something that a private landowner, at least under the conventions of Roman private law, could not do. By this time, however, in some sense every Mancian cultivator either inherited or otherwise acquired his or her rights from a predecessor or, alternatively, established these rights by bringing otherwise unoccupied land under cultivation. It is unknown whether the *lex Manciana* also continued as an arrangement for private estates.[13]

The inscriptions from the Medjerda valley estates allow us to trace the process that the Roman government followed in defining land-tenure rights of the *coloni*. In the Trajanic inscription from Henchir-Mettich, the imperial procurators were responding to a petition from the *coloni* over their rights to *subseciva*. The procurators established that *coloni* on the estate could occupy these lands in accordance with the *lex Manciana*, and they spelled out in detail what the obligations of *coloni* occupying these lands would be vis-à-vis the *conductores* (that is, the middlemen who collected the rent) or other putative owners or managers of the estate. The lease regulations in the HM inscription affirmed that the *coloni* were to have permanent rights to their land as long as they fulfilled basic obligations, including the provision of the share rent and the performance of six days of labor on the lands over which the *conductores* exercised direct control. What is especially significant for understanding the policy of the imperial administration is that the regulations offered incentives for *coloni* engaging in arboriculture. Accordingly, *coloni* planting fig trees were to enjoy an exemption from the obligation to pay rent for five years (HM 2.20–24). *Coloni* planting vineyards would likewise receive a rent-free period of five years (HM 2.24–3.2), while *coloni* planting new olive trees would be allowed a grace period of ten years before having to pay rent (HM 3.2–10). These rent-free periods corresponded roughly to the time that it would take the fig trees, olive trees, or vineyards to produce a substantial crop.

It seems certain that at least one of the purposes of the regulations in the HM inscription was to resolve disputes that had arisen between the *coloni* and the *conductores*. Thus the regulations recognize that *coloni* had already brought the lands in question under cultivation, and so the imperial procurators did not extend the privilege of the rent-free seasons for land that had fig trees or olive trees before the issuing of the current regulations (HM 2.17–20). In addition, the inscription addresses other areas of potential dispute, including the means for calculating the share rent owed by the *coloni* (HM 1.10–20), the precise level of the share rent for various crops (HM 1.20–2.17), the disposition of grazing lands and the conditions under which the *coloni* could set their own animals to pasture (HM 3.12–20), and regulations covering damage to the crops cultivated by *coloni* (HM 3.20–4.2). The inscription also defined the rights (termed *usus proprius* in the first part of the inscription, HM 1.9) that the *coloni* exercised over their land (HM 4.2–22), as well as regulations concerning the labor owed by the *coloni* to the *conductores* (HM 4.22–35).

If the HM regulations served to resolve potential ambiguities in the respective claims of *coloni* and *conductores*, the Roman government probably extended the extraordinary rights that the *coloni* exercised over their land gradually, responding to petitions from individual groups of cultivators.

This seems plausible when one considers the likely gradual process by which private estates passed into imperial control. Eventually, the rights created for *coloni* in the Henchir-Mettich inscription became part of a more general policy in regulating imperial lands in Africa. This policy received its most complete articulation under the emperor Hadrian (117–38) with the promulgation of the *lex Hadriana de rudibus agris* (Hadrianic law about the occupation of vacant lands). The *lex Hadriana* is known from a complex but fragmentary inscription, of Hadrianic date, found at a site called Ain-el-Djemala (*CIL* VIII 25943, AD).[14] This inscription contains parts of several documents, including an enactment issued by imperial procurators, called the *sermo procuratorum*, that announced the conditions under which the *lex Hadriana* would apply to a particular group of estates. Two other copies of the *sermo procuratorum* are known. One was published under Septimius Severus and discovered at a site called Ain-Wassel (*CIL* VIII 26416, AW). The second copy of the *sermo*, with the *lex Hadriana*, was recently discovered at a site called Lella Drebblia, some seven kilometers distant from Ain-Wassel.[15] The importance of the *lex Hadriana* for agriculture on imperial estates in North Africa is underscored by the fact that it was republished, presumably again and again, as is indicated by the survival of three fragmentary versions of this important enactment. This measure provided a mechanism to extend the terms of tenure established by the *lex Manciana* to additional lands.

The *lex Hadriana* established the general program allowing for the occupation of unused lands, but it was up to the local administration to outline the precise conditions under which the *coloni* were to occupy their land. This is at least the impression afforded by the Ain-el-Djemala inscription. This complex inscription includes two letters from imperial procurators, as well as a petition from *coloni* to cultivate vines and olives on forest land and swampland on an unnamed estate in accordance with the *lex Manciana* (AD 1.11). To support their petition, the *coloni* referred to the granting of similar rights on a neighboring *saltus Neronianus* (AD 1.7–8), and they also apparently included a document of wider import, the *sermo procuratorum* discussed in the following (cols. 2–3). This document, issued by imperial procurators, granted *coloni* the rights to occupy lands and cultivate them with vines, olives, and grain on a particular group of estates. These estates included the *saltus Blandianus et Udensis* and also lands from a *saltus Lamianus et Domitianus* that were joined to another estate, the *saltus Tuzritanus*; the basis for this decision was the general policy formulated in the *lex Hadriana de rudibus agris*. The *coloni* on these estates were granted the right to cultivate these lands as long as they were not being worked by *conductores*, and like the *coloni* in the HM inscription, they received the right to occupy the land in perpetuity and pass the land onto their heirs.

The documents in the Ain-el-Djemala represent at least three different requests to the imperial procurators on the part of *coloni* to occupy unused lands. The imperial government apparently responded to these requests on a case-by-case basis, even after the more general policy represented by the *lex Hadriana* was formulated. Perhaps the imperial government had no more efficient way to establish these rights than to respond affirmatively to the *coloni* who requested them. It is not likely that the *lex Hadriana* had any wider scope than state-owned land, since there is no parallel for the imperial government prescribing the rental arrangements on privately held land. There is no evidence that the *lex Hadriana* was applied in any area of the empire outside of Africa.[16]

The rights created by the *lex Hadriana* were similar to those that the procurators in the HM inscription accorded to *coloni* on the *fundus Villae Magnae Varianae*. Accordingly, the AD procurators authorized anyone to occupy any unoccupied lands within a particular group of estates, as long as these lands were not being worked by *conductores*. In addition, the *coloni* occupying these lands were to have permanent possession and enjoyment as well as the capacity to bequeath their rights over their land to heirs. These rights are spelled out in the *sermo procuratorum*, the document written by the imperial procurators that provided the basis for implementing the *lex Hadriana:*

> Speech of the procurators of the emperor Caesar Hadrian Augustus: because our Caesar [in keeping with] his tireless care, because of which he is assiduously vigilant for the interests of humankind, orders all parts of the fields that are suited for both olives or vines as well as cereals to be brought under cultivation; therefore by the permission of his providence the authority accrues to everyone to occupy even those parts which are in the leased out centuries of the estate of Blandus and Udens and in those parts which have been joined to the Tuzritan estate from the Lamian and Domitian estate, and are not being worked by the lessees; to those who have occupied them that right of possession and enjoyment and bequest to one's heir is given, which is included in the law of Hadrian concerning vacant lands and those which have not been cultivated for ten consecutive years.[17]

The Roman administration's efforts to exploit its valuable properties in North Africa centered around promoting long-term investment in the productivity of the land by establishing long-term rights to the land for small-scale farmers engaged in arboriculture and the cultivation of grain. Thus the *coloni* on the imperial estates enjoyed perpetual rights to their land as long as they kept it under cultivation, and they could bequeath these rights and also use them as security in loans. To encourage arboriculture, *coloni* received the benefit of rent-free seasons. So even if the planting of olive orchards or vineyards involved substantial investment on the part of the *coloni*, the imperial lease regulations gave them a long-term interest in the land.[18]

The *lex Manciana* and the *lex Hadriana*, however, did not give the *coloni* anything like full rights of ownership. The situation of the *coloni* was apparently similar to that of perpetual lessees of municipal lands (*agri vectigales*). These lessees had an in rem claim to their land, and they enjoyed full rights of possession against third parties, including the people of the town from whom they were leasing (Paul. *D.* 6.3.1, 21 *ad ed.*).[19] This was a much more secure form of tenure than enjoyed by conventional private farm tenants (see chap. 3). To make sure that its revenues from the imperial estates remained as stable as possible from one year to the next, the Fiscus employed middlemen, or *conductores*. The *conductores* held short-term leases, in all likelihood leases of five years' duration, as was the norm in conventional Roman farm leases. The Fiscus, then, exploited these estates by leasing to two distinct groups. Both the *coloni* and the *conductores* had direct contractual relationships with the imperial administration. The *coloni* leased perpetual cultivation rights in exchange for a share rent and some other duties. The *conductores*, by contrast, gained the right to collect the rent from the *coloni*, as well as to cultivate certain lands not occupied by the *coloni*. The *coloni* were required to provide a fixed number of days of labor (generally six) to keep this land cultivated. The *conductores* were landlords of the *coloni* only in the limited sense that they collected the rent; there is no indication that they sublet land to the *coloni*. Although the inscriptions do not inform us directly about the conditions under which the *conductores* leased the imperial estates, it is logical that they provided the imperial government with a fixed yearly quota of cash or foodstuffs and that the revenues from the *coloni* or from the lands under the *conductores*' direct management that exceeded this quota represented their profit. The imperial government's revenues from the imperial estates, then, depended on a delicate balance of encouraging the *conductores* to squeeze revenues from the imperial estates against the need to make sure that the *coloni*, who cultivated the bulk of the land, remained productive for the long term.

In effect, the Fiscus created limited rights to the land for several groups of people. The right of the *coloni* to dispose freely over their land was circumscribed by their obligation to keep it cultivated with a prescribed range of crops; they would forfeit their rights if the land ceased to be cultivated. At the same time, the Fiscus created other rights to the land, including the right of the *conductores* leasing the land to exact the share rent from the *coloni* and the right of the same parties to use the labor of the *coloni* to cultivate additional lands. Still, the security of tenure created by the imperial government's policy can be traced in the remarkable survival of land-tenure systems based on the *lex Manciana* in diverse regions of North Africa. Thus in the Vandal period, in the late fifth century, a group of documents called the Albertini Tablets indicate how tenants on a private estate in the predesert region of Roman Africa occupied their land under a tenure system called *culturae Mancianae*. On this estate, the major object of the lease consisted of olive trees, cultivated in wadi beds to capture water. This system of tenure involved rights that the holders of *culturae Mancianae* could buy and sell.[20]

The rights created by the *lex Manciana* and the *lex Hadriana* were jealously guarded. Certainly, the republication of the *sermo procuratorum* with the reference to the rights created by the *lex Hadriana* in the Severan Ain-Wassel inscription, some seventy years after the law's original promulgation, suggests that *coloni* still took advantage of its provisions and, more important, were ready to insist on the rights that it created.[21] Indeed, cultivating land in accordance with the *lex Manciana* accorded some status. This is at least the impression given by the dedication to Septimius Severus by an individual named C. Aufidius Utilis, who was a tenant on an imperial estate, the *fundus Tapp*(. . .). In his dedication, Utilis claimed the privilege of being a *Mancian(a)e cultor*, or a cultivator occupying his land under Mancian tenure (*ILTun*. 628, 629).[22] In Egypt and especially in Asia Minor, by way of comparison, it was also common for tenants on imperial estates to claim a special status by virtue of serving the interests of the imperial treasury when they were involved in disputes and petitioning to the government for protection.

THE CULTIVATION OF PUBLIC LAND IN EGYPT

In leasing imperial estates out to small-scale tenants, the Roman government was following a consistent policy that it implemented on imperial properties elsewhere, including in Asia Minor, as we will see, and in

Egypt.[23] In Egypt, the Roman state generally relied on individual farmers, many of whom held quite modest parcels, to cultivate public or imperial land. In contrast to imperial estates in North Africa or in Asia Minor, state-owned land in Egypt was not likely to form large, contiguous estates. Rather, agriculture in Egypt revolved around individual parcels of land. In any village, these individual parcels would include land in various juridical categories, including state land and privately held land. So the land belonging to the state in Egypt often consisted of individual parcels that were scattered among the privately owned lands. As a consequence, the people cultivating state land in Egypt often included private landowners and tenants leasing private land. Still, the state's policy of retaining direct control over this land suggests that it was seeking to accomplish goals comparable to those that it sought to accomplish with the imperial estates in North Africa.

State-owned land in Egypt could be divided into three broad categories: royal land (*ge basilike*), which was taken over from Ptolemaic times; public land (*ge demosie*), referring to state land that came into being under Roman rule; and ousiac land (*ge ousiake*). For the purposes of understanding the tenure of state-owned land, the first two categories can be treated together. The third category refers to land that made up the first-century *ousiai*, which were estates or at least complexes of agricultural properties placed at the disposal of members of the Julio-Claudian court.[24] After the demise of the Julio-Claudian dynasty, the *ousiai* became state land, and, although the land was formally classified as *ge ousiake*, it was largely assimilated with other categories of state land.

There was no single regulation akin to the *lex Manciana* specifying how state land in Egypt was to be cultivated, and there was probably considerable variation from one location to another. The allotments that Jane Rowlandson lists in her study of land tenure in the Oxyrhynchite nome mostly encompassed fewer than ten arouras (two to three hectares), although it was also apparently not unusual for a single person to cultivate much larger allotments, even some over one hundred arouras (about 25 hectares).[25] The most commonly cultivated crop was wheat. The rents were set as a fixed assessment in kind. At least in theory, state land was subject to continual oversight, which meant that the rent could be adjusted in accordance with changing local conditions. However, for the most part, rents seem to have remained consistent on a given parcel of land once they were set, and any adjustment that was made was likely to have been in response to a cultivator's request for a lower rent as a result of deteriorating conditions. There were many variations in rental amounts, but most documented rents fall between 3½ and 4½ artabs of wheat per aroura.[26] Since it is generally assumed that wheat yields in Egypt from annually cropped land were on the order of ten artabs per aroura (one thousand kilograms/hectare), the rent from state land might correspond to one-third of a typical crop.[27]

The cultivators of state land in Egypt seem to have enjoyed substantial security of tenure. If in theory the state could withdraw land from one cultivator and assign it to another offering a higher rent, in practice the administration seems to have been more concerned with finding and retaining suitable tenants.[28] As a consequence, cultivators (*georgoi*) could hold on to their land as long as they wished, and it seems to have been common for cultivators to pass their rights to their lands onto their heirs. These cultivators would include people who owned and leased in private land, so the cultivation of state land represented an additional source of income for them. Presumably, if the apparently fossilized rents became higher than the market would otherwise suggest, cultivators could withdraw their resources from state land and concentrate on private land instead. The difficulty that the state faced in finding cultivators is suggested by its occasional resorting to the practice of assigning otherwise uncultivated land to private landowners (*epibole*).[29]

In effect, the Roman administration in Egypt made private landowners responsible for shortfalls in the revenues that it sought to collect from state lands. It is not clear how widespread this practice was or whether the administration enjoyed any great success in garnering additional revenues from private landowners in this way. But the bottom line is that, in making adjustments for the very different geographical conditions that obtained in North Africa and Egypt, the Roman administration pursued broadly comparable strategies in exploiting state-owned land. So the responses of the Roman government to the conflicts documented as taking place on the North African imperial estates were not likely the result simply of an ad hoc reaction to an immediate crisis but part of a much broader approach to dealing with the problem of achieving stable revenues in kind for the long term.

AGENCY AND INCENTIVES

The land-tenure system that the Fiscus established on the North African estates represents a form of agency, in which the principal, namely the state, assigned the task of producing crops and revenues to the agent, in this case, the farmers on the imperial estates. In this respect, the tenure arrangements to be examined are like any tenancy arrangement. The chief factors affecting the choice of contractual arrangements in farm tenancy include providing the tenant with the proper incentives to maximize production and allocating the risk between landowner and tenant, or even structuring the contract in such a way as to reduce risk.[30] The Roman administration sought to keep its agency costs under control.[31] It offered the *coloni* substantial incentives to invest their labor and resources in cultivating land on the imperial estates. Probably the most important of these incentives, apart from the right to a perpetual leasehold, consisted of the rent-free periods offered for the cultivation of olives, which was one of the principal cash crops in North Africa. From the point of view of agency costs, it made good sense for the imperial administration to promote the cultivation of olive trees through *coloni* rather than, say, through a large landowner employing gangs of slaves.

Olive trees and vines are "care-intensive" crops, which require a great deal of attention over a long period of time before they can produce a crop. Such crops are to be contrasted with "effort-intensive" crops, which require a great deal of labor, but not necessarily skilled labor. Wheat could be viewed as such a crop.[32] When care-intensive crops are cultivated with slave labor, there is a need for substantial supervision to make sure that the slaves perform the appropriate tasks in a timely manner. In many circumstances, landowners could reduce their own costs of monitoring by assigning the task of cultivating olive trees to tenants. The tenants would then have a much greater incentive than slaves or even wage laborers to engage in sufficiently careful cultivation, since they would be able to profit from their investment of labor and resources. Indeed, as mentioned already, Mattingly and Hitchner have suggested that landowners in Roman North Africa used a tenancy system much like that documented as being used on the Medjerda valley imperial estates to create the large olive plantations that provided so much of the region's wealth.[33] By offering rent-free seasons for the cultivation of olive trees, the Fiscus sought to encourage *coloni* to make a long-term financial commitment to their land. *Coloni* who established plantations of olive trees could also be expected to cultivate other crops, especially wheat, which they might intercultivate with the olive trees.

Security of tenure provided the *coloni* with significant incentives. Indeed, there is some empirical evidence from the modern world that protection of tenure for tenants helps to promote agricultural productivity. In the Indian state of West Bengal in 1977, a left-wing state government undertook a program of agrarian reform, called Operation Barga, which was aimed at improving the lot of sharecroppers (for which *barga* is a local term). Sharecroppers are important to the agrarian economy of West Bengal, accounting for about one-fourth of the land devoted to rice production, the main staple of the region. The reform program involved enforcing existing but largely ignored protections for sharecroppers. Sharecroppers who registered with the government were now firmly protected in their tenure. They could not be evicted, as long as they continued to pay their landlords a share rent, which was set at a maximum 25 percent of the crop. Moreover, although they could not transfer their rights to their land, they could bequeath them. A recent study has found that this reform led to increased productivity on sharecropped land. The productivity of West Bengal, where approximately 65 percent of sharecroppers registered with the government, was compared with that of neighboring Bangladesh, where no such reform had taken place. The authors of the study attribute this increased productivity to the enhanced bargaining power of sharecroppers and their security of tenure. Both of these factors helped to increase the sharecroppers' incentives to invest in inputs that would lead to greater productivity. The reforms affecting sharecropping accounted for approximately 28 percent of the increased agricultural output in the period 1977–93.[34]

If security of tenure promoted cultivation by the *coloni*, the open-ended terms under which they occupied their land imposed substantial costs on the Fiscus. For one, because the *coloni* paid their rent as a share of the crops, the Fiscus shared with them the risk for the size of the harvest and the market price for the crops that they produced.[35] In addition, the Fiscus could only offer incentives to the *coloni* to cultivate lands on the imperial estates, and it had no means to enforce the requirement that *coloni* keep land cultivated, except by confiscating it when it was neglected for two consecutive years. The threat of confiscation was of limited value when there was a constant supply of unused land on the imperial estates, and the republication under Septimius Severus of incentives originally granted by Hadrian to cultivate vines and olives on unused lands suggests that the imperial administration faced the constant problem of finding cultivators for lands on its estates. From another perspective, the administration had few of the means available to it that landowners leasing to sharecroppers use to make sure that the land is cultivated productively. The Fiscus did not share the costs of investing in inputs with the *coloni*, and it did not restrict their access to additional land. These measures are commonly seen as essential to overcoming the inherent inefficiency of sharecropping and making sharecropping equally as productive as other forms of land tenure.[36] Under these conditions, the revenues of the Fiscus ultimately depended on its ability to capture a portion of the surplus produced by the *coloni*, who would have cultivated a variety of crops as they pursued their own self-sufficiency.

The establishment of a generally applicable share rent allowed the Fiscus to avoid the task of assessing the quality of the various types of land occupied by the *coloni* and setting the rent accordingly. Thus the share rent represented the solution of the Fiscus to a major problem in agency, in which the principal, in this case, the landowner, has much less information than the agent, in this case, the tenant, who has much better knowledge of the quality of the land and thus of the possibilities for cultivating various crops.[37] One could imagine that a landowner with firsthand knowledge would have been in a better position to develop a more-nuanced system of leasing, one in which the rents charged more accurately represented the quality of the land. But such an approach would have imposed on the Roman administration substantial costs that it was not prepared to bear. In this connection, the exaction of a share rent did not serve simply to reduce the risk that the *coloni* had to bear in cultivating their land. Rather, the sharecropping system allowed the Fiscus to establish a level of rent that would be generally applicable on lands that represented a wide range of quality, from rich land in an alluvial plain to rocky hillsides. The Fiscus gave up a good deal of flexibility, since the perpetual leases of the *coloni* prevented it from adopting in the future alternative methods of exploiting the estates. Yet maintaining the viability of the cultivators on the land remained the administration's priority.

The Fiscus sought to make the best out of this situation by setting up the *conductores* as middlemen to collect the rent from the *coloni*. This measure helped the imperial administration to overcome the asymmetries of information characteristic of tenancy arrangements. The *coloni* had full knowledge of the crops that they produced, whereas the administration had only the most rudimentary knowledge of this and little capacity to monitor the efforts of the *coloni*. Consequently, the *conductores*, as short-term lessees whose own profits depended on exacting as full a share rent as possible from the *coloni*, had a large incentive to monitor the production of the *coloni* and to exact the full share rent. In addition, the Fiscus sweetened the deal for the *conductores* by giving them the right to cultivate lands not occupied by the *coloni* and requiring the *coloni* to provide them with labor and the use of their draft animals.

The inherent conflict between the *coloni* and the *conductores* raises the question about the continuing investment in the infrastructure needed to sustain the productivity of the estates, such as olive presses. In North Africa, olives represented a major cash crop, and revenues from olive production helped to sustain the growing urban elite in the early empire. During this period, Roman North Africa saw the creation of numerous large estates in many regions, including the Kasserine plain on the Tunisian steppe, as well as the coastal region of Tripolitania. Both regions had estates with substantial olive-pressing facilities, which housed multiple presses to serve a large cultivated area. At Lepcis Magna in Tripolitania, stamps on oil amphorae from the second and early third centuries indicate that the wealthy elite of the city owned oil-producing estates in the region. These owners included some of the wealthiest and most powerful people in the empire, including the emperor Septimius Severus and his family and the praetorian prefect C. Fulvius Plautianus.[38] The olive-oil factories on these estates made use of the heavy and expensive lever-press, which provided landowners with a cost-effective way to produce olive oil from extensive holdings.[39] We have no direct information about the composition of the labor force on such estates, but it seems likely that many of them were divided among tenants. Since most of the labor in olive culture is required at the harvest, it seems likely that landowners or tenants recruited seasonal labor on a large scale, possibly from seminomadic pastoralists, who in later ages provided labor at the harvest in exchange for food.[40] The recent archaeological survey of the region in which the Medjerda valley imperial estates were situated reveals the presence of numerous olive presses and pressing facilities. Most of the sites were modest installations, with generally one, or sometimes two or three, presses.[41]

The question is how such pressing facilities were maintained on the imperial estates. The HM inscription seems to indicate that olive-pressing installations were housed centrally on the estate, since *coloni* were required to furnish their share rents in wine and olive oil after the pressing. Indeed, maintaining control over the pressing facilities would provide the *conductores* with the opportunity to monitor the production of the *coloni*. It thus seems likely that the *conductores* paid for and were responsible to maintain pressing facilities, but their incentives to do so would be increased to the extent that they had greater security of tenure than implicit in their short-term leases to the estates. From this perspective, it is easier to understand why the imperial administration would allow some *conductores*, like Allius Maximus, who is the target of the complaints by *coloni* in the inscription from Souk-el-Khmis (see the following), to renew their short-term leases routinely. At least this provided the *conductores* with some incentive to make the types of investment that only they, rather than the *coloni*, were capable of making to maintain the productivity of the estates. We can imagine that, without maintenance of olive presses and storage facilities, there would be little opportunity for *coloni* to produce olive oil at a surplus.

INCENTIVES TO COOPERATE AND TO RESOLVE CONFLICTS

The Roman administration's policy of privileging small-scale cultivation carried additional costs beyond those associated with monitoring the *coloni*. We can appreciate these costs by considering other means that the Roman administration might have used to protect the property rights of the *coloni*. It could have granted the *coloni* the equivalent of outright ownership over their land; that is, it could have enforced the rights of the *coloni* with a "property rule" so that they could have sold their rights to whomever they pleased at the price they found appropriate. Alternatively, the Roman administration might have protected the rights of the *coloni* over their land with something like a "liability rule," according to which anyone who violated the rights of the *coloni* to cultivate their land would have to compensate the *coloni* at an objectively determined price. This is the same type of compensation that Roman law provided as the basis for relief in all in personam claims involving contracts.[42]

In this connection, it might be useful to consider the concept of the "efficient breach of contract." This is a concept that lawyers use to denote the conditions under which it is economically efficient for one party to a contract to violate the terms. A breach of contract is deemed efficient only when the benefits of doing so outweigh the costs.[43] One party may choose to violate the contract because a much more lucrative opportunity appears. In a tenancy relationship, the landlord might choose to terminate the tenant's lease if he or she had a more remunerative use for the property held under lease. For instance, the landlord might choose to combine the tenant's holding with another parcel of land to achieve greater economies of scale. In Roman law, both the landlord and tenant could violate a lease contract, but they would both have to compensate the other party for his or her losses. The only compensation arising out of a breach of a consensual contract in Roman law would be monetary. Roman law had no provision to require specific performance by either party. Thus a tenant expelled from a tenancy before the expiration of the lease could not sue to be restored to the lease but only to receive compensation for his losses resulting from the premature termination of the lease.[44] Under ideal conditions, this liability rule of protecting entitlements would tend to induce both the landowner and the tenant to bargain continuously over all aspects of the lease, including the allocation of the costs of investment and of risk. This bargaining process would affect the rent that the tenant paid.

On the North African imperial estates, the Roman government seems to have endowed the *coloni* with rights to some extent similar to a property rule, but more limited in scope. The *coloni* could bequeath their cultivation rights or pledge them as security for loans. But there was no provision for selling their rights (even if later, according to the Albertini Tablets, *coloni* clearly could do this). This situation surely offered the *coloni* substantial protection against any inroads by other parties, such as the *conductores*, who might see an opportunity to profit from the investment that the *coloni* made by taking over their land. But this protection, at least potentially, represented a social cost, since it discouraged bargaining with the *conductores* or the Fiscus to alter in any significant fashion the conditions under which the *coloni* cultivated their land and paid their rent.[45]

Such bargaining could have been to share the costs of investment that might increase productivity, for example in pressing installations to increase the production of wine or olive oil, or in irrigation systems to cultivate marginal land.[46] Alternatively, one could imagine that, under certain circumstances, the *coloni* and the *conductores* might bargain to find a different arrangement to cultivate certain crops from the one established by the *lex Manciana* or the *lex Hadriana*. If such transactions could be carried out at low cost, the results could have been advantageous for all concerned.

As discussed in the next chapter, the Roman government's treatment of disputes involving private tenancy arrangements suggests its willingness to accommodate, within the conventions of Roman private law, the many arrangements that landowners and tenants might make to respond to the uncertainties surrounding agriculture in the Mediterranean. From this perspective, the contractual relationships between private landowners and tenants can be characterized as "relational," in the sense that landowners and tenants often went beyond the conventional terms of Roman lease contracts to perpetuate a mutually advantageous contractual arrangement in the face of contingencies, such as crop failure or changing market conditions for crops, that could not be anticipated when the lease was entered into. The point is that private landowners and tenants had some incentive to find mutually cooperative arrangements to resolve the differences that would inevitably arise.

On the North African imperial estates, however, the system of land tenure established by the Fiscus diminished any such incentives to cooperate. Since there was apparently little, if any, sharing of the costs of investment between the *conductores* and the *coloni*, each side was more or less pitted against the other in allocating these costs. If the conflicts represented in the petitions to Commodus suggest that the conditions under which the *conductores* leased the estates had become less favorable, the perpetual leases of the *coloni* effectively ruled out any prospect for renegotiating the relationship between the *coloni* and the *conductores* to adapt to changing circumstances. If one side endeavored to change the terms of the lease relationship, then either the other side had to put up with this or there would be an intervention on the part of a public authority to settle the dispute. Thus the *conductores* would simply use whatever means of compulsion they had at their disposal, including bribing imperial officials and violence, to exact as large a share of the surplus produced by the *coloni* that they could. For their part, the *coloni*, like their counterparts on imperial estates in Asia Minor to be discussed later in this chapter, sought to use the power of the state to promote their interests or to enforce what they interpreted to be their rights. Thus, whatever areas of dispute that might have been subject to bargaining between parties to a conventional contract would remain "externalities," in the sense that the costs for them would be allocated without bargaining. This situation is sometimes characterized as a form of "market failure."[47] The result was that both the *coloni* and the *conductores* had every reason to engage in the type of opportunistic behavior that would allow them to profit from the other party's efforts without contributing any investment of their own. This effort to capture the profit from the investment and efforts of others would result in a lower overall income and so would be detrimental to production, no matter which party engaged in it.[48]

We can see this market failure especially in the incentives created for the *conductores*, to judge by the complaints that the *coloni* made in their petitions to the emperor Commodus. Since the *conductores* had little legal capacity to cooperate with the *coloni* by sharing costs of investment, their only recourse to enhancing or even maintaining their revenues was to extract as much of the surplus produced by the *coloni* as they possibly could. In this effort, the *conductores* took advantage of the investment that the *coloni* made in their own crops by imposing extramarket burdens on them and essentially taking the lion's share of any surplus that the *coloni* produced. If the *coloni* committed their resources by planting olive trees or vines, this investment essentially represented "sunk costs," and the *coloni* could not simply react to adverse conditions on the imperial estates by moving elsewhere when their terms of tenure became unattractive. The *coloni* would thus be vulnerable to the efforts of *conductores* who, seeking to increase their own income, would endeavor extralegally to capture quasi-rents, that is, the profits from the investments that the *coloni* had made.[49] This happened even if there was, as was almost certainly the case, a shortage of cultivators on private estates. The *conductores* might do this, as revealed in the petition to the emperor Commodus to be discussed shortly, by conniving with the local administration on the estate to raise the share rent of the *coloni* and to impose additional labor services on them. In making their case against those parties whom they perceived as violating their traditional rights, *coloni* on imperial estates commonly threatened to abandon these estates to take up leases with private landowners. But this course of action was hardly practical for *coloni* who had invested all their resources in maintaining farms within imperial estates, since they would have to sacrifice all of their investment and essentially start from scratch. Under this circumstance, the *conductores*, if left unchecked, could use the sunk costs of the *coloni* as leverage against them to increase the charges that the *coloni* had to pay.

The Fiscus maintained a rather rigid system of managing imperial estates. Its efforts to protect the rights of the *coloni* inhibited the possibility that the *conductores* or others might simply exhaust the surplus produced by the *coloni* so that the *coloni* would have no capacity to reinvest in the continued productivity of their land. At the same time, the *conductores* had little capacity to influence how the *coloni* allocated their resources. In effect, the Fiscus relied on two sets of agents to achieve its revenues from its estates. It created incentives for the *coloni* to invest in the long-term productivity of the land, but at the same time it had to strike a delicate balance to make sure that these incentives were not defeated by the incentives with which the *conductores* were invested to exact the rents and other obligations due from the *coloni*. Only the Fiscus, not the *conductores*, had any incentive to ensure the *coloni* undertook investments that would only pay off in the long term.

RESPONDING TO CONFLICTS

These conflicting incentives help to explain the petitions that the *coloni* on several North African imperial estates sent to the emperor Commodus (180–92) and the consistent response that the Roman government made. Three inscriptions survive from the early part of the reign of Commodus that preserve petitions to the emperor by *coloni* about the conditions of their land tenure. Two of these inscriptions survive only in small fragments, but one is quite substantial. This inscription, discovered at Souk-el-Khmis

(SK, 182 CE), preserves a lengthy fragment of a petition by *coloni* from an estate called the *saltus Burunitanus*, as well as the emperor's response (*subscriptio*) (*CIL* VIII 10570, 14454).[50] In particular, the *coloni* complained about abuses that they had suffered at the hands of a procurator whose name does not survive and a *conductor*, Allius Maximus, who was his confederate. The basis of the complaint of the *coloni* was that the procurator had allowed Allius Maximus to raise their share rent and to exact greater labor services than permitted by lease regulations. The *coloni* had tried to counteract these actions by making frequent appeals to the imperial government (SK 2.a–3.4):

> Col. II: "[. . . collusion], which he has practiced without restraint not only with Allius Maximus our adversary, but with almost all lessees contrary to justice and to the detriment of your accounts, that he has not only failed to take notice despite our insistence and entreaties and petitioning your divine subscription, but he has also indulged in the devices of the same most influential Allius Maximus in this final outrage, that having sent soldiers onto the same Burunitan estate he has ordered some of us to be arrested and harassed, some to be bound in chains, and some, even Roman citizens, to be beaten with rods and clubs, apparently for this single merit of ours, that we had had recourse to an [unrestrained] letter as we were proceeding to implore your majesty in an [injury] so serious with respect to the measure of our [mediocrity] and one so manifest. By the evidence of this injury [to us], Caesar, it is possible to estimate [directly], what . . ." Col. III: "[This matter] has compelled us most wretched people [once] again to supplicate to [your] divine providence, and for this reason we ask, most sacred emperor, that you aid us."

The procurator in question not only turned a blind eye to the abuses of the *conductor* but also responded brutally to the attempts by the *coloni* to seek redress, sending soldiers onto the estate to arrest and beat *coloni*, several of whom were Roman citizens.

The legal basis for the appeal made by the *coloni* indicates their confidence in the rights that the imperial government granted them over their land. In making their appeal, they referred to a chapter (*kaput*) of the *lex Hadriana*, as well as letters written by procurators (SK 3.4–18). These documents, in the description of the *coloni*, established the norms under which the *coloni* were to cultivate their land, including the amount of the share rent as well as the provision of days of labor to the *conductores* and the use of draft animals. The description that the petitioners offer of the *lex Hadriana* and the letters written by the procurators corresponds to the documents referred to in the AD inscription, in which the *lex Hadriana* established the general conditions under which *coloni* occupied their lands and regulations written by procurators outlined the more specific conditions surrounding the payment of rent. The petitioners further claimed that these regulations had been inscribed in bronze and were universally observed in the region surrounding the estate. They characterize the regulations prescribing the conditions of land tenure as the *perpetua forma:* "and that matter should be without any controversy, since it has both been inscribed in bronze and has been provided by all our neighbors in every direction in the agreement perpetual up to this day, and also has thus been confirmed in the letters of your procurators, which we have written above."[51]

The resistance that the unnamed procurator offered would seem to indicate that the institutions that were designed to mediate between the *coloni* and the *conductores* had failed, with the result that the *coloni* were subject to the unilateral abrogation of their traditional rights and even violence.[52] But the very existence of this inscription indicates that the *coloni* were able to initiate a successful petition against the procurator who had caused them so much trouble. It has been suggested that the response of the emperor, that the procurators were to see that the *coloni* not be subject to demands in contravention of the *perpetua forma*, hardly gave the *coloni* what they sought, which was a stronger repudiation of the actions of the *conductores* and the procurator: "the procurators in the contemplation of my discipline and practice—[added by the *coloni*] 'not more than two days of labor three times'—will take care that nothing be exacted from you by way of injury in violation of the perpetual agreement."[53] But the point is that the emperor vindicated the interpretation that the *coloni* attached to the *perpetua forma* as defining the terms of land tenure on the imperial estate. In the emperor's response, the *perpetua forma* represented a right not subject to any infringement. The task of enforcing the *perpetua forma* fell upon the procurators responsible for administering the estate, and the fragmentary letter of the equestrian procurator Tussanius Aristo and his freedman colleague Chrysanthus presumably included more specific instructions for the implementation of the emperor's general policy. The very existence of the inscription suggests that the *coloni* interpreted the emperor's response and the procurator's instructions as upholding their rights. Elizabeth Meyer, in her study of written legal documents in the Roman world, argues that the publication of *tabulae* carried considerable legal authority. On the North African imperial estates, the publication of both the *perpetua forma* as well as the petition and the emperor's response provided the *coloni* with a lasting safeguard of their cultivation rights.[54] How well the emperor's decision was enforced on the ground is a different matter. But it hardly seems likely that the *coloni* of the *saltus Burunitanus* or many other petitioners in the empire, for that matter, would have taken the trouble to petition imperial authorities without some confidence in the efficacy of this process.

The inscription from the *saltus Burunitanus* emphasizes the claim that tenants of imperial estates had on the imperial administration for the protection of their rights. These *coloni* argued that the actions of their opponents interfered with the important contribution that they made to the imperial finances by cultivating their land.[55] In another petition to the emperor Commodus, preserved in the fragmentary inscription from Gasr Mezuar (GM), *coloni* made explicit the threat implicit in the petition from the *saltus Burunitanus* by mentioning the possibility of their quitting the imperial estate for private land (*CIL* VIII 14428).[56] This threat to abandon imperial land is common in petitions from imperial estates. This was a threat that the imperial administration had to take seriously, even if, as I have argued, there were substantial impediments preventing the *coloni* from taking this drastic step.[57] Replacing the *coloni* would be no easy task. Would a procurator administering an estate want to risk the departure of a substantial number of *coloni* on his watch?

The Roman government's response to the conflicts between the *coloni* and the *conductores* on the North African imperial estates was designed simply to try to restore the conditions of land tenure that its own regulations had created. As we will see, this is the same policy that the Roman government implemented in resolving disputes surrounding the cultivation of imperial estates in Asia Minor. This response suggests the limited extent to which the Roman government could formulate an economic policy in the face of uncertain information and high transaction costs. Rather than revise the system under which the imperial estates were leased out, the Roman administration instead resorted to its time-honored practice of privileging the tenure rights of the small-scale farmers actually cultivating the land. These farmers, after all, were the ones on whose production the revenues of the state ultimately depended, so it made sense for the imperial administration to do everything that it could to protect their tenure rights. At the same time, however, this policy did nothing to alleviate the tensions that existed within the imperial estates. The *conductores* or other tax officials continued to have the same incentive to engage in the practice of exacting "monopoly-rents" by using their influence to increase their exactions from the *coloni*. The result of all of this was that the revenues from the imperial estates continued to depend largely on the investment made by the *coloni* alone. The Roman government achieved revenues by balancing the traditional tenure rights of small-scale cultivators against the incentives on the part of their immediate landlords to exploit their position. When this delicate balance resulted in conflict, as we should expect that it definitely would, the consistent policy of the Roman government was to reassert the validity of time-honored tenure rights. The repeated publication of the *sermo procuratorum* suggests that, in general, these rights were observed.

COMMUNAL ORGANIZATIONS WITHIN IMPERIAL ESTATES

The Roman government's policy of privileging small-scale cultivation explains the steps that it took to foster the strength of peasant communal organizations within imperial estates. These communal organizations helped to protect the tenure rights of the *coloni* by providing them with the means to take unified action to gain access to the protection of the state's legal institutions.[58] For example, on the imperial estates in the Medjerda valley, the imperial government fostered the development of communal institutions as it sought to monopolize the services of the *coloni* cultivating the land and to isolate them from competition from private landowners or towns.[59] Commonly the African imperial estates included some kind of communal center, which provided facilities for processing crops and also markets. The *coloni* were organized under officials, generally called *magistri*, who apparently played some role in regulating relationships among the *coloni*, and who represented the *coloni* before the imperial authorities. Other officials are mentioned in the inscription, including priests.[60] Under Trajan, two individuals holding the offices of *magister* and *defensor* led the *coloni* on the *fundus Villae Magnae Varianae* (HM, base). It seems likely that the *coloni* on the various imperial estates in the AD inscription who petitioned the imperial government for rights to unused lands also had a similar communal structure. Later, the *coloni* who appealed to the emperor Commodus also depended on a communal structure within their estates. On the *saltus Burunitanus*, the *coloni* presented their petition through an individual named Lurius Lucullus, in all likelihood a *colonus* from the estate. The inscription commemorating the success of the *coloni* in vindicating their rights was inscribed under the direction of an individual named C. Iulius Pelops (son of Salaputus), who was serving in the post of *magister* (SK 4.28–29). It is not clear how the *magistri* or other leaders among the *coloni* were chosen. They could have gained their offices because of their relative wealth, or possibly the offices were passed down within families as part of a local social hierarchy that has vanished from the historical record.

Communal structures are also documented to have been on imperial properties in other regions of Roman North Africa. Most notable in this regard are the imperial domains in the plains surrounding the city of Sitifis. These domains included *castella*, which were quasi-municipal entities whose residents could be organized in communal building projects. The inhabitants of the *castella* cultivated imperial domains in the vicinity, and the *castella* provided these people with a civic center. The landlord was not some local landowner but the emperor, or the imperial administration. In the third century, many of these *castella* saw the construction of town walls, which provided military protection but which also signaled the importance of the estate as a community for the *coloni*.[61]

THE ECONOMIC IMPLICATIONS OF ROMAN LEGAL POLICY

Let us now consider the economic implications of the imperial government's policy in defending the cultivation rights of tenants on imperial estates. It is difficult to gauge the extent of imperial ownership of land in this region, but it is clear that the state in effect withdrew large tracts of land from private ownership and reserved this land for small-scale cultivation. This intervention in the economy certainly created opportunities for *coloni*, and it tended to promote a more egalitarian distribution of land than would have been likely without imperial estates. Although we have almost no information concerning the conditions under which private tenants in Roman North Africa occupied their land, it is likely that private landowners had to offer their tenants terms of tenure that would be competitive with what the Roman government could offer. Private landowners shared a common interest with the imperial government in promoting long-term investment in olive trees, and they had to overcome many of the same impediments to investment.[62] The repeated promulgation of the incentives in the *sermo procuratorum* to cultivate unused lands indicates that there was a chronic shortage of farmers with resources adequate to become independent, productive farmers on imperial estates. The same situation surely existed for private land as well. The imperial government offered a clear alternative to any tenants who might cultivate private land, and the security of tenure that the imperial government could guarantee would have been very attractive to farmers occupying their land under shorter or less secure tenure arrangements. Thus private landowners had to compete with the imperial government for the services and resources of potentially productive tenants. This certainly enhanced the bargaining position of private tenants and protected them against some of the bargaining power that the private landowners might otherwise have exercised by virtue of their superior social standing.

It is not known whether private landowners could offer perpetual leaseholds in the same way as the Roman government. Such a tenure arrangement would be at odds with conventional Roman lease law, which did not provide the tenant with the right of possession. This meant that, after an estate changed hands, the tenant had no right to stay in his tenancy, since Roman law did not recognize obligations imposed on third parties, such as subsequent owners of the land. Indeed, the Henchir-Mettich inscription provides evidence of the Roman government's concern about emphasizing its ironclad guarantee of the rights of the *coloni*, since it refers to future owners (*domini*) alongside the *conductores* as the potential landlords of the *coloni*. This phraseology would seem to indicate that the Roman administration envisioned the possibility that the estate in question would eventually revert to private ownership; in such a circumstance, the *coloni* would retain their perpetual rights to the land. Whether a private landowner could make such a guarantee is uncertain, but it does seem likely that many private landowners offered their own *coloni* de facto rights of possession, a possibility that is examined more fully in the next chapter. In any case, if the *lex Manciana* began as a private lease arrangement (perhaps without the same clearly defined right of possession, or *usus proprius*, that is the basis of the imperial regulations), then surely other estate owners offered their tenants comparable terms as they sought to exploit their lands.

If private landowners could not match the perpetual leaseholds that the imperial government offered, they would have to compensate in some way, perhaps by offering *coloni* better access to pressing facilities than available on imperial estates or by collecting lower rents. Of course private landowners could also seek to inhibit competition for the services of their *coloni* by restricting their access to markets and exchanges outside of the estate. Brent Shaw has traced such an effort in the creation of the periodic markets (*nundinae*) within the confines of private estates.[63] But ultimately, the juxtaposition of private and imperial estates meant that private landowners and the imperial government competed with one another for the services of *coloni*. The imperial government's creation of perpetual lease rights established the terms of this competition.

The Roman government's protection of the tenure rights of the *coloni* served a broad overall purpose despite the difficulties associated with it. From one perspective, this policy had a "distributional" aspect, in that it promoted a distribution of wealth that the Roman government presumably valued. At the same time, this system of land tenure may have also resulted from the Roman government's general sense of justice.[64] Thus the government preferred when possible to protect the tenure rights of small-scale cultivators against the possibility of forced expropriation by wealthier landowners. This concern can be traced in the government's solicitude for the plight of small farmers when they were unfairly matched against corrupt tax collectors or wealthy landowners who sought to shirk their own fiscal duties by imposing the burden of paying taxes on their poorer counterparts (see the following). But this protection also served a basic economic purpose, since it helped to achieve the overriding goal of access to revenues in kind, whether or not it promoted the most efficient allocation of resources. So even if the *conductores* or some putative group of wealthy landowners thought that they could make a handsome profit from the imperial estates by buying the land that the *coloni* were cultivating, the Roman government ruled out such an arrangement. The policy of the government suggests that, in the long run, in its view, allowing the control over this land to fall into the hands of large-scale private landowners at some point would begin to threaten the security of the revenues that the Fiscus collected from the imperial estates.

PROPERTY RIGHTS ON ESTATES IN ASIA MINOR

The Roman government applied a broadly similar approach in responding to conflicts involving cultivation rights on imperial estates in Asia Minor, although the actual disputes were somewhat more complicated than on the North African estates. These conflicts in Asia Minor are documented in a small corpus of inscriptions recording petitions from farming communities within imperial estates for redress against abuses by imperial procurators and other tax officials.[65] In Asia Minor, the issue that the Roman government faced was how to respond to efforts of imperial tax officials to impose on imperial tenants tax and liturgical obligations that the residents of nearby cities were required to fulfill. These liturgies included services such as the collection of taxes, the maintenance of roads, and the provision of draft animals. So, in general, these conflicts pitted the interests of imperial tenants against those of private landowners, who shouldered the bulk of civic tax and liturgy burdens. When, in the third century, the pressure on towns in the Roman Empire to find suitable candidates to perform liturgies became more intense, towns naturally looked to neighboring imperial estates, which were populated by farmers with resources comparable to those who cultivated land in the territory of the towns and on whom liturgical obligations generally fell. The inscriptions describing these conflicts thus suggest some of the problems that the Roman government encountered in defining the property rights of imperial tenants and other parties with an interest in the productive capacity of imperial lands.

As I argue in the following, the terms of tenure that the Roman government established on imperial estates in Asia Minor left uncertain the obligations of imperial tenants to perform civic liturgies. In effect, the costs of covering these liturgies became a kind of externality, and the property rights established by the Roman government impeded any possible bargaining between landowners in towns and imperial tenants to divide the costs. The result of all this was, at least in the view of the imperial tenants, repeated incursions by town officials and tax collectors into imperial estates, to which they responded by seeking the intervention of the Roman government to uphold their traditional rights. Thus the government was forced to intervene to specify property rights on imperial estates in reaction to crises. The costs of the civic obligations that the towns wanted imperial tenants to share were considerable, and each side sought to impose these costs on the other, or even on the state, by simply not fulfilling liturgical obligations. The surviving inscriptions represent the government's efforts to sort out these conflicting claims for property rights, but the consistent principle underlying the government's policy was to protect the tenure rights of imperial tenants. This policy, however, is not likely to have represented a lasting solution, since towns continued to be adversely affected by the privileges accorded imperial tenants.

The imperial estates to be discussed formed part of a network of large properties that developed during the first three centuries of Roman rule in central Anatolia. Some of this land was in the hands of large private owners, but a substantial portion of it was owned by the Roman state. As Stephen Mitchell suggests in his survey of landownership patterns in central Anatolia, much the land had been in the hands of pastoralists before Roman rule. With Roman rule came well-placed Romans, who were able to displace some of the pastoralists and create large estates. This was especially the case in the plateau land in Galatia. These large landowners, who begin to appear in Augustan times, represented the core of a developing provincial aristocracy. At the same time, land that had been made *ager publicus* (public land) as a result of wars under the Republic became imperial land, and the extent of imperial ownership increased substantially during the second century CE, as estates that had once been in private hands passed into imperial control. In other parts of Anatolia, especially the more urbanized areas of Phrygia, Bithynia, and Lydia, private estates owned by large émigré landowners developed alongside those owned by the local municipal elite, who were often the leading citizens of Roman colonies.[66]

There is some evidence for how these estates were managed. Inscriptions preserve the names of administrators of various types, including *epitropoi* (procurators), business managers (*pragmateutai*), and bailiffs of estates (*oikonomoi*, also *oikonomissai*), as well as lessees (*misthotai*). The presence of this last group suggests that some estates were leased out to large-scale middlemen, comparable to the *conductores* on North African estates, presumably to collect the rent from the small-sale farmers cultivating the land. We can gain some idea as to how estates in this region might be managed from a series of inscriptions from an estate belonging, from the second century until around 260–70, to the family of Annia Cornificia Faustina (the sister of Marcus Aurelius). This estate was located in the territory of Ormeleis, near the colony of Olbasa in the province of Asia. The farmers on this estate were collectively termed the *ochlos* (crowd), and they appointed representatives called *proagontes*. The *proagontes* were likely to have been comparable to the *magistri* on North African estates, or officials called *prostatai* who often represented the interests of farmers in agricultural communities in Egypt. The interests of the landowners were represented by a series of administrators, including *epitropoi* and *pragmateutai*. In addition, the mentioning of *misthotai* indicates that the estates, or parts of them, were leased out to middlemen. Presumably the other administrators supervised the work of the *misthotai* and possibly also managed lands that were not leased out to middlemen.[67]

The period from which most of the petitions to be examined date, the mid-third century, was characterized by increasing military unrest on Rome's eastern frontiers, and this unrest spilled over into Asia Minor.[68] Asia Minor itself, at least beginning in the 250s and 260s, was subject to incursions by the Sassanians and the Goths. For our purposes, Asia Minor had earlier been a scene of increasing military activity as armies were marshaled to campaign on the eastern frontier. Soldiers became a common presence in towns in Asia Minor as they traversed the region, and the Roman government had to deal with the difficult problem of reining in soldiers who might extort favors or bribes from local populations, not to mention requisition draft animals. Less dramatically, the military pressure on the eastern frontier surely created additional tax pressures, so the inroads by soldiers and Roman tax officials—of which villagers and imperial tenants complain in the documents discussed in the following—resulted to a large extent from the prolonged military problems that the Roman Empire faced in the third century.

The surviving inscriptions include petitions from imperial estates at Aga Bey and Güllüköy in Lydia, Aragua and Takina in Phrygia, and Tabala in Caria.[69] The common theme of the petitions was the efforts of tenants on imperial estates to resist the imposition of liturgies and other charges, in particular, the provision of requisitioned draft animals (*angareia*), which is the subject of a number of third-century petitions from Asia Minor.[70] Disputes over requisitioned transport were a continuing problem that the Roman administration had to address, from the establishment of Roman rule in Asia Minor into late antiquity.[71] In addition, cities and towns in the Roman Empire often engaged in boundary disputes over their territories to secure an adequate recruiting base for providing such services. These disputes frequently required the intervention of the provincial governor or other high-ranking official to resolve.[72]

Commonly, the petitioners sought to add special urgency to their claims by emphasizing their status as imperial tenants and so drawing attention to the vital service that they performed for the imperial treasury. Such claims often went hand in hand with appeals to the emperors' concern for justice. Thus the petitioners would contrast the outrageous injustices that they were suffering with the general atmosphere of justice and prosperity prevailing throughout the Roman Empire.[73]

Claiming a special status by virtue of being an imperial tenant was apparently a common practice throughout the empire, to judge by petitions from Egypt. For example, a farmer from the village of Theadelphia described himself as a *georgos ousiakos* (a cultivator of state-owned ousiac land) when he complained to the *strategos* (the official in charge of a nome, or administrative division) about the failure of certain officials to provide adequate irrigation for state-owned land that he held under lease (*P.Mich.* XI 617, 145–46 CE).[74] Another petitioner described himself as a farmer "useful to the most sacred treasury" in a complaint to the prefect of Egypt about being subjected to violent treatment (*BGU* XI.1 2061, 207/208 CE).[75] Around the same time, in 207 CE, twenty-five farmers from the village of Soknopaiou Nesos involved in a dispute over cultivation rights to shore land made the basis of their claim that the efforts of their rivals to deprive them of the land in question would threaten their ability to pay revenues to the state (*Sel.Pap*. II 289; *P.Gen*. 16). To support their complaint, the petitioners referred to an edict of the prefect Subatianus Aquila concerning the return of Egyptians to their *idia* (village of origin) to perform their customary agricultural labors.[76] We might also consider the claim that a wealthy landowner in fourth-century Hermopolis, Aurelius Adelphios, made over rights to ousiac land that had allegedly been in his family's hands for generations (*CPR* XVIIA 9b, 320 CE).[77] Adelphios, a councilor and officeholder at Hermopolis, was angered that, when seeking to enter his land, he was prevented by certain villagers' "boorish stubbornness." To underscore his importance to the state, he described at some length how the substantial expenditures that he had made in cultivating the land allowed him to contribute the financial well-being of the imperial treasury (lines 5–10).

To return to Asia Minor, the petitions from the imperial estates could spark a considerable response from the government. For example, the imperial tenants at Takina in Phrygia complained to the emperor Caracalla about harassment by soldiers, who requisitioned transport under the pretext of making preparations for visits by the provincial governor.[78] The emperor responded by sending instructions to the procurator in charge of the imperial property in question, Aurelius Philokyrios. The emperor instructed the procurator to protect against unauthorized incursions by soldiers and to make sure that the soldiers pay the appropriate charges for the use of wagons and draft animals belonging to the affected farmers. This procurator, in turn, sent a letter to the current proconsul of Asia, C. Pompeianus Tranquillus, requesting that the governor instruct that the imperial tenants be paid appropriately for providing transport. Finally, the proconsul sent a letter with his own instructions about the decision to the magistrates and people of Takina. In this very fragmentary document, the proconsul acknowledged the violations of the law and ordered publication of the emperor's response so as to prevent for all time any further violations.

The farming communities on imperial estates were using the petition process in the same way as towns to defend themselves against harassment by soldiers and other imperial officials. Perhaps the most famous example of a town using this process is the efforts of the people of Skaptopara in Thrace to prevent soldiers and other visitors from exhausting the town's resources by demanding *hospitium* (lodging).[79] In this case, the town provided an inviting target for unwanted visitors, since it was near the site of a festival and also had hot springs. The Skaptopareans endeavored to gain the intervention of the governor of Thrace by petitioning the emperor,

Gordian III (238). The petitioners were successful in gaining a rescript from the emperor, which led to a presumably successful hearing before the provincial governor. The surviving inscription includes the petition by the town's spokesperson, the praetorian soldier Aurelius Pyrrhus; the emperor's *subscriptio*, in which he ordered the provincial governor to examine the facts of the case; and part of a speech before the provincial governor made by representatives of the city of Paulatia, in whose territory Skaptopara lay.[80]

We can appreciate the nature of the conflicts created by the government's fostering of special tenure arrangements within imperial estates by considering in detail an inscription from a site called Aga Bey, in ancient Lydia. This inscription from Aga Bey preserves a large part of a petition submitted by the farmers on an imperial estate. This petition is addressed to two emperors, either Septimius Severus and Caracalla (197–211) or, as seems more likely, Philip the Arab and his son and coruler (244–249).[81] In this petition, the tenants (*georgoi*) complained about oppression that they had suffered at the hands of imperial tax officials (*kolletiones*), as well as military personnel (*frumentarii*).[82] According to the petitioners, the *kolletiones* interfered with the performance of the agricultural work on the estate. They went so far as to bring soldiers into the estate and arrest nine people, putting them in chains. They then turned eight of these farmers over to the provincial governor for trial, releasing one in exchange for a ransom or bond of 1,000 drachmae (lines 1, 4–8). The size of the ransom suggests that many of these farmers had considerable wealth, or at least that the community as a whole could raise a substantial sum on short notice. The result of these abuses, in the words of the petitioners, was that they would be unable to attend to their farming duties and to fulfill their obligations to the state by paying their rents (*despotikai apophorai*) (lines 27–30): "since we are unable to comply for the future with our imperial rent obligations and decrees as a result of being prevented from cultivating the land." As tenants on an imperial estate, the tenants first turned toward the procurators administering imperial property in Asia Minor, including Aurelius Marcianus, the local procurator, as well as higher-ranking equestrian procurators.[83] Having failed to gain redress from the procurators, the petitioners now turned to the emperors, whom they entreated to instruct the proconsul and the procurators to pass judgment on the outrageous behavior of the imperial officials. Specifically, the petitioners wanted to stop the inroads into the estate made by the *kolletiones* and unspecified other parties under the pretext of offices or liturgies (lines 30–36).

The conflicts standing behind this petition were in many ways more complicated than those in the inscription from the *saltus Burunitanus* in Africa, with which it shares a number of parallels. In both cases the tenants sought relief against what in their description was abusive and violent treatment. But whereas on the African estate the *coloni* directed their complaint against changes in their terms of tenure, the farmers in the Aga Bey inscription were primarily concerned with safeguarding the special status that they enjoyed as cultivators of land within an imperial estate. What was at stake for the Aga Bey farmers was not simply that imperial tax officials were applying increasing pressure on them. Rather, the actions of the *kolletiones* stemmed from a larger conflict over the allocation of taxes and liturgies between landowners and cultivators in municipal territories and farmers on imperial estates.

It was a long-standing controversy in the Roman Empire whether—or rather, to what extent—tenants of imperial estates were exempt from the duty to perform civic liturgies. Thus Frontinus (*de contr. agr.* 53, Lachmann) discussed disputes between municipalities in Africa and imperial estates for services of *coloni*.[84] In Egypt, certain cultivators on Julio-Claudian *ousiai* apparently enjoyed a privileged status. The *ousiai* were estates that belonged to the emperor or were assigned to various members of the imperial family or associates of the imperial court to provide them with a source of income.[85] On certain of these estates, the cultivators were denoted by the term *apolysimoi*, which suggests a dispensation from certain liturgical obligations. These same cultivators might band together to perform liturgical and even social functions, and they selected leaders, on a basis no longer known.

The imperial government apparently was never successful in developing a definitive policy on the liturgical obligations of imperial tenants, and as a result emperors repeatedly issued constitutions on this contentious issue. Accordingly, the emperors Marcus Aurelius and Lucius Verus issued a rescript requiring *coloni* of imperial estates to perform civic *munera* (liturgies) if they could do so without compromising their obligations to the Fiscus ("sine damno fisci," Pap Iust. *D.* 50.1.38.1, 2 *de const.*). The provincial governor was charged with making this determination while consulting with the procurator.[86] Later, the third-century jurist Callistratus wrote that imperial *coloni* were to be exempt from such obligations, since their resources could more suitably be used for fiscal purposes (*D.* 50.6.6.11, 1 *de cognit.*).[87]

In addition, the Roman government granted privileged groups exemptions from certain types of liturgies. For example, citizens of the Greek city of Antinoopolis in Egypt were exempt from performing liturgies in other areas where they might own land. The exemption of Antinoites from liturgies might be the subject of bitter dispute, as is suggested by a petition by an Antinoite citizen named Sempronius during the reign of Marcus Aurelius to the *epistrategos* (a high-ranking official in the administration of Egypt of equestrian status). In this petition, Sempronius appended an array of previous decisions concerning the exemption of Antinoites from performing liturgies, including letters to Antinoopolis by three emperors, Hadrian, Antoninus Pius, and Marcus Aurelius and Lucius Verus (jointly), as well as two letters on this issue, one from the prefect or governor of Egypt and the other from an *epistrategos*.[88] The earlier documents that Sempronius included in his petition to strengthen his case indicate that the requirements of Antinoites to perform liturgies had often been the subject of litigation.

The situation that existed on the imperial estate at Aga Bey and on other imperial estates in Asia Minor suggests why it was very difficult to establish a definitive policy on the obligations of imperial tenants to perform civic liturgies. The petitioners from Aga Bey apparently resided in a village near the territory of the city of Philadelphia.[89] It was possible that some of the imperial tenants owned or cultivated land outside of the imperial estate but within the territory of the town, land that—from the city's point of view—formed part of its resource base for taxes and civic liturgies. Certainly the town, when its own resources were extenuated, would find the temptation to impose a share of its burdens on nearby imperial tenants hard to resist. In the inscription from Aga Bey, the "outrages" committed by the *kolletiones* may have consisted primarily of cooperating in this effort to impose on imperial tenants some portion of the obligations that the people of the town would otherwise have had to bear. That such an effort formed the basis of the dispute is strongly suggested by the imperial tenants' horror at the prospect of taking up offices or liturgies in the town.

The petitioners, however, framed the issue in a different way. It was for them not so much a question whether they should be asked to fulfill new obligations but rather whether the imperial administration would countenance the violation of the long-standing terms of tenure that they enjoyed as farmers on an imperial estate. Thus the petitioners from Aga Bey described the *kolletiones* and the putative representatives of the town who tried to impose offices and liturgies as "harassing and annoying farmers who are yours by virtue of all our possessions being reserved from the time of our ancestors to the most sacred treasury in accordance with the right of cultivation" (lines 35–40). The basis of the petitioners' claim was the special right of cultivation (*to tes georgias dikaion*) that for generations had established the conditions under which they cultivated their land. This arrangement had significance comparable to that of the *perpetua forma* in the SK inscription from North Africa, which both the *coloni* and the emperor Commodus understood as establishing the basic tenure arrangements of the *saltus Burunitanus*. It is impossible to determine the origin or scope of the arrangement on the Aga Bey estate, but it is clear that the tenants viewed it as establishing their rights and duties as tenants of imperial land and, for the purpose of the petition, their exemption from any other duties except for those specified by it.[90] To emphasize their claim to be exempt from any duties other than those specified by the cultivation agreement, the petitioners threatened to abandon their homes that they had occupied for generations, leave behind their burial places, and seek refuge on private land (lines 43–54):

> It is necessary for us who have been abandoned, not enduring the outrageous behavior of the *kolletiones* and of our adversaries for the reasons we have stated, to abandon both our ancestral hearths and our grandfathers' tombs and to migrate to private land to be saved—for those living the evil life are more likely to spare those dwelling there than your farmers—and to become refugees from the imperial estates, in which we have been born and have been raised and, remaining there from the time of our ancestors as farmers, maintain our obligations to the imperial treasury.[91]

The conflicts from Asia Minor arising over disputes about the provision of draft animals are also vividly illustrated in an inscription that farmers on an imperial estate at Aragua in Phrygia sent to the emperor Philip.[92] In their petition, the imperial farmers complained that soldiers, certain imperial officials called *Caesariani*, and powerful people from the city had departed from the public roads to invade the estate and requisition the oxen that the farmers of the imperial estate used for plowing. The surviving inscription preserves several documents, including a petition to the emperor, the emperor's response to the petition, and, as a supporting document to the petition, a *subscriptio* that the emperor Philip had written to a similar petition when he was still serving as praetorian prefect. The petition was presented by an individual named Aurelius Eclectus through a soldier named T. Ulpius Didymus, both of whom were acting on behalf of a community of farmers. The exact nature of this community and the relationship among the various groups involved in the submission of the petition are not clear. The petitioners are styled as "the community of the Aragueni, residents and your [sc. imperial] farmers of the deme in the city of Appia of the community of the Moiteani and Soeni in Phrygia" (lines 6–8). The most likely explanation is that the petition came from farmers on an imperial estate that included the village of Aragua and apparently several other villages as well. This estate, in turn, was situated within the territory of the city of Appia.[93]

In the inscription from Aragua, the issue there was largely the same as for the tenants on the imperial estate at Aga Bey. The actions of the soldiers and imperial tax officials violated what they understood to be their traditional rights to the land. Thus, when describing the lack of success in achieving results by petitioning Philip in his previous capacity as praetorian prefect, the farmers state that they were forced to make payments that the terms of their tenure did not require them to (line 29). As they insisted on their traditional tenure rights, the Aragueni linked their own welfare with the financial stability of the state. Accordingly, in the petitioners' description, the harassment that they were suffering was resulting in the desertion of their farms (line 32). Implicit here is the threat of abandoning the estate that was made explicit in the Aga Bey inscription. The response of the imperial government was to uphold traditional tenure arrangements in favor of the petitioners. Accordingly, the emperor referred the matter back to the proconsul, not because the proconsul exercised any responsibility over the internal workings of the estate but because he had the responsibility to resolve disputes between the estate and the town. As was the case for many petitions, the higher authority, in this case the emperor, instructed the lower authority to take appropriate action after ascertaining the veracity of the petitioners' claims.[94] The general phrasing of this response should not disguise the policy of the imperial government in protecting the cultivation rights of imperial tenants.

The threat that the farmers on estates in Asia Minor made to abandon their ancestral estate provides an important clue to understanding the enormous consequences of the Roman government's policy in defining property rights. To be sure, this appeal underscores the long-standing claim that the imperial tenants had on the protection of the emperor, as well as the failure of the imperial procurators to provide the type of protection that they deserved. But this threat could only be taken seriously if there was real competition between the imperial government and private landowners for the services of suitable tenant farmers. The competition affected the situation of both private and imperial tenants. The attractive terms of tenure that the state offered certainly forced private landowners to make concessions to attract and keep tenants. More important, the competition from private landowners induced the imperial government to play an active role in resolving disputes involving its own farmers. The imperial government also had a vested interest in checking the power of patronage that private landowners might exercise.[95] The petitioners' assessment of their chances under the protection of private landowners is a forerunner to the situation in the fourth century, when the imperial government struggled against the patronage offered by large landowners that tended to undermine the authority of the institutions of the state (see chap. 5). In the present case, the imperial government's response to this situation was to defend the traditional tenure rights of its tenants. The very publication of the petition and, presumably, the now lost response of the emperors on a large marble stele in the central village of the estate suggests that the petitioners viewed their efforts to defend their traditional rights as successful.

At the same time, the inscriptions discussed here also demonstrate the imperial government's readiness to intervene to offer imperial tenants the same type of protection that large landowners were able to obtain. For example, a large landowner from the Phrygian Pentapolis petitioned to protect his estates against incursions by soldiers.[96] We learn of this petition from an inscription, dated to the years 187–191, preserving a letter written by a military tribune to the administrator of a group of private estates belonging to a single owner. In this letter, the military tribune quoted the response that the governor of Asia, T. Flavius Sulpicianus, gave to a petition from the landowner.[97] The landowner complained of disturbances caused by soldiers passing through the estates and demanding meals. In this case, the landowner could deal with the imperial administration on an individual basis, and the letter from the tribune was apologetic in tone and promised an end to the inappropriate behavior of the soldiers. This landowner could approach the imperial government on much the same basis as the recipients of the so-called *sacrae litterae*, a rescript of the emperor Septimius Severus in which the emperor refers to a *senatus consultum* (decree of the senate) exempting Roman senators from the obligation to house soldiers.[98] The point is that the institutions of the state did not serve the interests of large landowners alone.

CONCLUSION

The imperial responses to these petitions allow us to trace the bases on which the Roman government adjudicated disputes involving the rural economy: first, the reliance of the imperial government on small-scale cultivation to gain revenues from imperial estates; second, the tendency of the government to support vested property rights (especially of *coloni* on imperial estates); third, the ideology of the government to champion the rights of imperial tenants over the interests of large private landowners or officials. The imperial government seems to have been quite conservative, defending established property rights and avoiding any innovation. This policy of guaranteeing property rights established years or even generations in the past surely offered small farmers some degree of protection against inroads by larger landowners. If landowners forced small farmers off their land to incorporate it into a larger estate, it was not with the active support of the imperial government.

The inscriptions concerning the tenure rights of *coloni* on imperial estates in North Africa and Asia Minor help us to understand how the legal and social concerns of the Roman government coincided. In the decision-making process of the Roman government, a legal policy of respecting time-honored land-tenure arrangements was inseparable from a method of exploiting agricultural resources that relied on small-scale cultivators. The Roman government's policy of privileging the tenure rights of small-scale cultivators on imperial estates was a response to the many uncertainties surrounding the market for agricultural products and the atmosphere for long-term investment in agriculture. The long-term goal of the imperial administration was to safeguard a supply of foodstuffs that it could use for various crucial purposes, including supplementing the food supply for the city of Rome. Rather than trust the free market to produce food for the city of Rome, the administration intervened in the rural economy and simply reserved for its own use some portion of the surplus produced by numerous small-scale farmers.

This policy resulted in a fairly rigid system of tenure that precluded other potentially more efficient allocations of resources, but it can be understood as a response to the high transaction costs that are likely to have accompanied alternative contractual arrangements. The Roman government's insistence on the rule of law in the countryside tended to support the interests of imperial tenants, even when doing so compromised the interests of locally powerful people. Thus the situation for the farmers on the estates in Asia Minor may not have been as bleak as described by Stephen Mitchell, who suggests that the landowners exercised control over whatever portion of the harvest might be marketed in the cities, leaving the peasant farmers themselves with little beyond subsistence and seed.[99] Upholding the tenure rights of imperial *coloni* may have been an economically sound policy, to the extent that the administration established tenure rights for a group of farmers from whom it could always capture some portion of the surplus that they produced. At the same time, to the extent that revenues from the imperial estates funded food distributions in Rome, they can be seen as productive from the perspective of supporting a public good, albeit one from which the cultivators on the imperial estates themselves did not benefit.[100] But this policy also fostered its own continuation, as the government responded to conflicts not by devising a new property rights regime that might correspond better to current economic realities but by insisting on the observance of established policy. In effect, the Roman government's maintenance of time-honored property rights became a major part of the economic reality, influencing the distribution of wealth between landowners and cultivators. In the next chapters, I examine how the Roman government, in developing rules for private farm tenancy, confronted the same economic factors that created the institutional path dependence inherent in the government's policies in administering imperial estates.

CHAPTER 3

Roman Legal Policy and Private Farm Tenancy

The formal and informal institutions surrounding farm tenancy played a fundamental role in shaping the Roman agrarian economy, in particular, the distribution of wealth between large landowners and the small farmers who cultivated the bulk of the land. In this chapter, I clarify the likely economic effects engendered by the Roman government's legal policies surrounding farm tenancy by analyzing how the jurists dealt with two areas of the law crucial to the Roman agrarian economy: the risk in agriculture caused by weather and the tenant's security of tenure. My focus in this chapter is on the formal institutions surrounding tenancy. They encompass the laws surrounding land tenure, in particular the classical Roman law of farm tenancy, as well as the institutions that served to enforce these laws, including the law courts and the Roman state. Informal institutions, such as social values and local traditions, are more difficult to detect in the legal sources but probably also played a significant role in defining the conditions surrounding land tenure.[1]

Farm tenancy was an institution crucial to the financial interests of upper-class Romans.[2] It provided Roman landowners with a means to simplify the difficult task of managing diverse properties that were often scattered geographically.[3] In addition, tenancy gave landowners a means of organizing labor, a consideration that might be especially important in exploiting properties that were isolated or for other reasons could not be cultivated in common with a larger set of properties.[4] In some cases, tenancy provided an additional advantage as well, in that it allowed landowners to share the costs of investing in agriculture with their tenants.

The managerial and investment-sharing advantages of farm tenancy might be very attractive for upper-class landowners who could reduce their own managerial costs and exposure to risk by relying on tenants for the day-to-day management of their land and for the continued investment in its upkeep that was needed to ensure its productivity for the long term.[5]

By examining the formal institutions surrounding farm tenancy, we can trace certain broad principles that guided Roman legal policy. The Roman government did not prescribe systems of land tenure but instead reacted to legal issues put before it as it responded to the needs of the empire's subjects. To some extent Roman legal policy was guided by a legal conservatism, since the government was reluctant to cast aside time-honored legal categories as economic and social conditions in the empire changed. But the very efforts of the Roman legal authorities to use conventional Roman private law as a way to interpret the rights and duties of the empire's subjects often allows us to glimpse at the underlying economic relationships. At the same time, however, I would argue that the government was guided by an understanding of the economic realities of the empire that it shared with upper-class Romans. This is the class, of course, from which the Roman legal authorities were recruited.[6] In the conception of the jurists, agriculture represented primarily a form of security rather than an investment in the modern sense. Many upper-class landowners would have managed their holdings in such a way as to achieve stable and predictable incomes that would help maintain their privileged social position. Such landowners would not have been interested first and foremost in choosing among various options for investing their wealth, since the Roman economy offered them few investment choices that could be expected to provide stable returns for the long term.[7]

In its efforts to adjudicate legal issues connected with the agrarian economy, the Roman government faced the difficult problem of interpreting in a consistent manner the rights and duties of the empire's subjects, who lived under a wide variety of land-tenure arrangements. This problem became more acute as the imperial government was called upon with increasing frequency to settle legal disputes. Thus, when we analyze the government's legal policy in the rural economy, we won't be examining the tenure arrangements of any particular locality but rather the way in which the Roman legal authorities defined such tenure arrangements as they imposed a legal order that facilitated the adjudication of disputes. Their policy was to foster, to the extent that the adjudication of legal disputes allowed them to do so, tenure arrangements that promoted bargaining between landowners and tenants.[8] Such bargaining, all things being equal, could help to create incentives for the type of investment needed for greater productivity in agriculture. However, the realities of the Roman economy involved the government in another effort as well: to protect farm tenants against the opportunistic behavior of large landowners who might take advantage of tenants in long-term tenure arrangements by imposing greater burdens on them.

ROMAN LEGAL POLICY AND THE RELATIONAL CONTRACT

As discussed in the previous chapter, in administering its imperial estates, the Roman government clearly recognized the usefulness of creating and defending the rights to the land of small-scale cultivators. Private landowners also benefited from the long-term presence of tenants, and they could be more flexible in devising labor and land-tenure arrangements on their estates. So the question now arises whether the Roman government applied any of these considerations when it addressed legal questions surrounding private farm tenancy. When we examine their treatment of certain crucial areas of tenancy law, it seems clear that the legal authorities were ready to modify the conventional Roman private lease terms to suit the realities of the agrarian economy by recognizing as legally binding long-term tenancy relationships based on local, customary tenure arrangements rather than on Roman law.

Let us begin by considering the terms of the conventional Roman farm lease.[9] As indicated in the previous chapter, the Roman farm lease represented a solution to a problem of agency, in which the principal, or landowner, had to rely on an agent, the tenant, to perform the necessary tasks to keep the land productive and thereby provide an income. The problem that landowners faced was to establish incentives for appropriate investment by the tenant and to monitor the performance of the tenant.[10] At first sight, the classical Roman farm lease seems ideally designed to serve the interests of upper-class Romans who sought stable, long-term income from their estates. In the Roman farm lease, the tenant paid a cash rent (*merces*) for the farm held under lease (*fundus*), and the lease period was conventionally set at five years.

This type of leasing was advantageous to the landowner, since it allowed the landowner to achieve a predictable income from the farm. The landowner's costs were largely established at the outset, as he or she was generally obliged to provide the fixed capital, such as buildings, storage facilities, and olive and wine presses that the tenant needed to have a usable farm (*frui*). The tenant, in turn, provided movable capital, including tools, draft animals, and even slaves. Because he paid a rent in cash, the tenant could keep any proceeds that exceeded the rent agreed upon in the contract, and so he had every incentive to manage the farm well. At the same time, the tenant had the responsibility to sell the crops that he raised to pay the rent, and he bore the risk both for the size of the harvest and for the market price of the crops. Finally, the landowner had ample means to enforce the tenant's performance of his contractual obligations. Whatever property the tenant brought into the farm (*invecta aut illata*) was pledged as security for the rent and for the tenant's proper performance of his contractual obligations. In addition, the short-term duration of the conventional lease gave the landowner the option of dismissing an unsatisfactory tenant and leasing out the farm to someone else.

If, in developing rules for the classical farm lease, the Roman jurists envisioned the landowner and tenant as freely contracting to share resources in pursuit of a common economic goal, in the real world the relationships between landowners and tenants were likely to have been far more complex. One problem was providing tenants with an incentive to invest their own resources in maintaining the productivity of the farm. This could be a crucial issue with vines and olives, which were common cash crops and in many parts of the empire represented a major source of income for upper-class landowners. But here private landowners faced the same difficulty as the Fiscus did on imperial estates: vines and olives required substantial investment of labor and resources and, when newly planted, a long period of time before they produced any income. The Roman administration addressed this problem on its North African estates by giving the *coloni* perpetual leaseholds, but on private estates matters were not so straightforward. Occupying his land under a short-term lease, the conventional Roman tenant had little incentive to make long-term improvements that would only realize profits after his lease ended. This problem was exacerbated by the tenant's lack of legal possession, in that he was subject to eviction when the land that he cultivated changed ownership. The compensation to which he would be entitled for improvements that raised the value of the land could hardly make up for the uncertainty of being able to reap the profit of years of investing labor and other resources in the planting of crops such as olive trees.

The formal allocation of rights under classical Roman lease law had important economic implications, not all of which were particularly welcome to either landowners or tenants. On the one hand, the absence of any provision for specific performance in Roman lease law can be viewed as economically efficient, in that a Roman court would not compel either the landowner or the tenant to fulfill the contract, and thus to engage in wasteful activity, when it was advantageous to breach the contract and to pay the other party the resulting damages.[11] Specific performance would involve the landlord's being required to retain the tenant, even when it was to his or her advantage to put the farm to another use, while it would require the tenant to remain on the farm, even if he could gain by leaving the lease. On the other hand, if the tenant lost a lease on which he placed a high value, this situation could also represent a loss to society, since the compensation that he would gain through a lawsuit would probably not match the value of the lease to him. This is because of the so-called endowment effect, which represents the difference between the value that an owner of a piece of property (or a right) might place on it and the market price that society places on it. In Roman law, the market price would represent the basis for any legal settlement. Although the endowment effect is a very controversial subject among economists, it is likely to be appreciable when a commodity is not easily replaced with money.[12] In other words, a farm tenant in the Roman Empire, with few alternatives to making a living, would in all likelihood not be willing to surrender a lease at the market price but would require a premium. The loss to society is more apparent if the tenant were deterred from suing for compensation of the lease, because of his lack of access to a court or because of the social power of his landowner.

So the lack of security of the tenant in the conventional Roman farm lease represented a disincentive to investment, and Roman landowners and tenants had strong incentives to bargain around this. Since tenants with resources adequate to cultivate the farms of upper-class Romans productively were in short supply, landowners had an incentive to accord their tenants greater security of tenure than would be implicit in the conventional Roman lease.[13] Accordingly, it seems a likely hypothesis that landowners were willing to give up some of the advantages that the allocation of resources in the conventional lease gave them to safeguard what was really more important for their interests, namely, the continued productive cultivation of the land by the tenant. Likewise, tenants had every incentive to adjust the conventional terms of the Roman farm lease to make their tenure more secure.

From this perspective, it may be useful to consider the concept of the *relational contract*, which contemporary legal scholars have developed to analyze long-term, dynamic business relationships.[14] The term denotes long-term contracts in which much of the conduct of both parties is subject to flexibility, change, and thus renegotiation because of the uncertainty surrounding the original negotiation of the contract and the inability of the parties to anticipate future contingencies. To quote the definition of relational contracts offered by Charles Goetz and Robert Scott: "A contract is relational to the extent that the parties are incapable of reducing important terms of the arrangement to well-defined obligations. Such definitive obligations may be impractical because of inability to identify uncertain future conditions or because of inability to characterize complex adaptations adequately even when the contingencies themselves can be identified in advance."[15] In contemporary legal literature, this concept serves as an analytical tool to explain how parties bound together in business relationships that they have every desire to maintain constantly adjust the terms of the contractual relationship in response to changing circumstances.

The concept of the relational contract is rooted in the neoinstitutional approach to legal and economic analysis, which posits that people make economic decisions on the basis of limited, costly information. In neoclassical economics, by contrast, contracts can be viewed as "discrete transactions," that is, transactions that take place at a specific time for a specific purpose. In this mode of analysis, the parties only have a relationship with one another for the immediate purposes of the contract. Disputes can be appropriately settled in courts or other institutions providing legal enforcement, in strict accordance with legal rules. The purpose of any judgment is simply to satisfy the legal claims of the parties, without considering any ongoing or future relationship between the two parties, because no such relationship is anticipated.[16] The notion of a contract as a discrete transaction, moreover, presupposes complete knowledge on the part of the contracting parties. As Goetz and Scott describe the neoclassical contract: "All relevant risks can thus be assigned optimally—either by legal rule or through individualized agreement—because future contingencies are not only known and understood at the time the bargain is struck, but can also be addressed by efficacious contractual responses."[17]

The neoclassical conception of the contract as a discrete transaction, however, seems inadequate to explain long-term relationships that characterize much of the contemporary business world and surely characterized the agrarian economy of the Roman Empire, in which tenancy relationships often involved the tenant's long-term occupation of the land. The recourse to a court to settle a dispute had the effect of ending the contractual relationship, or, as Ian Macneil notes in discussing legal doctrines according to which courts settle disputes, of "picking up the pieces of broken contracts and allocating them between the parties on some basis deemed equitable."[18] The point is that business relationships are established in an uncertain world and no contract can anticipate all the future contingencies that might affect the business climate and the ability of the parties to a contract to continue to fulfill their obligations. So the concept of relational contracts, by contrast, explains how contracting parties will make adjustments to the contract, many of which could hardly have been anticipated at the outset, to maintain a relationship that is mutually profitable. Although this concept has been developed to explain the evolving contractual relationships in modern businesses, in particular in franchises and in employer-labor relationships, it seems that many of the considerations raised by this approach to contracts can be applied appropriately to the landlord-tenant relationship in the Roman world.

The Roman law of contract, in particular the classical law of farm tenancy, can be understood formally in terms of neoclassical analysis. Contracts in the classical law of farm tenancy were of short duration, and when a dispute arose, the courts simply functioned to allocate monetary damages to one party or the other. There was no provision for specific performance by either the landowner or the tenant, and the resolution of a dispute through a court of law effectively ended the contractual relationship. However, in my view, this neoclassical approach is inadequate for analyzing farm tenancy in the Roman Empire, since many, if not most, tenancy relationships were characterized by the tenant's long-term occupation of the land. As I argue in the following, the Roman legal authorities recognized the inadequacy of certain areas of classical Roman lease law as they struggled to adapt the law to the realities of the Roman agrarian economy. We will see this in their treatment of many areas of farm tenancy law, and in particular in their treatment of risk in agriculture. As they applied conventional Roman lease law to legal disputes representing a wide variety of tenure arrangements, the Roman legal authorities were guided by the desirability of preserving the contractual relationships between landowner and tenant in the face of contingencies that otherwise would have resulted in the termination of the lease.

The modern concept of the relational contract provides us with an important analytical framework within which to understand the Roman legal authorities' regulation of farm tenancy. Since, in general terms, neither the landowner nor the tenant could anticipate all the future contingencies that might surround the cultivation of land, both parties had every incentive to be flexible and to develop mechanisms to resolve disputes before the ultimate step of going to court might be taken. The flexibility that both landowners and tenants desired took many forms. In some cases, restricting the length of the lease contract served to preserve flexibility. This is likely to have been the case in Egypt, where many lease contracts were set for between one and three years.[19] The duration of these leases in and of itself tells us very little about the relative bargaining power of the landowner and the tenant or about the tenant's security of tenure. Rather, limiting the duration of the lease allowed both landowners and tenants to renegotiate key terms to the lease as circumstances changed. In Egypt, these circumstances included the changing levels of the Nile flood or the condition of dikes and canals and of the facilities designed to channel the flow of the Nile flood. Typically, the extent of the Nile flood had an especially important effect on land cultivated with grain, whereas vineyards and orchards were located on higher ground and required artificial irrigation.

In other parts of the empire, limiting the duration of the lease was not the primary means to adapt to changing circumstances; landowners and tenants found alternative means to accomplish this goal. The contractual relationship between landowners and tenants remained dynamic. What guided its development included both the formal legal institutions of the state and the more informal institutions, the latter of which were rooted in the expectations that both parties had about their respective rights and obligations. To be sure, the social relationship between landowners and tenant influenced the legal and economic one.[20] Indeed, Alfons Bürge argues that a social asymmetry was an inherent aspect of many Roman contracts, particularly those involving farm tenancy. Landowners may have entered into contractual relationships with tenants, but lurking behind these contracts was the social and economic dependence of the tenant, which gave the landowner wide latitude in exercising self-help to resolve disputes. Bürge sees such social dependency as establishing the ground rules for the ways in which Columella and Pliny the Younger treated their tenants, which I discuss in this chapter.[21] The likelihood of such social dependency in many tenancy arrangements does not mean that the legal relationship between landowner and tenant was inconsequential for the ability of both parties to defend their interests. Still, given the incentives that both landowners and tenants had to preserve the lease relationship, it is likely that most disputes were not resolved by resorting to the exact wording of the contract, if such wording even existed, let alone by going to court. Thus what we see in some constitutions concerning lease law in the Code of Justinian is the result of the occasional and total breakdown of the process, when no informal resolution of a dispute could be reached.

Such breakdowns were most likely to happen when one party or another wanted to withdraw from the lease.[22] The resulting legal settlement was designed simply to allocate resources in an equitable fashion to parties who would no longer seek to do business together.

This is not to say that the formal terms in accordance with which lease relationships were legally defined were irrelevant to the efforts of landowners and tenants to preserve relational contracts. On the contrary, the formal terms of the contract and the existence of viable institutions to enforce them provided an incentive for landowners to reach mutually satisfactory resolutions of disputes. The degree to which legal remedies were readily available would have enhanced the bargaining power of tenants, who could use the possibility of seeking the protection of the state to offset some of the advantages that the landowner exercised by virtue of his or her greater wealth and socially superior status.

The precise legal terms of the Roman lease, then, do not tell us how disputes were generally resolved. Instead, they represent the terms according to which the law would allocate resources if the lease arrangement broke down beyond recovery. We can trace the limitations of the neoclassical conception of the lease contract as a discrete transaction in the famous rescript that the emperor Antoninus Pius issued to a tenant seeking remission of rent on the grounds that the vines on the farm that he was leasing had become aged and were no longer productive (Ulp. *D.* 19.2.15.5, 32 *ad ed.*). The emperor rejected the tenant's claim for a remission of rent in this case; indeed, the age of the vines was certainly a circumstance that any tenant could be expected to foresee upon entering into a tenancy contract. But as I have argued elsewhere, the tenant making this unusual claim for a remission of rent was in all likelihood involved in a long-term tenancy relationship, and the costs of renewing the vines on the farm under lease were something to be negotiated if the landowner and tenant both desired to prolong the lease relationship.[23] The fact that the tenant in this case petitioned the Roman government for a legal remedy to what ordinarily would have been a matter for negotiation strongly suggests that the lease relationship had broken down beyond repair. In view of the advanced age of the vines, the tenant probably sought a reduction of his rent, and having failed to obtain this through negotiation with his landlord, he took the ultimate step of resorting to the courts. This involved refusing to pay his rent and, having been sued for it and lost, appealing to the emperor.

We can put the decision of Antoninus Pius in rejecting the petition of the tenant in broader terms by considering how American courts tend to resolve disputes involving long-term contracts. In this situation, such contracts are likely to be "incomplete," in the sense that the parties have not bargained to cover all contingencies. Legal scholars have often envisioned people as leaving contracts incomplete because they are deterred by the prohibitive costs involved in negotiating significant contractual terms. As Alan Schwartz describes the situation, "certain contracts are incomplete not because the parties overlooked or failed to understand the issue that came to divide them but because they are unwilling to bear the strategic-behavior risk that a complete contract would create."[24]

So the courts, when faced with litigation on contracts involving such gaps, often try to resolve them by establishing default rules, that is, the rules to cover nonnegotiated terms of a contract. The effort to establish default rules typically involves determining what the parties would have wanted had they negotiated the term in question. This can take two forms: an untailored default rule, in which the typical party is imagined, or a tailored default rule, in which the court seeks to determine what the individual parties in the present contract would have wanted. Untailored default rules are said to "mimic the market."[25]

The efforts of parties to a contract to account for future contingencies are complicated by asymmetries of information. For example, in a lease contract, the tenant would in all likelihood have much more specific information about the factors affecting his ability to complete the terms of the contract by farming the land productively. In his analysis of the role of American courts in adjudicating disputes involving such contracts, Schwartz argues that the courts tend to avoid filling the gaps in incomplete, long-term, relational contracts.[26] In Schwartz's analysis, the courts, when confronted with such cases, will tend to judge them "passively"; that is, the courts will tend to avoid devising terms to the contract that the parties themselves have not negotiated. Modern American courts, then, will tend not to adapt or alter the contractual terms to preserve a long-term relationship by filling in the gaps to cover contingencies that the parties themselves left unresolved. Instead, the courts will seek to interpret the contract according to the parties' intentions, rather than substituting their own judgment in making contractual terms for those of the original parties to the contract. In other words, the courts will tend "to treat incomplete contracts *as if* those contracts were complete."[27] This means that the courts will not be in a position to impose economically "efficient" solutions, since the courts are constrained to judge cases in accordance with commonly accepted principles. It seems unlikely that the Roman courts were in any better position to impose economically efficient default rules. Rather, the Roman legal authorities seem to have imposed default rules, at least in lease contracts, that facilitated the courts' ability to adjudicate disputes.[28]

To return to our case about the advanced age of the vines, let us suppose that this case did originate from a long-term lease relationship, and the struggle really was about allocating the costs of the upkeep of the vines that were crucial to the profitability of the lease. In this case, we could imagine that there would by a substantial asymmetry of information between the tenant and the landowner. Of course, the tenant might have more specific knowledge than the landowner about the age and condition of the vines, but it would not be difficult for the landowner to verify this information. The real asymmetry of information would involve the effort the tenant had made in maintaining the vines. We cannot know what type of understanding, if any, the tenant had made with the landowner about the upkeep of the vines.

But even if the landowner and tenant had agreed that the tenant would take certain steps to maintain the vines and receive some consideration from the landowner in return, it would be difficult for either party to prove his or her own adherence to the contract or the noncompliance of the other party.[29] So the tenant attempted to resolve a gap in the contract by appealing to traditional lease law, and thereby to impose a substantial share of the costs of maintaining the vines on the landowner. The court (i.e., the emperor) responded in the same terms that the tenant used to make his claim. The emperor was in no position to issue a ruling on the basis of any private understanding that the landowner and tenant might have reached about maintaining the vines, but he instead interpreted the rights and responsibilities of landowner and tenant in terms of a purely conventional Roman lease, which contained no provision for the gradual replacement of aging vines. In effect, the Roman government was not interested in determining whether there was a gap in the individual contract that led to the appeal to the emperor. Rather, the government fell back on a default rule that did not take into account what the parties to the contract were likely to have wanted.[30] This is likely to have been the way that the Roman courts commonly responded to disputes between landowners and tenants. The background to such cases is almost always certain to have been far more complex than we might conclude from the brief reports accompanying rescripts in the Digest or the Code of Justinian to petitions that came to the emperor.

This particular tenant's lack of success should not, however, undermine the overall importance of legal institutions in setting parameters for the informal avenues of dispute resolution available to Roman landowners and tenants. The availability of the legal institutions of the state as a realistic option to resolve disputes influenced the behavior of the countless landowners and tenants who never set foot in a court of law or sent a petition to the emperor or any other Roman official. Certainly most disputes were likely to have been resolved through informal means that did not directly involve the law. To appreciate the role of informal mechanisms, we might consider the crucial role that they play in resolving disputes in other societies, where they often function alongside of the courts. Robert Ellickson's analysis of relationships between ranchers and farmers in rural Shasta County, California, provides an instructive comparison.[31] One major issue in this setting was the damage done to property by livestock that were allowed to roam freely in search of pasture.

In Ellickson's analysis, both ranchers and farmers were interested in preserving long-term relationships with their neighbors based on cooperation and reciprocity, and so they would use informal means to resolve disputes, and when these failed, they would sanction the offending party informally, relying on various means of self-help, rather than going to court. Only in extreme cases would people resort to formal means of redress to address grievances, such as formal petitions to county agents. Indeed, residents of this county were generally poorly informed about the state laws regulating liability for damage caused by livestock, and they tended to settle such cases in terms of their own sense of fairness and reciprocity rather than in strict conformance with the law. Still, resorting to the law courts remained an option, especially when the stakes were high.

We should expect that in the isolated rural society of the Roman Empire, informal means of resolving disputes would have played an even greater role. But at the same time, petitions preserved on papyri in Roman Egypt and those preserved in the Code of Justinian suggest strongly that, even in the Roman world, the law always stood in the background, providing one means of resolving disputes. So it is likely that as the state intervened in local affairs by responding to petitions, relationships between landowners in the Roman Empire developed "in the shadow of the law."

This phrase has found its way into discussion of law and economics from a famous study of divorce settlements in the United States by Robert Mnookin and Lewis Kornhauser.[32] In the view of these two scholars, the legal rules surrounding divorce settlements establish the basic conditions under which negotiations are conducted: "In other words, the outcome that the law will impose if no agreement is reached gives each parent bargaining chips—an endowment of sorts."[33] The final negotiated settlement in divorce settlements is a product not simply of the law but also of the two parties' attitudes toward risk, of transaction costs, and of the strategies that they adopt in negotiating.[34] In the Roman Empire, the law set the basic parameters within which tenancy relationships might be negotiated, but social factors also influenced these relationships.[35]

If, as I argue in the following, the Roman government tended to adjudicate disputes in terms of conventional Roman law, this does not necessarily mean that landowners and tenants saw themselves as formulating lease arrangements in accordance with these conventions. Rather, Roman law provided a set of rules to allocate the resources of landowners and tenants when irreconcilable differences made continuation of the lease arrangement impossible. Indeed, a dispute over rights to land from an imperial estate at Beth Phouraia in Syria (discussed in the introduction) suggests strongly that farmers in many locations in the Roman Empire were able to obtain, when circumstances warranted, sufficient knowledge about how to approach the Roman law courts and to present their cases effectively in terms of Roman legal categories. In this case, the cultivators of the imperial estate asserted their claim to their land on the basis of Roman legal norms. The extent to which legal conventions provided landowners and tenants in the Roman Empire basic starting points for negotiating their ongoing relationships depended on how real the possibility was of ultimately resorting to a court to settle disputes. The case from the imperial estate at remote Beth Phouraia in Syria suggests that this was a real possibility.

At the same time, other factors influenced the relationships between landowners and tenants. As M. Galanter suggests, legal relationships among parties can also be shaped by what he terms *indigenous law*, that is, the "other normative orderings that pervade social life."[36] Indeed, parties in a potential conflict might not fully or accurately understand normative legal rules. On occasion, the courts may even function to impose solutions that respect "indigenous" rules.[37] For our purposes, indigenous law would include customs, including the traditions of respect for hierarchy and status. These varied from region to region but shaped the relationships between landowners and tenants. Such relationships, of course, are difficult to reconstruct from the legal sources.

To return to the relational contract, we can gain a sense of how this concept helps to explain Roman lease relationships by examining how Columella and Pliny the Younger, our two principal literary sources for farm tenancy in the early empire, defined and endeavored to solve the principal difficulties that they encountered in dealing with their tenants. Both writers assume that the formal rules surrounding farm tenancy guided landowners as they entered upon lease relationships with tenants, but that the legal recourse that landowners had hardly represented a viable solution to many of the disputes that might arise with tenants.

In his recommendations about the proper management of tenants, the first-century agronomist Columella was particularly concerned with making sure that the tenant remained on the land, cultivating it productively for the long term.[38] The careful cultivation of the land, in Columella's view, was the most important contribution that the tenant made, and it was more important than the tenant's timely payment of rent or performance of other services (*De re rust.* 1.7.1–4). For Columella, careful stewardship on the part of the landowner meant avoiding being placed in a position of having to go to court to enforce lease terms. So it was best not to lease to a "city tenant," who did not cultivate the land personally but employed his own slaves, because such a tenant would be less likely to have a commitment to the land and a personal relationship with the landowner. Ideally, the landowner could avoid being forced to grant a remission of rent except in the most extreme circumstances, such as a climatic disaster or an attack of brigands, extreme circumstances that are precisely those under which tenants in conventional Roman lease law were entitled to seek a remission of rent.[39] For Columella, a tenant making a legal claim on the lease was a real possibility; such a claim was only enforceable to the extent that the tenant could seek the relief provided by a court of law. The possible recourse to the courts certainly influenced how Columella's putative tenants might have dealt with him, but it seems clear that Columella envisioned the best solution to a dispute with a tenant was one that left both parties standing at the end of the day. Columella preferred a tenant who would be less likely to view the lease as "'transactional," that is, oriented toward the immediate realization of a profit. He instead sought a tenant with whom it would be possible to establish an ongoing and mutually beneficial relationship. To do this, Columella had to remain flexible, since the tenant's continuing productive cultivation of the land was his priority. The wide social and economic gulf that separated a landowner like Columella from his tenants does not alter this situation.

The interplay of formal and informal institutions surrounding farm tenancy is also apparent in the case of Pliny, whose published correspondence allows us to trace how a senatorial landowner dealt with problems connected with the leasing of his estates to tenants.[40] The question that is important for our purposes is how problems would be resolved when the *coloni* cultivating land belonging to a larger landowner did not perform their contractual obligations. To judge by Pliny's description of the plight of the impoverished tenants on the estate at Tifernum Tiberinum, whose purchase he was contemplating (*Ep.* 3.19), landowners always had the option of following established legal procedures to enforce the tenants' contractual obligations. On this estate, the tenants had chronically fallen behind on their rent, and the previous owner of the estate had addressed this situation by confiscating the tenants' pledges. The fact that this pledged property included slaves indicates that the tenants, their arrears in rent notwithstanding, had considerable resources at their disposal. What is unclear is whether (1) the previous owner exercised this right by taking unilateral action against the tenants in arrears or (2) the confiscation of the tenants' pledges was conducted under the scrutiny of the courts, a procedure on whose observance the Roman legal authorities insisted, at least beginning in the second century (see chap. 4).

In dealing with his own tenants, Pliny seems to have eschewed these drastic legal steps in favor of a more accommodating relationship. Thus he granted his tenants substantial remissions of rent on several occasions (*Ep.* 10.8.5),[41] and when this measure did not solve the problem, he replaced the traditional system of cash leases with sharecropping (*Ep.* 9.37). In Pliny's case, and no doubt in the case of many other landowners, transaction costs played a major role in influencing the way in which he dealt with his tenants. Pliny depended on his tenants to cultivate his land productively, and they invested their own considerable resources in this endeavor. Even if there were tenants capable of taking over the leases for the ones who had fallen chronically behind in their rent, replacing sitting tenants would have been a very costly step. Given the likelihood that most tenants cultivated a variety of crops and the fact that the growing and harvest seasons for these crops varied over the course of the year, a landowner who evicted an unsatisfactory tenant would certainly face the possibility that the land would be uncultivated for an inconveniently long period of time. So the landowner had an incentive to take steps to prolong the relationship, that is, to find cooperative ways to resolve disputes. For their part Pliny's tenants also had an incentive to keep the lease relationship intact. To the extent that they invested their own resources in the cultivation of Pliny's land, they had many sunk costs that they could not recover if they lost their leases.

The many steps that Pliny took to alleviate their problems of indebtedness indicate his strong desire to maintain a relational contract with his tenants. His decision to institute sharecropping (*Ep.* 9.37) shows the leverage that tenants could apply. In Pliny's description, the impoverished tenants had given up on the idea of ever getting out of debt, and so they cultivated their land in what Pliny considered to be a destructive manner (*Ep.* 9.37.2). Concerned with preserving what was most valuable for him in the lease relationship, Pliny sought out a permanent solution to the costly risks that his tenants faced by instituting a system of tenure in which risk would be shared more equally between landowner and tenant. Sharecropping represented for Pliny a contractual arrangement better designed to deal with future uncertainty than the traditional system of leases for cash rents. As discussed in the following, the decision to adopt this form of land tenure resulted from a complex bargaining process between Pliny and his tenants.

It seems likely that a landowner like Pliny would resort to a court action against his tenants only under the most extreme circumstances. Part of the difficulty, of course, was that Pliny and other landowners faced a great deal of trouble in finding new tenants, as Pliny complains in a letter about his Tuscan estates (*Ep.* 7.30.3). When Pliny visited his estates, the possibility of taking tenants to court probably ranked low on his agenda. Instead, he went to his estates to negotiate and settle the disputes of others. Thus Pliny complains that when he visits his estates, he has difficulty finding the time for his studies (*Ep.* 7.30). Instead, in his description, he was often called upon to serve either as a judge (*iudex*), presumably in a traditional formulary procedure, or as an arbiter (*Ep.* 7.20.2). In addition, Pliny was called upon to settle complaints of farmers in the area (*rustici*).[42] Whether these *rustici* were Pliny's own tenants or other small farmers in the area is not clear; since Pliny refers in the next sentence to leasing his estates to lessees (*conductores*), the former possibility does not seem likely.

This letter suggests Pliny's status as a large landowner placed him in a position to settle a variety of disputes involving small farmers in the neighborhood of his estates. Given the matter of fact way in which Pliny reports these activities, his service as judge or arbiter appears to be a completely conventional duty for upper-class landowners in regions in which they owned substantial property. If landowners regularly played such a role, then it seems very likely that they would exercise a great deal of influence over the adjudication of disputes involving landowners and tenants, and this local influence would give landowners a great deal of leverage in disputes with their own tenants.

Pliny's concern in his letter to Trajan with exploring the possibility of remissions of rent after continued poor crops suggests the role that strict legal norms could play even when Pliny was engaging in more informal negotiations with his tenants (*Ep.* 10.8.5). Certainly the remissions of rent that Pliny contemplated granting are to be understood as "social remissions." After all, Pliny was taking the initiative in granting these remissions; he does not seem to have reacted to any legal claim lodged by his tenants but rather to the tenants' apparent inability to pay the agreed upon rent.[43] At the very least, Pliny's strict adherence to legal norms in dealing with his tenants meant that, in the event of a serious dispute, Pliny could call upon the full protection of the legal institutions of the state to support his claims. Based on this evidence, it is not possible to conclude that Pliny's tenants could likewise claim this protection. But Pliny's letters do suggest that Roman law defined the rights and obligations of landowners and tenants in the countryside, and Pliny's concern with legal forms suggests that he could not simply exercise self-help to enforce the obligations of his tenants. The rights that the tenants theoretically had did play some role in their relationship with their landlord.

But the most important conclusion from Pliny's experience with his tenants was that he frequently adjusted the terms of tenure for his tenants in order to maintain a mutually beneficial contractual relationship. Certainly Pliny exercised a great deal of power in setting the terms of this relationship, as the substantial social and economic gulf that separated him from his tenants would make us expect. For their part, the tenants were not completely powerless to adjust the terms of tenure to their own advantage, as is indicated by the fact that their methods of cultivation compelled Pliny to adopt sharecropping. The drastic step of replacing the traditional and more convenient system of cash rents with sharecropping demonstrates clearly the relational nature of Roman lease contracts. The institution of sharecropping adjusted the contract to circumstances that neither party to the lease anticipated at the outset. But more important, sharecropping offered Pliny a way to keep adjusting the contract to keep pace with future contingencies. Sharecropping may or may not have been the optimal allocation of resources for Pliny, but since he had no way of foretelling the future market for agricultural products, sharecropping represented a relatively low-cost solution to the problem of maintaining a system of tenancy on his estates that he found beneficial.

THE ALLOCATION OF RISK

The example of Pliny suggests how a Roman landowner might be flexible in interpreting contractual arrangements to preserve a long-term tenure arrangement that he or she found advantageous. In my view, the Roman government also recognized the desirability of preserving long-term tenure arrangements, despite the short-term nature of the classical Roman lease contract as it adjudicated disputes involving a wide variety of tenure arrangements throughout the Roman Empire. We can trace how the government responded to this challenge by considering its treatment of risk in agriculture.

Agriculture in the Mediterranean area was subject to substantial risks, especially those posed by the irregularity of rainfall, which on average might be sufficient to allow for the production of wheat and other basic staples, but which also might vary considerably from one year to the next.[44] Classical Roman law imposed the bulk of the risk upon the farm tenant, who, since he paid a rent in cash, was responsible both for the size of the harvest and for the market price of the crops. In the formulation of the late-Republican jurist Servius Sulpicius Rufus, Roman law granted the tenant relief only when an unforeseeable disaster (*vis maior*) made it impossible for him to fulfill his contractual obligations (Servius apud Ulp. *D.* 19.2.15.2, 32 *ad ed.*; cf. Gaius *D.* 19.2.25.6, 10 *ad ed. prov.*).[45] The types of disasters that qualified as *vis maior* included an invasion of an army, an unusual infestation by predatory birds, or an unforeseeable natural disaster like an earthquake or an unaccustomed heat wave. But Roman law granted the tenant no relief for the foreseeable risks associated with agriculture (*vitia ex re*), such as the infestation of a grain crop by birds or weeds, or theft by a passing army. In contrast to an unaccustomed heat wave, seasonal variations in rainfall that could produce drought were foreseeable disasters.

To some extent this allocation of risk promoted productivity, since it induced landowners and tenants to "internalize" the costs of the risks associated with agriculture, in that these costs were factored into the bargaining process between landowner and tenant. The alternative was that the risks inherent in Mediterranean agriculture would remain an "externality" so that tenants could recover the costs of a disastrous harvest without bargaining for them, which is sometimes interpreted as a form of "market failure."[46] Thus the traditional allocation of risk in Roman tenancy law made the landowner responsible only for the most unpredictable risks, which were not necessarily the most extreme risks, since drought, resulting from annual variation in rainfall, or other foreseeable disasters could ruin the crop just as badly as a disaster classified as *vis maior* and leave the tenant equally unable to pay his rent. Because the tenant was responsible for most of the risks associated with weather, he had every incentive to take steps to reduce his exposure to the irregularities of Mediterranean agriculture. Accordingly, tenants might take measures to shield themselves from risk, such as storing surpluses, diversifying their crops by engaging in polyculture, cultivating crops such as barley that are more resistant to drought, or reducing their investment in inputs in each unit of land cultivated and instead using their resources to farm additional land elsewhere.[47] Under these circumstances, the costs that the tenant bore in taking these steps to reduce risk would be included in the bargaining surrounding the lease contract. Indeed, the existence of default rules that impose the risk for serious contingencies on one party or the other have been seen in contemporary contract law as providing the parties with an incentive to develop cooperative strategies to reduce risk.[48]

From the perspective of law and economics, the allocation of risk in the classical Roman farm lease promoted efficiency, in the sense of achieving the greatest product from the exchange resulting from the contract. This issue characteristically arises when one party seeks discharge from its obligations on the grounds that performance of the contract is no longer economically feasible. The grounds typically presented in such cases include (1) "impossibility of performance," when it is no longer "physically possible" for one party to fulfill the contract; (2) "frustration of purpose," which refers to the situation in which it is still physically possible to perform the contract but the purpose for which the contract was entered into in the first place no longer obtains; and (3) "impracticability," which refers to a situation in which unexpected developments will make the performance of the contract a severe economic hardship on one of the parties.[49] Discharge will be efficient when the savings generated to the party seeking to withdraw from a contract outweigh the costs that result for the other party. Otherwise, failure to perform will be treated as a breach of contract.

It is a continuing controversy in the scholarship on the relationship between law and economics whether American courts should, let alone can, adjudicate contracts in such a way as to promote economic efficiency. In a now classic article on the subject, Richard Posner and Andrew Rosenfield have argued forcefully that the courts would serve the interests of both parties to a contract by promoting efficiency:

> If the purpose of the law of contracts is to effectuate the desires of the contracting parties, then the proper criterion for evaluating the rules of contract law is surely that of economic efficiency. Since the object of most voluntary exchanges is to increase value or efficiency, contracting parties may be assumed to desire a set of contract terms that will maximize the value of the exchange. It is true that each party is interested only in the value of the contract to it. However, the more efficiently the

exchange is structured, the larger is the potential profit of the contract for the parties to divide between them.[50]

Critics of this view have raised doubts whether courts are capable of identifying the solutions to disputes that would promote efficiency, and so they argue that the courts will judge cases on quite different grounds, including fairness or equity.[51] Thus, as discussed previously, Alan Schwartz sees courts as hesitant to opt for economically efficient interpretations of contracts. Instead, the courts interpret contracts "passively," in the sense of interpreting the explicit terms of the contract strictly, rather than, say, filling in the gaps, or supplying terms, in incomplete contracts. The courts are especially likely to adjudicate contracts in this way when the information required to fill the gaps is difficult to substantiate in court.[52]

This discussion may seem somewhat abstract, but it does shed some light on the approach that the Roman legal authorities took to the issue of remission of rent in farm leases. In the view of Posner and Rosenfield, the courts promote economic efficiency by considering which party is the "superior risk bearer." The ability to bear risk is measured in terms of economic efficiency, and the superior risk bearer is the one who (1) can take the actions that will "prevent the risk from materializing" and (2) can more cheaply insure against the risk, either by being in the better position to assess the costs and risks connected with a contract or by taking steps to cover the costs associated with the risks (self-insuring), by diversifying portfolios, or even by purchasing insurance.[53] So the courts will promote efficiency by holding liable the party that is in the better position to minimize or bear the costs for the circumstances that prevent the contract from being fulfilled. Considering the superior risk bearer promotes efficiency, because doing so provides incentives to take the steps to minimize the effects of risk and thus ultimately secures the largest product.

To apply this approach to the Roman law of tenancy, the tenant is clearly the superior risk bearer for the normal hazards of farming, since the tenant is in a position to decide on inputs and can take the steps necessary to prevent losses from the foreseeable hazards. Likewise, the landowner is the superior risk bearer for the unforeseeable catastrophic hazards, such as *vis maior* as defined in classical Roman lease law, since the landowner is in a much better position than a tenant to ride out such a disaster by diversifying holdings (e.g., by owning estates in different regions or by storing up savings sufficient to withstand a sudden loss of income). In fact, the landowner is also the superior risk bearer for catastrophic drought, which might destroy the crop or prevent the production of a crop, but which is not included among the unforeseeable hazards classified as *vis maior*. The issue is not simply, or even at all, whether the landowner has more resources and so can ride out the storm, so to speak. But since the landowner is likely to have larger holdings than the tenant, the landowner is in a better position to take steps to mitigate the losses that climate might impose. The classical Roman law of risk, then, seemed to encourage the type of activities on the part of landowners and tenants that could be viewed as efficient from an economic perspective. Roman law would hold the tenant liable when circumstances subject to his control resulted in a loss, no matter how catastrophic, whereas it would hold the landowner liable when the circumstances resulting in the loss were beyond the control of the tenant.

The problem with this approach is that it imposed on tenants a larger portion of the risk than their relative bargaining power with landowners would suggest that they would have to bear. This situation can be seen in Pliny's experience. Pliny's tenants encountered continuing difficulties in paying their rent, and this was a problem that was apparently not confined to his own estates. Thus when he was considering the purchase of an estate adjacent to his existing property at Tifernum Tiberinum, the poor condition of the tenants, who had fallen behind on their rent and seen their pledges confiscated by the previous owner, led Pliny to hesitate to complete his purchase (*Ep.* 3.19). Pliny's solution to the problems of the "continuing poor crops" (*continuae sterilitates*) experienced by his own tenants was to grant social remissions of rent, ones not required by a strict interpretation of Roman lease law (*Ep.* 10.8.5, 9.37.2; see the preceding). This measure did not solve the problems besetting his tenants but instead had the undesirable consequence of allowing his tenants to externalize the costs of risk, in that they left these costs for Pliny to bear. But Pliny did not allow this undesirable situation to endure for long, and instead of granting further remissions, he replaced the traditional and convenient system of cash rents with sharecropping on his property at Tifernum Tiberinum. The establishment of sharecropping meant that the costs of risk in agriculture were again internalized, in this case with both the landowner and tenant sharing them, much as they were on the North African imperial estates. Pliny made a substantial sacrifice by adopting sharecropping, since he faced greater costs of enforcement and no longer had the convenience of receiving his rent in cash. But the advantage was that he could maintain a tenure system that gave his tenants an incentive to cultivate their land productively for the long term.

To return to the imperial estates in North Africa, the costs arising from the risk in agriculture were also internalized, since the sharecropping system in force there divided the risk between the *coloni* and the *conductores* and, by extension, the imperial administration. But there were limits to the extent that the imperial administration could induce the *coloni* to cultivate their land productively. Since they bore some of the costs arising from risk, the *coloni* had an incentive to practice the type of agriculture that minimized their risk. Accordingly, the regulations in the HM inscription indicate that the *coloni* cultivated a variety of crops, not only olives, vines, and wheat but also other cereal crops such as barley, figs and other fruit trees, and even honey. Since the HM inscription includes regulations about the pasturing of animals, it is likely that the *coloni* on the estate maintained their own flocks of sheep, which allowed them to produce food from land not otherwise suited for agriculture, and which also represented a form of food savings in lean years.[54]

In other parts of the Roman Empire, it is difficult to assess how the risk in agriculture was allocated, except in Egypt, where documentary papyri offer a great deal of detailed information about farm leases. There, the costs of risk were internalized much as in the Roman farm lease. The tenant was normally responsible for all risks, and only in the case of the most extreme risk, the failure of the Nile flood (*abrochia*), was the tenant entitled to any relief from the obligation to pay rent.[55] For grain land, the rent was generally exacted in fixed amounts of produce for each unit of land. Consequently, the tenant bore the risk for the size of the harvest and so had an incentive to take measures to reduce his risk. Since agricultural production depended on the annual flood of the Nile, the range of fluctuation in crop yield was much less than in the parts of the empire subject to a Mediterranean climate. Essentially, the Egyptian tenant faced much more of an all-or-nothing situation: if the Nile flood did not reach his land or if it receded too slowly, making it impossible to plant his crop, then the tenant would have no crop at all. But farmers in Roman Egypt did not face the risks associated with the highly irregular rainfall that characterized Roman agriculture. Consequently, farmers in Egypt reduced their exposure to risk by leasing land in a variety of locations, thereby minimizing the effects that fluctuations in the Nile flood might have on production. In addition, farm tenants in Egypt combined the cultivation of wheat with other crops, including figs, vines, and olives. These crops were often cultivated on land irrigated artificially, which further diminished the possibility of crop loss resulting from climatic conditions.

It should be emphasized that there is nothing inevitable about the distribution of risk in Roman lease law and the jurists' treatment of this issue. For example, in emphyteutic possession (an arrangement in late antiquity in which the emphyteutic possessor gained quasi-ownership rights over land in exchange for a yearly rental paid to the owner, whether the state or a private individual), the owner bore the cost for the complete destruction of the land held under emphyteutic right, but the emphyteutic possessor was responsible for all other risks (*CJ* 4.66.1, 476–84; Just. *Inst.* 3.24.3).[56] To put the Roman regime in some perspective, it is worth comparing it with the norms that existed in classical Greek law, as revealed by fourth-century BCE leases preserved on inscriptions from Attica and other parts of the Greek world.[57] Most of the leases seem to make no provision for risk whatsoever, which suggests that the risk for events that made the farm impossible to cultivate fell entirely on the lessee. Occasionally, however, provision was made for the difficulties caused by warfare, in which case the lessor would be entitled to one-half of whatever crop was left, instead of the standard rent in cash.[58] There seems to have been some room for negotiation on this issue. Thus the arrangements that a certain Xanthippos made in a perpetual lease for land belonging to the Attic deme of the Teithrasioi probably represented the best terms a tenant could gain, since he gained this lease in reward for services that he had rendered (*SEG* XXIV 151).[59] In this case, in the event of a hostile incursion, Xanthippos had the choice of paying half of the crop or withdrawing from the lease. A somewhat different approach to sharing risk can be seen in an arrangement, probably from 216 BCE, struck between the city of Anaktoria and the Akarnanians over the management of the festival of Apollo at Actium. The Akarnanians were now taking over responsibility for the staging of the festival (*IG* IX^2 583). The two parties were to share in equal portions the revenues from the festival. The Akarnanians were released from their obligation to organize the festival in the event of war or the presence of a friendly army (lines 44–46).

To return to the Roman world, the government confronted the same problems that Pliny faced as it adjudicated claims for remission of rent initiated by small-scale tenants. The problem that the Roman legal authorities faced was that there was a fine line between an unforeseeable risk that could be classified as *vis maior* and a climatic disaster, falling under the category of *vitia ex re*, that could be equally deleterious to the tenant's crop and leave the tenant equally unable to fulfill his contractual obligations. In adjudicating tenants' claims for remissions of rent, the Roman government did not prescribe a particular division of the substantial costs imposed by risk. Rather, it was concerned with defining the rights and obligations of landowners and tenants in the event that landowners granted social remissions, that is, remissions that were granted as a result of economic circumstances such as a poor crop (*ob sterilitatem*). This type of remission became an important issue for the Roman government, which was most concerned with the legal implications of something granted socially, as well as the social pressures that it might put on other landowners.[60] In effect, at issue is whether a landowner who granted a social remission was "estopped" from pursuing his or her claims for back rent in the future.

In this circumstance, the Roman courts had to confront the asymmetries of information that would have obtained between landowners and tenants. The concept of *sterilitas* (a poor crop) is sufficiently ambiguous that there could be a wide range of interpretation as to what constituted a disastrously poor harvest, and whether the tenant's own poor cultivation of the land might have contributed to the disaster. In this case, it might be "observable" that the tenant had or had not made a good-faith effort in cultivating the farm, but the tenant's effort would not be something that was easily "verifiable" in a court of law, in the sense that either party could prove claims made about the way in which the tenant cultivated the land.[61] The Roman courts did not interject themselves into this issue or even attempt to define what constituted *sterilitas*. Doing so would have placed the courts in the position of determining fact situations on which the litigating parties would not agree. Indeed, in his discussion of the circumstances allowing a remission of rent, Gaius only describes the crops as being damaged "more than was tolerable" (*si plus, quam tolerabile est, laesi fuerint fructus*). Otherwise, the tenant was to be prepared to tolerate a moderate loss (*modicum damnum*) (*D.* 19.2.25.6, 2 *ad ed. prov.*). Indeed, the lease contract could call for remissions of rent in the event of *sterilitas* to be established on the judgment of a third party (*boni viri abritratu*), as discussed in the *Opiniones* attributed to Ulpian (*D.* 50.8.3.2, 3 *opinionum*).[62] In addition, the landowner and tenant could bargain to shift the risk for *vis maior* entirely on the latter party, and such an agreement would be recognized in a court (Jul. apud Ulp. *D.* 19.2.9.2, 32 *ad ed.*).[63] So instead of entering into the issue of defining what was tolerable for the tenant, the role of the Roman courts was simply to define what legal rights and obligations arose when a landlord did grant a social remission of rent on the basis of *sterilitas*.

The principle that guided the Roman legal authorities in dealing with this issue was that the tenant's long-term occupation of the land was of paramount importance for the estate economy of the Roman Empire. Hence the Roman legal authorities devised solutions to the problem of defining the rights and duties of landowners and tenants that preserved the lease contract.[64] This was the principle guiding the early third-century jurist Papinian, for instance, when he addressed the legal questions surrounding the landowner's grant of a remission of rent on the basis of a poor crop (*ob sterilitatem*) (Papin. apud Ulp. *D.* 19.2.15.4, 32 ad ed.). In Papinian's response, the grant by a landowner of a remission in a poor year did not compromise his claim to a full rent in a later, more bountiful year. Papinian did not envision the termination of the lease contract as a remedy but rather assumed that the contractual arrangement would endure beyond the individual growing season:

> Papinian says in his fourth book of Responses that if someone has granted a tenant a remission in one year on account of a poor crop, and then an abundant harvest occurs in subsequent years, the remission does not prejudice the claims of the landlord, but the payment is to be demanded also for the year in which he remitted the rent. He made the same response concerning the loss of a *vectigal*. But if the landlord remitted the rent on account of the poor crop of a year as a gift, the same thing will have to be maintained, as if it were not a gift, but a transaction. What happens, however, if the last year of the lease, in which he granted the tenant a remission, was sterile? It will be more truthfully maintained that if the previous years had abundant crops and the lessor knows, this year should not be included in the computation.[65]

In Papinian's interpretation, the landowner's loss in income represented by the remission of rent could be balanced against his continuing claim for the rent due for the lease period in its entirety.

The principle formulated by Papinian guided the imperial government in its subsequent treatment of requests for remissions of rent. For instance, the emperor Alexander Severus, in responding to a tenant's claim for a remission of rent, would only allow such a remission if the tenant could demonstrate that the poor crops caused by a weather-related disaster were not balanced out by plentiful crops in other years (*CJ* 4.65.8, 231):

> Assuming that you have leased a farm for fixed annual payments, if, however, it has not been expressed in the lease or the custom of the region does not require that, if any losses had occurred because of disastrous weather or another climatic problem, they should be your burden, and the poor crops that have happened will be proved not to have been balanced by the abundant crops of the other years, you will rightly demand that your request be considered in accordance with good faith, and the judge who will hear the case on appeal will follow this principle.[66]

This insistence on the continuing validity of the landowner's claim provided an incentive for tenants to internalize the costs associated with agricultural risk. They stood to gain by pursuing risk-reducing strategies in cultivating their crops, including saving up surpluses for a bad year, since they could not simply impose these costs on the landowner. Papinian's ruling, then, could be interpreted as designed to allow the landowner to respond to the problems besetting his or her tenants much as Pliny did, while at the same time preserving the convenience of maintaining the traditional leasing system based on cash rents.

From the perspective of NIE, the doctrine formulated by Papinian and followed by Alexander Severus tended to reduce transaction costs by defining property rights more specifically. According to the Coase Theorem, people will bargain to achieve the most remunerative allocation of resources, as long as transaction costs are zero and property rights are fully specified.[67] In the classical or Servian interpretation of *remissio mercedis*, according to which the tenant was entitled to a remission only in the case of an unforeseeable disaster, property rights could be considered to have been fully (or almost fully) specified. The tenant bore the risk for all the normal hazards of farming, whereas the landlord bore the risk for only those hazards that were unforeseeable and made it impossible for the tenant to complete his lease obligations. So within this scheme, it would seem possible for landowners and tenants to bargain to alter the distribution of risk and costs to meet their respective needs.

In fact, however, since the distinction between fully foreseeable risks (*vitia ex re*) and an unforeseeable hazard (*vis maior*) was artificial at best, it would be uncertain as to what constituted suitable grounds for a tenant to claim a remission of rent. The legal authorities acknowledged that landowners might be forced to grant concessions that would then make the delineation of rights for themselves and for other landowners and tenants ambiguous. The government sought to remove some of this ambiguity by carefully defining the legal obligations that arose from a landowner's granting of a remission of rent outside of the Servian scheme, that is, for *sterilitas*. Thus the government did not seek to regulate relations between landowners and tenants but instead sought to establish new rules of the game under which private bargaining could take place.

So when the state stepped in to define what the rights and obligations of landowners and tenants would be when the landowner granted a remission for a poor crop, it was providing both parties, but especially the landowner, with the assurance that what amounted to a renegotiated contract would be legally enforceable. As Alan Schwartz has observed, it is when the new terms of a contract are legally enforceable that renegotiation is most likely to take place in the light of conditions that neither party could have completely foreseen at the outset of the contractual relationship.[68] Such renegotiation provides an incentive for the type of investment needed for productivity in agriculture that often represents one of the most important reasons for entering into a long-term contract.[69] The possibility of renegotiating in response to changing circumstances reduces the risk for both parties to the contract. This could be a particularly important concern for landowners in long-term tenancy relationships in which the level of rent was set by custom and was fixed. As we will see, the Roman government encountered this situation and, when seeking to define what rent landowners could legally claim, established that landowners could not raise the rents that tenants had customarily been paying. The government's policy in treating landowners' grants of remissions of rent provided some balance to this situation. If the state limited what landowners could claim from their tenants, it also prescribed that landowners did not give up their rights to this rent when poor crops kept tenants from paying their full rent. This approach, then, provided a legal basis for continued flexibility on the part of landowners, since when they granted remissions in response to poor harvests they would not be giving away their rights and weakening their position with their tenants. Whether landowners could actually collect the rent that was theoretically owed them after a remission of rent resulting from a bad harvest is another matter. Indeed, the continuing claim on the debt owed by the tenant granted a remission may have enhanced the bargaining power of landowners considerably.[70]

CUSTOMARY TENURE ARRANGEMENTS AND INFORMAL INSTITUTIONS

In adjudicating tenants' claims for remissions of rent, the Roman imperial chancery was confronted with the problem of resolving legal issues arising in tenure arrangements that were foreign to classical Roman law. The Roman government often responded to these claims by interpreting the rights and obligations of landowners in terms of the conventions of Roman private law while at the same time respecting as much as possible the customary arrangements of the region concerned.[71] To return to the rescript of Alexander Severus discussed earlier in the chapter, the emperor was responding to a petition from an individual named Sabinianus Hyginus, a tenant who was apparently appealing an unfavorable ruling. In responding to this petition, the emperor allowed the tenant's request for a remission and instructed that the judge hearing the case on appeal would rule accordingly, as long as the specific terms of the lease or local custom did not require that the tenant bear all the losses caused by weather.[72] This rescript does not necessarily indicate ready access to legal institutions on the part of a tenant, since Sabinianus could have been a large-scale tenant rather than a more modest farmer leasing from a large landowner. But the emperor's insistence on the contractual validity of the custom of a given region suggests that the imperial government did in fact confront the problem of remissions of rent on a widespread basis.

This involvement on the part of the imperial government in sorting out legal issues arising from such tenure arrangements becomes more apparent in two rescripts from Diocletian. In the first, Diocletian responded to a lessor whose tenant had withheld rent for the period in which the crops on the farm under lease had been devastated by a plague of locusts (*CJ* 4.65.18, 290). Diocletian ruled that the tenant was not obligated to pay rent for this period but that the tenant would have to pay the rent for the rest of the lease in accordance with past custom, "iuxta praeteritam consuetudinem."[73] In a case like this, it might be difficult to determine when the devastated farm would again be suitable for cultivation. The tenant in all likelihood was occupying the farm in a long-term lease arrangement, given the phrase used above to denote the rental obligation. Unable to raise a crop, the tenant ceased paying rent, and the landlord was initiating proceedings against him to recover his losses; the rescript obtained to this petition would strengthen the landlord's case in the future court proceedings.[74] In view of the apparent long-term tenancy relationship standing behind this rescript, it seems likely that the landowner was of a substantially higher economic status than the tenant. Even so, the landowner followed established legal norms in proceeding against the recalcitrant tenant.

The importance of following legal norms can be seen especially in a second rescript from Diocletian (*CJ* 4.65.19, 293):

> Concerning leases the faith of the contract is especially to be observed, if nothing specific should be expressed against the custom of the region. But if some landowners have remitted rent payments in contravention of the terms of the contract and the custom of the region, this should not be able to prejudice the claims of other landowners.[75]

In this text, Diocletian was concerned with making sure that remissions of rent granted in contravention of the contract did not compromise the rights of landowners. The emperor emphasized the primacy of the lease contract, itself apparently based on the custom of the region, in determining the obligations and rights of landowners and tenants. The emphasis on the custom of the region as creating contractual obligations indicates that the government was concerned with the relationships between landowners and a broad range of tenants, and not simply with an upper stratum of economically advantaged tenants. In the government's view, when one landowner granted a remission of rent in contravention of local customary tenure arrangement, the other tenants in the region would be in a position to demand similar remissions of rent from their landowners and to defend their claims in court. To judge by the rescript of Diocletian, the imperial government had to perform a delicate balancing act as it interpreted the rights and duties of landowners and tenants operating under a variety of tenure arrangements. The government recognized the legal validity of remissions that landowners granted under various circumstances, but at the same time it also sought to protect the interests of landowners by defining the customary practice of the region involved as a contract enforceable under conventional Roman lease law.

The imperial rescripts that we have examined in connection with tenants' requests for remissions of rent were published in response to petitions made when one party or the other sought to achieve through legal action what could not be attained through negotiation. But even when we examine this evidence for "broken" lease relationships, it seems clear that the Roman government recognized the existence of informal institutions through which disputes involving land tenure could be ironed out without recourse to law courts. The key text in this respect is the second rescript of Diocletian discussed in this chapter (*CJ* 4.65.19). In this rescript, the imperial chancery recognized that many landowners would go beyond what might be interpreted as their legal obligations in sharing the costs for disastrous harvests with their tenants. In the understanding of the chancery, many landowners would gain little by pressing legal claims in court against tenants, and these landowners were finding an informal means to allocate the risks in farming. But the task of the Roman chancery was not to find informal solutions to disputes involving land tenure but to establish what legal rights and obligations arose as a result of the informal solutions that landowners and tenants themselves found.

To solve this problem, the Roman government pursued a consistently conservative legal policy that avoided creating new law, or at least avoided the appearance of creating new law. Instead, it recognized local customary arrangements as lease contracts defined in terms of conventional Roman private law. In some cases, these arrangements may have simply represented informal means of establishing the terms of land tenure. Landowners who went beyond these customs, now enforceable as law, could not be seen as prejudicing the rights of other landowners who were less generous in dealing with tenants.

Behind these few rescripts lurks a whole series of disputes and solutions that were not decided in court but, in the interpretation of the imperial government, helped to establish the legal rules in accordance with which disputes involving land tenure would be mediated. To use the terminology of NIE, landowners and tenants had recourse to informal arrangements, or "private ordering," as a way to cooperate to resolve differences without going to court. The whole reason for such private ordering was to preserve a lease relationship that presumably both sides found advantageous.[76] Indeed, recent analysis of the relationship between custom and law suggests that customary arrangements that are adopted as law are often the result of market forces. Thus parties to a contract might find a more efficient means to establish their mutual rights and obligations than would be possible under existing law. From a different perspective, customs that become enshrined as law often reflect changing moral standards or social practices of a society.[77] At the same time, in many cases, the parties to a contract can devise more satisfactory solutions to disputes than courts, since they can take into account information not available to the courts.[78] We clearly have very little information about the customary arrangements that lurk behind the rescripts preserved in the Code of Justinian, but it is likely that they were the result of both the market forces and the more informal institutions surrounding landowner-tenant relationships. In its legal policy, the Roman government made into law what society deemed to be acceptable in the relationship between landowners and tenants.

The practice that the Roman government followed in adjudicating these cases could be regarded as "gap filling," in the sense that the government supplied contractual terms to vaguely conceived agreements. As we have seen, Roman courts were not likely to have resolved ambiguities in contracts in such a way as to promote economic efficiency (see the preceding). The terms that the Roman government supplied only imperfectly took account of the likely interests of the parties involved in litigation. Instead, the Roman government consistently interpreted lease contracts in terms of the conventional Roman lease, in which the good faith of both landowner and tenant was paramount. This practice delineated the rights and obligations of landowners and tenants and so provided a starting point for negotiation between the two parties. Such a delineation of rights, in turn, facilitated the type of private negotiation that could lead to economically advantageous situations for both landowners and tenants. Accordingly, the Roman government's practice served what seems to have been its broader social policy (i.e., to preserve lease arrangements between landowners and tenants).[79]

Any negotiations between wealthy landowners and tenants were almost certainly to have been tilted in favor of the former group, who because of their wealth, social privileges, and ready access to governmental authorities enjoyed distinct advantages in negotiating terms of tenure with small farmers. Indeed, landowners undoubtedly used the economic and social control that they exercised over tenants, whether through patronage or through the indebtedness of the tenants, to achieve more favorable terms of tenure for themselves. Still, landowners did not enjoy an entirely free hand in negotiating with tenants, constrained as they were by the need to achieve stable, long-term revenues from their estates in an economy offering limited growth and few options for investing their wealth. So upper-class landowners were likely to have sought to maintain tenure arrangements that best ensured their ability to gain stable incomes from their land. The state assisted in this process by establishing legal rules that promoted the tenant's long-term tenure of the land.

As I argue in the next chapter, however, the Roman government took some steps to mitigate the power that landowners could exercise, particularly because of the tenant's debt. It would thus be overly optimistic to view tenants as anything approaching equal partners with landowners in the negotiating process. Still, the involvement of the Roman government in settling disputes indicates that the tenants were not powerless and that they were able to affect the outcomes of negotiations. The viability of imperial legal institutions to adjudicate disputes meant that landowners could not simply dictate terms of land tenure. Indeed, the readiness of the Roman government to recognize customary law as legally binding afforded tenants and other smaller farmers some measure of protection against arbitrary actions by landowners who might seek to impose much less generous terms of land tenure.

SECURITY OF TENURE AND ROMAN LEGAL POLICY

In dealing with the contentious issue of risk associated with agriculture, the Roman government demonstrated a combination of flexibility and conservatism as it recognized the existence of informal institutions surrounding land tenure and then endeavored to accommodate these institutions within the conventions of Roman private law. These informal institutions involved the various arrangements that landowners and tenants struck to maintain long-term tenure arrangements. The tenant gained from such arrangements much greater security of tenure than would be recognized under conventional Roman law.

The capacity of Roman private law to accommodate customary tenure arrangements was especially strained when something occurred to disrupt the tenant's undisturbed occupation of the land. The papyrological evidence from Roman Egypt suggests that legal disputes were especially likely to arise when one party or the other considered the lease to be terminated. In this situation, both landowner and tenant might make claims against the other party, with the landowner seeking to keep the tenant in the lease or to exact overdue rent payments and the tenant seeking compensation for improvements that he had made on the farm.[80] Now in classical Roman law, the tenant, lacking the right of possession, was subject to eviction if the land that he was leasing was alienated. The reason for this is that the lease created a contractual obligation only between the tenant and the original lessor; Roman law did not generally recognize contractual obligations imposed on a third party, in this case the new owner of the land.[81] So the tenant only had recourse against his original landlord.

However, there is also evidence suggesting that the imperial chancery was flexible enough to modify this principle to accommodate the unique circumstances of other tenure systems. One example is a rescript from the emperor Alexander Severus concerning the rights of a sitting tenant when the land that he was leasing was sold (*CJ* 4.65.9, 234):

> The purchaser is indeed not required to allow the tenant to whom a previous owner has leased to remain, unless he purchases under this condition. But if he should be proved to have given his consent under some sort of an agreement, even without it being in writing, that the tenant should remain in the same lease, he is compelled in a judgment of good faith to comply with what has been agreed upon.[82]

In this case, the tenant sued apparently after losing his lease when the land that he was cultivating was alienated, and the rescript, issued either to him or to the new owner of the land in question, was to decide the issue. In the first part of the rescript, the emperor upheld the classical law, allowing only for the possibility that the contract of sale might have included a clause to allow the tenant to remain in his holding. But in the second part of the rescript, the emperor, apparently recognizing the inadequacy of such law, included the remarkable condition that the tenant must be allowed to remain on his farm if there was a general agreement with his original landlord that he could do so, even if this agreement was not formalized in writing. This understanding could simply be an arrangement between an individual landlord and tenant, but conceivably it could also represent the tradition of the region involved. In any case, the emperor's recognition of it as an enforceable contract under Roman law suggests the concern of the chancery to accord the tenant security of tenure when possible.

The Roman legal authorities seem to have faced time and again the difficulty of reconciling with recognized legal conventions tenure arrangements whose duration was not clearly defined in terms of classical Roman law. For example, the emperor Philip referred to frequent rescripts prohibiting lessors from retaining tenants or their heirs after the expiration of the original lease (*CJ* 4.65.11, 244). The landowners affected by these rescripts surely expected that their tenants would remain on the land indefinitely. We can see the Roman government's effort to establish general principles by which to judge such disputes in the emperor Gordian's ruling that lease obligations pass to the heirs of the original lessee, whether the lease was perpetual or for a fixed period (*CJ* 4.65.10, 239).[83] In long-term tenancy relationships, the obligations of the tenant or the heirs depended on how the imperial administration defined the period of the lease, whether it was for a fixed period or perpetual.

We can also trace the Roman government's efforts to accommodate long-term lease relationships within conventional Roman law in its flexibility in applying the principle of the "tacit renewal of the lease" (*relocatio tacita*). According to this principle, the lease terms under which the tenant cultivated the land were considered to be continued for one year by the implied consensus of the landowner and tenant if the tenant remained on the farm cultivating it without any specific objection on the part of the landowner. The tenant would be obligated to pay the same rent as before, and likewise, whatever property the tenant had brought into the farm would remain pledged to the landowner, as it had been previously. This principle provided a convenient framework for accommodating diverse systems of tenure within conventional Roman legal categories, since tenure arrangements in which the tenant occupied the land for indefinite periods of time without a written formal contract could be defined as one-year leases tacitly renewed year by year.[84]

A classical statement of the principle of *relocatio tacita* can be found in a rescript issued by Valerian and Gallienus (*CJ* 4.65.16, 260):

> The terms of the lease must be maintained and nothing more should be demanded as rent than what has been agreed upon. But if the time in which the farm had been leased should be completed and the tenant has

remained in the same lease, it seems that by tacit consent he has renewed the same lease together with the bond of pledging.[85]

The possibility of a legally recognized tacit renewal of the lease encouraged the tenant to make investments in maintaining the productivity of the farm. This was something clearly desirable for landowners—and for the Roman state, to the extent that its tax revenues ultimately depended on the production of small-scale farmers, including tenants. But to make such investments, tenants needed to be protected against the possibility that landowners might use their superior economic position to expropriate their value. In this situation, the landowner could use the possibility of ending the contractual relationship as a way to win greater concessions from the tenant. A tenant who had made substantial "relation-specific investments" could be especially vulnerable to a landlord seeking to rewrite the rules of the lease.[86] To be sure, the tenant in classical Roman lease law was entitled to compensation for unexhausted improvements, that is, improvements to the farm that had raised its value when the lease ended. This entitlement provided the tenant with some formal protection against a landlord who wanted to appropriate the value of his relation-specific investments. But this compensation could only help the tenant when the lease relationship ended, or when the tenant could use the possibility of withdrawing from the lease and receiving compensation as leverage against the landowner.

In enforcing this principle, the Roman government was promoting the tenant's long-term tenure of the land, much as it did in recognizing the enforceability of long-term tenure arrangements. As Yoram Barzel argues, a government is likely to enforce those rules that it finds advantageous, and protecting the tenant against landowners who would take advantage of the tenant's sunk costs by changing the terms of the contract was consistent with its other policies in interpreting lease law.[87] At the same time, the Roman government had little interest in deciding how landowners and tenants would allocate the costs of investment. Roman law established a basic template, according to which the landlord provided the fixed capital, such as buildings, storage facilities, and presses, while the tenant provided the movable capital, such a tools, livestock, and even slaves.[88] In the real world, we would imagine that landowners and tenants would make all sorts of agreements over allocating the costs of investment, especially when they were bound together in a long-term tenure arrangement. The role of the Roman government was to establish the broad guidelines under which this private ordering might take place, and that role is represented in the rule about unexhausted improvements.[89]

But most tenants depended for their livelihoods on their leases, and the compensation to which they were theoretically due would be cold comfort if the landowner decided to take advantage of the tenant's investment. The Roman government was aware of this situation, and it was apparently faced time and again with protecting the rights of tenants in long-term tenancy relationships. The problem was to find a contractual form that would allow landowners and tenants to adjust the terms of their relationship in the light of changing conditions. Providing specific terms in the contract to cover all foreseeable future contingencies would have been quite impractical. To use the terminology of Oliver Williamson, landowners and tenants in the Roman Empire required appropriate "governance structures" in their contractual relationship to address problems posed by the "opportunism" that each party might exploit to take advantage of unforeseen contingencies to exact better terms from the other party. In the Roman Empire, we would imagine that this would especially be a problem if the landowner, by virtue of a superior economic and social standing, sought concessions from the tenant after the latter had made "idiosyncratic" investments in improving the farm, meaning that the investments could not be taken elsewhere if the tenant reached some sort of impasse with the landowner.[90] Often this type of opportunism is called a "holdup." In this situation, one party can take advantage of the other's investment by appropriating a substantial portion of the "quasi-rent" for the asset in question. The term *quasi-rent* refers to the difference between the value of the asset and its salvage value, or its value in its next-best use.[91] In the case of a farm lease, it is doubtful that any of the investments that a tenant made in the productivity of a farm, such as by planting vines, would have any salvage value whatsoever, since the tenant could not take them to another farm. On the other side of the coin, any governance structure would ideally serve not simply to diminish the effects of opportunism but to encourage ongoing cooperation between landowner and tenant. The basic legal principles of the classical Roman farm lease could not accomplish this purpose.

So what mechanisms existed to promote such cooperation in the Roman agrarian economy? Simply relying on the market was no solution in an ongoing tenancy relationship, since it was not always practical for landowners to dismiss unsatisfactory tenants and hire better ones, and since tenants could only at great expense leave an estate where they had invested their resources and take up a lease elsewhere. Adjudication of contractual disputes by a court of law, on the basis of a strict interpretation of the terms of the lease, would also not represent much of a solution, since this would usually involve either ending a contractual relationship or, at the very least, pitting landowner and tenant against one another in such a way that would make future cooperation difficult. In fact, there was probably little that a Roman court could do to foster such cooperation, which is in contrast with the role that the courts today play in promoting long-term cooperation in relational contracts.[92]

The limited ability of the Roman courts to adjudicate disputes in long-term tenancy relationships is suggested in the rescript of Valerian and Gallienus concerning *relocatio tacita*. In adjudicating disputes between landlords and tenants, a court would find it difficult to verify claims made by either party. Changing circumstances, such as increasing demand for land in light of more favorable market prices, might make landowners think that the terms of tenure had become less advantageous to themselves, and they might respond to this situation by imposing additional charges on their tenants. The rescript from Valerian and Gallienus does not offer any details about the background to the dispute to which the emperors responded. Still, it seems plausible that the issue concerned the efforts of a landowner to impose a larger rent on a tenant in a long-term lease arrangement without a formal contract. In the second part of the rescript, the two emperors used the classical principle of *relocatio tacita* to define the rights of the tenant in question.

But if the rescript represents the Roman government's position on the issue, this still leaves unanswered the question of how landowners and tenants might enforce the terms of their tenure arrangements. This was especially a problem if the landowner could take advantage of the investment that the tenant made in the farm and demand more advantageous terms. One tactic that has been identified as a means of enforcement in such situations in the contemporary world is self-enforcement.[93] This means that the long-term nature of the relationship will provide an incentive for each party to make the appropriate investments. The sanctions enforcing compliance in a self-enforcing contract include the termination of an otherwise advantageous relationship or even the compromise to one's reputation that will make doing business in the future more difficult.[94] How well this latter type of sanction would have worked in the Roman world probably depended on the relative equality of the landowner and tenant. It seems unlikely that a small-scale tenant could inflict a social sanction on an elite landowner who took advantage of the tenant's investments by altering the terms of land tenure. Consequently, as in the rescript of Valerian and Gallienus, the Roman government might be called upon to reassert the tenant's rights.

CONCLUSION

The Roman government's treatment of lease law suggests both some of the most important factors affecting the empire's rural economy and the limited capacity of the state to implement a legal policy that would affect the economy. The primary interest of the government when adjudicating legal disputes connected with private land tenure was not to promote the interests of either landowners or tenants. Rather, the legal authorities struggled, to the extent possible, to make sure that such disputes were resolved in accordance with existing law, which they used to impose solutions that encouraged private bargaining on the part of both landowners and tenants. Ideally, such bargaining could lead to a dynamic rural economy with resources finding their highest-valued use. Such private bargaining could be especially important in creating incentives for landowners and tenants to share in the costs of investing in more productive forms of agriculture, include viticulture and olive culture, which required substantial investment.

But it would be a simplification to see the role of Roman law and legal institutions as simply smoothing the way for economically efficient bargains, even if the law to some extent accomplished this purpose. However, the tenure arrangements that Roman law recognized as involving some degree of equality between landowner and tenant in fact were often characterized by substantial inequality. In this circumstance, landowners often relied on tenants in long-term tenure arrangements to carry out the work of improving the land and to shoulder the cost for doing so, and they could use their superior economic and social standing to exact a larger portion of the tenants' production than would have fallen to them in a freely negotiated contract.

This situation created a degree of path dependence for private landowners, just as relying on small-scale *coloni* created path dependence for the state in its efforts to secure revenues from imperial estates. When private landowners derived their incomes largely by exacting a share of the surplus produced by tenants occupying their land under customary terms, they had little incentive to invest in greater productivity. The challenge that the Roman legal authorities faced, under this circumstance, was not so much to facilitate bargaining as to interpret the law to protect tenants against the efforts of private landowners to squeeze excessive rents from them.

CHAPTER 4

Legal Order in the Rural Economy

My investigation of the law of farm tenancy in the previous chapter suggests both the flexibility of the Roman legal institutions and the limits of their authority in defining the conditions under which landowners and tenants participated in the agrarian economy. The Roman government displayed considerable flexibility as it endeavored to accommodate within the conventions of Roman private law a wide variety of tenure arrangements, many of which were probably in origin quite foreign to Roman practices. The flexibility that the government demonstrated in such a key area of tenancy law as the allocation of risk suggests its recognition of the importance to the Roman estate economy of the long-term, uninterrupted occupation of the land by productive farmers.

In this chapter, I approach Roman legal institutions from a somewhat different perspective, by examining in greater detail the limits on what the government could accomplish in its efforts to establish a basic legal regime governing the agrarian economy. In the first two sections of this chapter, I focus on imperial constitutions concerned with some of the difficult legal questions raised by the significant role that long-term tenure played in the Roman economy. In the latter part of the chapter, I examine other areas of the law important for the rural economy, in particular, the adjudication of legal issues surrounding debt, as well as disputes over possession and ownership of property.

The evidence to be examined includes imperial constitutions preserved in the Code of Justinian and the Theodosian Code from the third and fourth centuries, and even later. These texts provide us with some hints about the complexities of the contemporary agrarian economy and of the difficulties that the government faced in adjudicating disputes. Although the focus of my book is on the early empire, I think that it is justified to consider material from the third and fourth centuries together. Recent scholarship has moved away from the notion of a sudden break in agrarian relationships in the fourth century with the development of the late antique fiscal system and instead has traced the origins of this institution to conditions in the third century and earlier.[1] Accordingly, constitutions from the fourth century and sometimes later help us to trace some of the issues that the government had to confront in the earlier period as it developed a legal policy.

As I argue, the state's power to regulate the rural economy was quite limited, and as it faced some of the contradictions raised by its policy of favoring long-term tenure, the state struggled to define property rights of landowners and tenants more precisely. This effort suggests that the real-world tenure arrangements were a good deal more complicated than what was envisioned in the legal authorities' responses to petitions.

The government responded to this situation by carefully defining property rights when they were either vaguely defined or defined in such a way that it found unacceptable. Usually, the property rights that the government would reject gave too much power to the tenant and compromised the interests of landowners. In facing the difficult task of defining the rights and obligations of landowners and small farmers in diverse tenure arrangements, the government struggled to balance the interests of these groups as it sought to impose a kind of legal order over the rural economy. This legal order rested on the principle that the Roman law courts were the authoritative venue through which to settle disputes. The efforts of the government to impose this legal order did not mean that private means of dispute settlement ceased to function. Rather, the government's legal policy provided both landowners and smaller farmers consistent legal norms that helped to shape the private arrangements that both parties would make. Ultimately, the existence of viable state institutions to settle disputes accorded the economically weaker party some protection. This tended to strengthen the hand of smaller farmers in the Roman economy, with significant effects for the incentives for investment by large landowners as well as the distribution of wealth between city and countryside.

LEGAL ISSUES ARISING FROM LONG-TERM TENANCY ARRANGEMENTS

To begin with local tenure arrangements based on custom, the government tended to recognize them as enforceable in its courts. Much of the task of the imperial chancery was to sort out key issues in tenancy law as they pertained to such arrangements, such as the allocation of risk. The rulings issued by the legal authorities in response to petitions were designed to protect stable tenure arrangements against the most unhealthful effects of opportunistic behavior by landowners and tenants. For tenants who had invested their own resources in the lands, this meant that the state provided some protection against landowners who would take advantage of the commitment by seeking to impose a higher rent without making any corresponding investment on their own part. For landowners, protection against opportunism by tenants meant preventing this group from infringing on their rights by claiming the right to alienate the land, such as by pledging it as security for a debt, selling it, or bequeathing it to heirs.

We can see the efforts of the government to protect tenants against the worst effects of opportunistic behavior by landowners in the rescript of Valerian and Gallienus discussed in the previous chapter concerning *relocatio tacita* (*CJ* 4.65.16, 260). This text shows the government's efforts to offer some protection to tenants whose long-term tenure was formally described in terms of leases tacitly renewed year after year. This concern with protecting against opportunistic behavior is also apparent in a constitution of Constantine (*CJ* 11.50.1, 325). In Constantine's decision, landlords were enjoined not to raise the customary rent, which indicates that Constantine's government interpreted a traditional lease arrangement as contractually binding:

> Whenever a tenant is required by the landlord to pay more than had been customary and he had been compelled to pay in previous times, he should approach the first judge whose audience he will be able to gain and should prove the crime, so that the one who is convicted of demanding more than he had been accustomed to receive should be prevented from doing this in the future, first having given back what he is known to have extorted by his demand for an extra payment.[2]

In addition, Constantine established a procedure for tenants to take their landlords to court if they illegally raised their rent.

To judge by this constitution, landowners in Constantine's time saw their interests compromised by the traditional terms of tenure under which many tenants apparently occupied their land. But any claims about changing conditions that landowners might make to defend their raising of the rent would be difficult to verify, and Constantine followed the well-established principle of the government in interpreting contracts conservatively. It seems unlikely that in developing this policy Constantine's government considered the role of the market, because doing so was beyond its capacity of establishing the factual situation underlying countless lease arrangements. As Alan Schwartz argues in his analysis of the role of American courts in contract law, courts tend to enforce what is verifiable and will be very cautious when confronted with unverifiable claims, refusing to apply their own judgment to situations in which the facts are likely to be in dispute by the litigants.[3] In the case of the constitution of Constantine, what was verifiable was the customary rent, and to establish clear rules of tenure, Constantine ruled that customary rents had the force of a contract. Constantine's conservatism in interpreting customary obligations favored tenants in long-term relationships. On the other side of the coin, by this principle, tenants would have a hard time making the case for lower rents if circumstances increased demand for their services. But the concern of Constantine was to protect tenants against exploitation by landowners who were in a position to take advantage of the relation-specific investments the tenants had made.

These texts indicate the imperial government's willingness to enshrine custom as creating legal rights and obligations that could be enforced in Roman courts. As Walter Goffart argues, the constitution of Constantine does not presuppose the existence of a formally bound colonate associated with the later empire.[4] Rather, the imperial government recognized that tenants commonly remained on their land indefinitely, and it considered the rent paid as the result of a traditional arrangement to have the force of a contract. The fact that a "customary rent" was a meaningful concept for Constantine suggests not only that tenants occupied their land in open-ended lease arrangements but also that society had long since established basic norms defining the conditions under which tenants occupied their land. As Ernst Levy points out, Constantine's interpretation of a customary long-term arrangement as binding indicates his willingness to depart from the practice of Diocletian's government of insisting on classical legal categories. This willingness suggests an early stage of the Roman government's incorporation of local practices, or "vulgar law," into the legal principles that it enforced.[5] Constantine afforded tenants occupying their land under such traditional arrangements an added degree of protection by establishing a legal procedure for them to seek redress when their landlords violated their customary obligations. But the most important protection that tenants enjoyed was the recognition of their traditional rights by other landowners in the vicinity. The task of the government was to come to the rescue of tenants when landowners exceeded the rights that tradition granted them.

We can trace a similar conception of traditional tenure arrangements later in the fourth century in a constitution of Valentinian I addressed to the governor of Tripolitania (in Africa, *CJ* 11.48.5, 365). This constitution required landowners to accept rents in kind and only allowed them to demand cash rents if the customary arrangement of the estate in question (*consuetudo praedii*) so required.[6] In this enactment, the imperial government recognized custom as binding law and in doing so upheld the traditional rights of *coloni*. Much later, Justinian ruled that "ancient custom" (*vetus consuetudo*) would be dispositive in establishing the rent that *coloni*, here *coloni* bound to the land, would have to pay (*CJ* 11.48.23.2, 531–34).

LEGAL ORDER AND TRADITIONAL TENURE ARRANGEMENTS

The government's power to control the contract norms adopted across the empire was limited, however much it sought to promote the smooth functioning of long-term tenure arrangements.[7] The limits on the government's power can especially be seen in the fourth century, when its fiscal policy involved restricting the mobility of farmers (see chap. 5). During the fourth century, there was a substantial disparity between the insistence of the state on viewing the *colonus* as one type of legal person, defined in terms of fiscal obligations, and the economic reality surrounding the conditions under which people actually occupied their land. But these limits on the government's power are also apparent in the second and third centuries, when it found itself in the position of having to sort out disputes arising from tenure arrangements that involved little if any cooperation.

The difficulties that the government encountered in defining property rights in traditional tenure arrangements are particularly apparent in a series of imperial responses to petitions. These responses limited application of the *longi temporis praescriptio*. This principle, first referred to in a rescript of Septimius Severus and Caracalla, established that a possessor of provincial land (as opposed to Italic land, which was subject to usucapion) who had acquired it on a lawful basis could be protected against lawsuits by rival parties claiming ownership. The principle stated that no suit claiming ownership could be heard from a plaintiff living in the same community as the defendant if the latter held the land for ten years, and that no suit could be heard from someone living elsewhere if the defendant occupied the land for twenty years.[8] As Dieter Nörr argues, it is likely that the imperial administration developed the *longi temporis praescriptio* as an emergency measure to restore legal order in areas of the Roman Empire ravaged by plagues (notably the Antonine plague beginning in 165), loss of population, and social disorder. This measure would have served to safeguard property rights in a period in which it might be especially difficult to establish them in courts of law. In the third century, this one-time emergency measure became a permanent legal institution.[9] During this same period, the prescription began to be applied to moveable property, but under Diocletian its application was apparently restricted to land.[10] Property over which the Fiscus held a lien, however, was not subject to this prescription.[11]

One major purpose that the prescription took on was to protect landowners against inroads by creditors. Without the *longi temporis praescriptio*, creditors or their heirs who viewed themselves as exercising a right of pledge might raise in rem claims against property years or even generations after the original loan had been made. The property in the meantime could have changed ownership, and the new owner's rights to the property could be jeopardized by the claims of past creditors. If the *longi temporis praescriptio* removed the in rem claim of a creditor against a particular piece of property, the creditor still had a claim against the debtor, but this was a weaker claim, one in personam, which was not secured by any property. That the legal authorities were primarily concerned with the claims of creditors in developing this principle is suggested in a rescript of the emperor Gordian, who asserted that a "long silence" barred the claims of creditors pursuing property pledged as security (*CJ* 7.36.1):

> A long silence corroborated by the *longi temporis praescriptio* has made the action ineffective for creditors pursuing a pledge, except when the debtors or those who have succeeded in their rights continue in possession of the pledged property. When however the *longi temporis praescriptio* is raised against the creditor by the possessor, a personal action still lies open to him against the debtor.[12]

The protection offered by this prescription would be especially helpful in settings where the records of transactions and liens on land would have been imperfectly kept. Without the prescription, landowners would have had a diminished incentive to acquire and invest in land, since even after years of lawful possession they might lose their entire investment when a third party registered a claim. So in establishing a prescription against claims to land, the government was seeking to define the property rights of landowners in a workable way that balanced competing claims.

However, to judge by a series of imperial rescripts on this issue, the *longi temporis praescriptio* also had unintended consequences for property rights, since parties clearly not envisioned in the original legislation used this principle to claim rights of ownership. The effort of the government to safeguard the rights of people whom it saw as lawful owners created an ambiguity about the rights of other parties occupying the land on a long-term basis but not exercising ownership rights as defined in classical Roman law. These parties, in all likelihood, occupied their land under local arrangements that were foreign to classical Roman law. However, as Levy argues, such arrangements formed the basis for the vulgar Roman law of late antiquity that simplified Roman categories and incorporated many elements of local practice into the law of the empire.[13]

Accordingly, the possibility of establishing ownership in accordance with the principle of the *longi temporis praescriptio* seems to have led to disputes between tenants and landowners, with tenants on occasion asserting ownership of the land that they had cultivated for long periods of time without interruption. Such a claim, of course, had no legal basis under the terms of conventional Roman lease law. Not only were tenants not owners of their land in any sense in classical Roman law but they lacked the rights of possession and so could be evicted from their land at the will of the owner, subject of course to compensation in accordance with the good-faith basis of the Roman lease contract. Accordingly, the emperor Alexander Severus ruled that a tenant, without the right of possession, could under no circumstances claim ownership of the property held under lease (*CJ* 7.30.1, 226):

> Whoever possesses on the basis of a lease, although he might physically hold the property, nevertheless he is believed to possess not for himself, but for the property's owner. Nor is the prescription on the basis of long possession sought for a tenant or a lessee.[14]

However, as is suggested by a rescript from Diocletian on the same issue from late in the third century (*CJ* 7.32.5), disputes about the tenant's rights under the *longi temporis praescriptio* may well have been common. In this case, the emperor ruled that a tenant could not sell the land that he held under lease:

> Since no one can alter the terms of possession for himself and you assert that the tenant without the intervention of any external cause has jumped from an opportunity to cultivate the land into the vice of a fraudulent sale, the governor of the province, having examined the truth of your claim, will not allow your right of ownership to be torn asunder.[15]

In the fourth century, Valentinian I reasserted the principle that tenants could not establish rights of possession when he ruled against the right of tenants and farmers occupying their land under the institution of *precarium* (a form of tenancy in late Roman vulgar law in which occupation was at the discretion of the landowner) to establish prescriptive rights to their land (*CJ* 7.39.2 pr.-1, 365).[16] In the wording of the constitution, people described as possessing "precariously" (*precario possidentibus*) were not to benefit from a prescription that prevented the owners from asserting their rights. Likewise, lessees (*conductores*) could not lawfully establish possession. Those excluded from the possibility of establishing possession were defined as paying a customary rent.[17] The danger for landowners would be that they would have to turn away potentially useful tenants if, by leasing their land to them for long periods of time, the landowners ran the risk of losing their title to their land or face having to vindicate their rights in a court of law (sec. 1).

But the distinction that this constitution drew between those who might establish rights of possession and farmers paying customary rents seems artificial at best. In the later empire, there were clearly categories of farmers who did exercise rights over land ultimately belonging to another party that went well beyond those accorded by conventional Roman law to a tenant. In the early empire, the *coloni* on the imperial estates in the Medjerda valley in Africa could bequeath or pledge as security the land that they cultivated under perpetual leaseholds.[18] Whether *coloni* occupying private land in North Africa during the early imperial period enjoyed these same rights is unknown, but it is clear that in the later empire they might. Thus, in the Vandal period, the cultivators documented in the Albertini Tablets bought and sold rights to land situated within a large estate.[19]

The Albertini Tablets, dated to the years 493–96, are an archive of documents, maintained by two brothers, Geminius Felix and Geminius Cresconius, who were tenants on an estate, called the *fundus Tuletianos*, owned by a landlord named Flavius Geminius Catullinus. The *fundus Tuletianos* was located in the predesert region of North Africa, on the Algero-Tunisian border. The Albertini Tablets include a number of sales of parcels of land (*particellae agrorum*) carried out over a four-year period. The documents record a series of purchases that the brothers made from other tenants within the estate of the rights to cultivate trees, especially olive trees. The cultivation rights are termed *culturae Mancianae*. Thus the tenants held their land under terms ultimately based on the *lex Manciana*, the lease regulation that had established land tenure on imperial estates in North Africa in the early imperial period.

In the present circumstance, it seems likely that the cultivators within the *fundus Tuletianos* enjoyed perpetual rights to their lands planted with trees but in exchange were required to pay a share rent to the landowner. According to the recent analysis of these documents by David Mattingly, these trees were likely to have been cultivated in wadi beds. Cultivating the trees in this way allowed the farmers to make use of the water from the infrequent but sometimes violent rainstorms that are characteristic of the predesert region in North Africa. Capturing the runoff from such rainstorms provides the main source of water for agriculture in these regions.[20] Whatever the precise conditions were on the estate that precipitated these sales, the Albertini Tablets indicate how a tenant exercised long-term rights to land that could be exchanged or sold without changing the ultimate rights of the owner.

On the *fundus Tuletianos*, the state recognized two sets of legal rights to the land, those of the owner, who certainly could sell, bequeath, or otherwise alienate the rights that he exercised over the cultivators, or *coloni*, and those of the *coloni*, who could freely dispose of the rights that they exercised over their land. Moreover, as H. Weßel points out, there is nothing in the Albertini Tablets to suggest that the cooperation of the owner of the estate was required to transact the sales.[21] This situation seems to be at variance with the late antique legal principal that *coloni* bound to the land could not alienate their property without the consent of the landlord or patron. Thus in the fourth century, the emperors Valentinian I and Valens addressed a constitution to the governor of the province of Asia in which they prohibited *coloni* from selling any property that they owned without the permission of the landowner (*CTh* 5.19.1, 365): "There is no doubt that *coloni* lack the right of alienating lands that they cultivate to this extent, that even if they have some property of their own, they are not permitted to transfer it to others if their patrons have not been consulted and are unaware."[22] The concern of the imperial administration in this constitution was to define the rights of *coloni* legally bound to their land. As Jean-Michel Carrié argues, it was completely logical that bound *coloni* should require the consent of their landlords to sell property, since the landlords held a lien over this property to cover fiscal obligations, not to mention the private obligations of the *coloni* to pay rent.[23] It is noteworthy that the *coloni* in this constitution were expressly prohibited from alienating the land that they cultivated. Surely what this means is that the *coloni* were not to sell or otherwise alienate the rights to cultivate the land that they held. This restriction logically follows from the general prohibition against *coloni* alienating property without the consent of the landowner.

To judge by imperial constitutions from the fourth century, the efforts of the government to draw a neat distinction between tenants on the one hand and landowners on the other continually ran up against the economic reality of land tenure in the Roman Empire, since many estates were cultivated by people with long-term rights to their land. The rights that such tenants exercised over their land did not conform to the definitions of classical Roman law, and the challenge faced by the government was to define these rights in a consistent manner that respected Roman conventions. What was at issue here was not simply what we would regard as sales of land but any type of alienation, including the efforts of tenants to pledge the land that they were cultivating as security for loans. Apparently, ambiguities about the rights of ownership could become a thorny issue for imperial estates, which, as we have seen, were customarily occupied by tenants with long-term rights. The problem was that any efforts to alienate such land might create a tangle of claims by private individuals against the state for rights to the land. To address this situation, the emperors Valentinian II, Theodosius, and Arcadius in 387 issued an edict rescinding sales by *coloni* of imperial or temple land, and in so doing the emperors emphasized that individuals purchasing land from such *coloni* would receive no protection from the *longi temporis praescriptio* (*CJ* 7.38.2):

> We order that all lands, which have been sold or alienated in any other way by imperial tenants under the authority of the state or a temple in any province, should be restored by those who hold them wrongly and in contravention of the laws, with no *longi temporis praescriptio* intruding, in such a way that the unjust purchasers not be permitted to demand back the price.[24]

It is unlikely that the sellers envisioned by the emperors saw themselves as full owners of the property in question in a conventional understanding of the term; instead, they were probably selling rights to cultivate the land or pledging them as security. This supposition draws support from a constitution issued thirty-five years later at Ravenna by Honorius, which listed tenants among other groups as excluded from the right to pledge landed property (*praedia*) as security (*CTh* 2.30.2; *CJ* 8.15.8, 11.48.17, 422): "It is repeated by the authority of the law and the statutes that a lien prejudicial to the owner's rights may not be imposed through a slave or a procurator or a tenant or an *actor* or a lessee without the willingness and knowledge of the owner."[25]

If *coloni* could alienate their rights to their land, then it is logical that, under certain circumstances, they might purchase rights to their land. Apart from the activities of the brothers Geminius on the *fundus Tuletianos*, this situation is at least envisioned in a constitution of the year

425 issued in the East. In this constitution, *coloni* purchasing imperial land, that is, belonging to the *patrimonium privatum*, were required to provide mutual sureties (*CTh* 5.16.34; *CJ* 11.68.6).[26] Perhaps some of the *coloni*, viewed as claiming rights to which they were not legally entitled, had taken over land that they judged to be derelict. For example, the emperor Theodosius I recognized the rights of farmers who had occupied state land and improved it without a formal lease contract (*CJ* 11.71.2, 383).[27] Clearly, the precise nature of the rights that various groups of farmers had over their land was open to interpretation, and the imperial government had to balance the rights of landowners against the desirability of keeping land under cultivation. The imperial government sought to address this problem by establishing a two-year prescription for owners of abandoned land to claim ownership when new cultivators had taken over the land in question and, at their own expense, restored it to productivity, as is indicated in a constitution Theodosius I issued to the praetorian prefect for the East (*CTh* 5.11.12; *CJ* 11.59.8, 392).[28] The landowner reclaiming the land had to compensate the new farmer for the expenses that he bore in improving it. One could imagine that the farmers taking over land in this way included some formally classified as tenants, and sorting out the rights of these farmers and their putative landlords could have been no easy task.

Shortly afterward, however, in a constitution issued in the East, the emperor Arcadius asserted the absolute property rights of the state against anyone occupying state land illegally; such farmers would not be protected by the prescriptions against claims of ownership available to the possessors of private land, including the *longi temporis praescriptio* (*CTh* 10.1.15; *CJ* 7.38.3, 11.67.2, 396).[29] In the fifth century, the emperor Zeno issued an edict imposing penalties on tenants, *conductores*, and other "invaders of other people's property" who resisted landowners trying to reassert their own possession (*CJ* 8.4.10 = 4.65.33, 484).[30] Under this edict, the party who attempted to assert possession illegally would be forced to restore the property in question as well as pay a penalty equal to the property's estimated value. This enactment was intended to protect the rights of property owners, in that it added a significant financial penalty for those who would dispute ownership.[31]

To return to the rescripts of Alexander Severus and Diocletian (*CJ* 7.30.1, 7.32.5), at first sight it might seem strange that the possibility of the tenant's selling the land that he was only leasing could even be a legal issue, since doing so was completely at variance with conventional Roman lease law. But these texts can be viewed in an altogether different light when we consider the apparent ambiguities that surrounded the property rights on many types of land in the later empire. The rescripts from the third-century emperors suggest that the government was struggling at that time to accommodate such tenure arrangements. Perhaps these tenure arrangements resembled those established by *lex Manciana* for imperial estates. This possibility becomes all the more likely if, as seems likely, imperial estates were occasionally returned to private ownership. In these arrangements, what was subject to dispute was probably not whether a conventional farm tenant could usurp the prerogatives of a landowner but rather what rights a long-term tenant might exercise over the land that he occupied. In some private tenure arrangements, tenants may have traditionally exercised the right to sell or otherwise alienate their rights to their land, but the question is what status such rights would hold in Roman law. Could they be recognized formally?

The response of Alexander Severus, and later of Diocletian, in adjudicating disputes about the tenant's rights under a long-term lease relationship is instructive about how the government dealt with the complications of reconciling conventional law with traditional practices. In tenancy law, as we have seen, the government recognized as legally binding tenure arrangements that derived from local custom but were in origin at variance with Roman conventions. The responses of Alexander Severus and Diocletian, however, show that the legal authorities would go only so far in accommodating such tenure arrangements within Roman law. In these cases, they decided disputes over private land precisely in terms of Roman private law. They deemed one party to be a tenant in the conventional understanding of the term and the other to be the landlord and ruled that the duration of the tenant's occupation of the land could in no way mitigate the landowner's rights.

But the constitutions from the later empire suggest some of the complexities that the emperors Alexander Severus and Diocletian faced in the third century. Whereas the imperial government defined the rights and duties of landowners and tenants neatly in terms of conventional legal categories, in the real world the relationships between these two groups might be far more complex. There were clearly situations in which the precise legal rights of owners and tenants over their land were not well defined, at least in terms of Roman law. To judge by the third-century rescripts, some farmers designated as tenants attempted to use the legal institutions of the state to assert their own rights against those that a landlord might customarily exercise, and also to protect themselves against inroads by their landowners. The response of the government to this circumstance favored the interests of landowners, since the government was not willing to recognize the legal validity of the tenants' claim to alienate rights to their land. So if the government sought to foster the long-term occupation of the land by productive tenants, this policy could not be stretched beyond what was recognizable in conventional Roman legal categories. The government's priority was not to favor the interests of either large landowners or the farmers cultivating their land but to impose a legal order in which Roman law would remain authoritative in delineating property rights in the rural economy.

This effort of the government to impose a legal order on a rural economy raises the question about the reach of Roman legal institutions in the countryside. On the one hand, the approach of the government was consistent with what it displayed in adjudicating other aspects of tenancy law. This policy, at least in theory, sought to define property rights more precisely and so helped to lower the costs of negotiating and enforcing contracts. If the government's definition of property rights established the rules in accordance with which disputes would be adjudicated in courts of law, this was only part of the problem that the legal authorities faced. Since very few disputes between landowners and tenants were likely to have found their ways into Roman courts, the real task was to establish rules that would guide landowners and tenants as they engaged in the private ordering needed to adjust to changing conditions in long-term tenancy relationships.[32] On the other hand, the continuing concern of the government during the third and fourth centuries with the principle that tenants could not establish possession suggests the difficulties of imposing any sort of legal order on the diverse agrarian economy of the empire. Claims based on the assertion of rights foreign to Roman law would likely meet little success in the courts. But the likely reality is that tenants did assert their rights to buy and sell or otherwise alienate cultivation rights, and landowners had to recognize these rights unless they desired to take the costly steps of going to court, which in all likelihood would result in the termination of tenure arrangement that otherwise provided them certain advantages. So the "governance" structures surrounding farm tenancy in much of the empire, to use the phrase of Oliver Williamson, resulted in a type of private ordering quite different from what might be defensible in Roman courts.[33]

If certain farmers claimed quasi-ownership rights to lands to which other, presumably distant landowners also claimed ownership rights, in what sense could these two groups engage in any sort of cooperation to reach mutually beneficial goals? In other words, could land-tenure arrangements involving two disparate parties each with its distinct claim to the land be "relational"? It seems likely that the farmers cultivating the land under such arrangements were responsible for covering most of the costs of cultivation, and that the role of the landowner consisted largely of exacting a rent that had been established by custom. If the landowner made few other contributions to the actual working of the farm, it would not be surprising that tenants would claim ownership rights over their land. The concern of the government with tenants' asserting ownership rights, then, represents another aspect of the problem that the emperors Valerian and Gallienus and, later, Constantine encountered in restraining landowners who raised customary rents (as discussed already). Such tenure arrangements were likely to have been characterized not by cooperation but by opportunism, with landowners asserting their rights to collect rents and using the sunk costs of the tenants as leverage to achieve this goal, and the tenants asserting their de facto rights to the land against landowners who were effectively more tax collectors than partners in a contractual relationship. Thus private landowner-tenant relationships were often subject to the same strains as existed on imperial estates, with two groups set against one another, battling to control the surplus produced by the small farmers. The interest of the government in regulating such private tenancy relationships was somewhat different than with imperial estates, since its main role in private tenancy was to facilitate the adjudication of cases by defining property rights in a consistent fashion.

Indeed, recognizing traditional rights within a normative legal framework raised complex issues for the Roman legal authorities. We can trace how they confronted such issues in a dispute over water rights addressed by Constantine (*CJ* 11.63.1, 319). As Yoram Barzel points out, water rights are crucially important "economic rights" in agriculture, but they are notoriously difficult to define and enforce by the state. The water that various parties rely on to irrigate their crops may come from communally held property or may be situated within the land belonging to one party.[34] In this constitution, issued in Carthage, the conflict was between certain *coloni* in North Africa, perhaps imperial tenants occupying their land in accordance with the *lex Manciana*, and emphyteutic possessors.[35] Emphyteutic possessors held perpetual rights to land granted to them by the state in exchange for the payment of a fixed yearly rent (*canon*). The emperor noted that *coloni* had violated the rights of emphyteutic possessors by exploiting the water sources on certain uncultivated lands (*CJ* 11.63.1 pr.):

> The *coloni* are burdening the *emphyteuticarii* by usurping lands, in violation of custom, that they have not improved with any cultivation, although imperial authority allows them only to touch what has been planted by their own labor with olives or vines. But they also endeavor to usurp irrigation water from springs, whose fruits are owed to the *emphyteuticarii* alone.[36]

The response of the imperial government was to allocate the water rights over these lands to the emphyteutic possessors, and to allow limited water rights to *coloni* specifically to cultivate vines and olives. The *coloni* would have to pay the *emphyteuticarii* a fee for any water that they might use for other purposes (e.g., for raising livestock):

> Therefore it has been decided that from now on the right and power over the waters should remain with the *emphyteuticarii*, and that the *coloni* are to be permitted only so much water as manifestly sufficient for the cultivation of those lands that they themselves cultivate. The *coloni* should offer payments and additional services to the emphyteutic possessors for the amount of the remaining water that they have usurped for purposes other than the cultivation of their crops.[37]

Admittedly, this constitution only allows us to draw inferences about the conditions under which the two groups in question occupied their land. It is noteworthy that custom played a crucial role in determining legal relationships. In this case, the emperor drastically restricted the water rights of the *coloni*, because, in using water from land that they had not cultivated themselves, the *coloni* were judged to have exceeded the rights that were accorded to them by custom. In other words, the rationale behind the restriction of the *coloni*'s water rights was based largely on the imperial government's interpretation of custom. This interpretation may have been prejudicial against the interests of the *coloni* and against what they would consider to be their legitimate rights. But the important point is that, to balance out customary rights against the newly defined rights of the *emphyteuticarii*, the Roman authorities approached this problem by respecting to the extent possible land-tenure arrangements enshrined by custom and, when this was not possible, by designating the *emphyteuticarii* as owners of the water and requiring the *coloni* to pay for the use of this scarce commodity. In taking this latter step, the government provided some incentive for private negotiations between the *coloni* and the *emphyteuticarii* over the costs of the water rights. The government had neither the interest nor the capacity to establish what the costs of the water rights might be. Perhaps, with the encouragement of the Roman government, these two groups reached an accord comparable to the one recorded in the famous inscription from Lamasba in Africa, which records water rights for the members of a farming community.[38] In any case, the constitution that Constantine issued to the governor of Africa would have the effect of encouraging the *coloni* and the *emphyteuticarii* to bargain over the externality represented by the depletion of water resources, a process that would ideally reduce the transaction costs involved in accommodating agriculture and livestock raising in a region with scare water resources.[39]

The government's efforts to define property rights in a consistent manner led it to confront other types of legal claims that were the products of local tenure arrangements but had no basis in conventional Roman law. For example, Diocletian ruled unlawful a creditor's efforts to collect a debt owed by a landowner from the tenants who were making their agreed upon rent payments (*CJ* 4.10.3, 286). The creditor had no legal basis to proceed against the tenants of the debtor, since Roman law did not allow parties to a contract to impose obligations on third parties. The effort of this creditor to make good the loan by taking the rents paid by the tenants may have originated in a situation similar to the one that seems to stand behind another decision of Diocletian. In this case, it was ruled that a landlord could not be held responsible for his tenants' debts (*CJ* 4.10.11, 294).[40] Apparently, a woman had made a loan to some *coloni* in the presence of the landowner's *actores* (business managers). The woman had, in all likelihood, arranged credit for the tenants with the understanding of the landowner; the purpose of this credit was presumably to make it possible for the tenants to cultivate their land and to pay their rent, or alternatively to allow them to pay their back rent. When she sought repayment of her loan, it does not seem unreasonable that she should turn to the landowner, who stood to benefit from the credit advanced to the tenants. Her actions certainly make sense if the tenants occupied their land under a long-term tenure arrangement and so were not likely to depart from the farm in question at the end of a short-term lease. Admittedly, other explanations are possible: the creditor may have turned to the landowner simply because the tenants were in no position to pay her back.

The woman who submitted this petition may have sought to enter into an arrangement like the one that stands behind another rescript of Diocletian (*CJ* 4.65.27). In this case, an individual had advanced money to cover obligations to be paid by the tenants of an estate, and the landowner had made a formal promise through a stipulation to pay back the funds advanced.[41] Accordingly, the stipulation obligated the landowner, but barring such an arrangement, a loan to a tenant could not result in any obligation on the part of the landowner. Thus the response of Diocletian in these cases was to recognize only the original relationship between the creditor and debtor, even when doing so in all likelihood ignored the complex relationships between the landowners and the tenants that led to the credit being extended in the first place.

The loans involving tenants long remained an issue that the imperial government had to adjudicate, if we can judge by a later constitution issued by the emperor Honorius at Ravenna (*CTh* 2.31.1; *CJ* 4.26.13 pr.-3, 422). In this constitution, the emperor upheld the classical Roman principle that a creditor lending money to a slave could only collect from the slave's owner if the latter had authorized the loan. In this case, the creditor could recover under the *actio quod iussu* (action on the basis of the slave owner's authorization).[42] But the constitution goes on to prohibit creditors from pressing landowners for debts contracted with estate personnel, including slaves, tenants, large-scale lessees, procurators, and *actores*. The creditor could only collect if he or she had made the loan with the specific authorization of the landowner, and ample proof was required for this. Any creditor making such a loan without the landowner's permission was to pay a fine equal to the sum of money lent out.

In this constitution, the imperial government, concerned with preventing landowners from being bound by obligations that they themselves had not expressly entered into, stringently applied the time-honored principle of classical Roman law that obligations could not be imposed by the actions of third parties. But what was the most probable scenario under which a creditor would make a loan to a farm tenant or other manager of an estate? As far as loans to a tenant are concerned, in many cases they provided funds needed to cultivate the land and pay the yearly rent, so they were in some sense advantageous to the landowner. Surely the creditor making such a loan had every expectation that the landowner was in agreement, and the creditor's willingness to extend credit depended on his or her assurance of the tenant's long-term tenure and the landowner's cooperation. When the tenant failed to pay back the loan, the creditor reasonably tried to recover from the landowner. But the imperial government did not consider these factors as it sought to protect the full rights of landowners.

The final section of this constitution shows the imperial government making a gesture to economic reality. If the manager of the property in question was autonomous in keeping the accounts, creditors could recover under an *actio utilis*, that is, an analogous action granted by the praetor for situations that did not exactly correspond to the strict letter of the law but still matched the law's general principles. In this case, the landowner's authorization of any loans would be implicit (*CTh* 2.31.1; *CJ* 4.26.13.4). The imperial government apparently was called upon time and again to adjudicate the liability for debts incurred by *coloni*. In the late fifth century, for example, the emperor Zeno declared the illegality of making villagers mutually liable for debts (*CJ* 11.57.1).[43] In this same period, contracts for mutual sureties in Egypt indicate that landowners sought to ensure repayment of loans by requiring their debtors to provide additional sureties.[44] The emperor Zeno outlawed the logical extension of this practice, that is, that landowners would unilaterally impose the obligation to pay the debts of *coloni* on all those farmers residing in the villages that formed part of the estate.

The rescripts concerning loans involving farm tenants from the reign of Diocletian suggest the nature of the private ordering that took place under the shadow of Roman law. These rescripts, when seen against the continuing difficulties that the government in the later empire encountered in dealing with loans involving farm tenants, indicate that complex arrangements were undertaken to provide tenants with credit. Often these arrangements involved the cooperation of the landowner. But these arrangements, sensible as they might have been to facilitate agriculture, were not enforceable in Roman courts, at least not in the way that some of the creditors envisioned that they would be. Of course, very few disputes arising from such loans ever reached the Roman courts, and we should imagine that creditors, landowners, and tenants developed their own private means of enforcing such loans that did not involve the state. What the rescripts represent are situations in which these private methods of enforcement broke down, when one party turned to the state for support in a dispute that private means of enforcement could not resolve. The issues that Diocletian confronted offer us a hint about the complex ways in which credit might have been provided in agriculture, and they should likewise alert us to the likelihood of a wide variety of ways in which land tenure might have been arranged. Even if many of these arrangements were maintained outside the reach of Roman law, it is also apparent that the presence of viable legal institutions of the state provided a last resort for both landowners and tenants to defend their interests.

DEBT AND LEGAL CONTROL

One area of the law that had significant impact on agrarian relationships was the right of a creditor to take over the property of a defaulting debtor.

In any agrarian society, small-scale farmers often require credit to achieve the production that allows them to pay their rent, meet their fiscal obligations, and provide for the nutritional needs of their households.[45] In the Roman Empire, the crucial question surrounding debt is to what extent the need for credit placed small farmers in an economically dependent position vis-à-vis upper-class landowners. According to M. I. Finley, the economic dependence resulting from chronic indebtedness enabled Roman landowners to exercise a great deal of control over tenants. A continuing cycle of rental arrears and indebtedness from which *coloni* had no capacity to escape allowed landowners effectively to bind *coloni* to the land and to impose terms of cultivation on them unilaterally.[46] Compounding the economic dependence of small farmers was the practice of creditors to use self-help to enforce debts.[47] Indeed, under extreme circumstances, creditors could imprison debtors and use other types of violence to compel the repayment of debts. Even if the state tended to discourage the maintenance of private prisons to house debtors, these institutions nevertheless continued to exist throughout antiquity. The policy of the state was to assert its own authority in determining when someone could be imprisoned for a private debt. In addition, fiscal debtors were often subject to arrest as a means of compelling repayment.[48] Small farmers could clearly fall prey to powerful landowners who could call upon the institutions of the state to support their unilateral measures against defaulting debtors.

The credit that might be extended to small-scale cultivators could take many forms. We are best informed about such credit in Roman Egypt, thanks to documentary papyri. One form of credit was a loan of seed or cash during the sowing season. Such loans were to be paid back at the harvest, generally in the form of wheat. When the loans were in kind, the amount paid back at harvest would generally be substantially higher than what was borrowed to begin with, since the value of wheat and other products was highest before sowing and decreased substantially after the harvest.[49] Credit might also be extended to people who would repay the loan through various types of work contracts. A type of purchase contract, called a "sale on delivery," often represented a way of repaying a loan. In this arrangement, the debtor would repay the loan by agreeing to turn over to the creditor a specified volume of a crop. Contracts such as this seem to represent loans particularly when they do not specify a price for the crop.[50] Another type of credit can be seen in antichretic leases, in which the debtor, instead of repaying the capital of the loan, allowed the creditor to lease a property in question without paying a rent.[51] Finally, credit in the rural economy might also involve more conventional mortgages. The

Roman legal sources provide evidence mainly for loans secured against the property of the debtor. This means that many credit arrangements, often between landowners and tenants, were conceived outside the ambit of the law. Sometimes the landowner and tenant might simply have bargained to include any credit extended to the tenant in the rent due each year. This type of credit might be crucially important to the financial interests of landowners and especially tenants, and it might well place tenants in economically dependent positions, but it represented the type of private ordering that the Roman government fostered but did not seek to regulate.

We can, however, trace the efforts of the government to exercise control over one aspect of the credit market, namely, when loans were secured against real property and the creditor confiscated the property held as security to make good a defaulting debtor's obligation. In classical Roman law, the creditor might hold property pledged as security as *pignus* (property over which the creditor exercised possession). Alternatively, the debtor might retain possession of the pledged property, but the creditor still exercised considerable rights to it. In a lease, the lessor could have recourse to an interdict from a magistrate, in this case the Salvian Interdict, through which the lessor could establish his or her possession rights to the property that the tenant brought onto the farm under lease. This interdict would give the creditor immediate protection against other claimants to the tenant's property, including not just the tenant but any third party who might also be a creditor to the tenant. Strengthened by this interdict, the lessor could then sue the tenant for the pledged property through the *actio Serviana*, which gave the lessor an in rem claim on the tenant's property.[52]

The Roman legal authorities seem to have especially been concerned that the creditor's disposing of the pledged property proceed under the control of the courts. In classical Roman law, the nature of the rights that a creditor exercised over the property pledged as security has been subject to considerable debate. Max Kaser's influential view is that the creditor originally gained ownership of the property in the event of the debtor's default.[53] In the classical period of Roman law, the creditor typically satisfied his or her claims by selling the pledged property. Andreas Wacke has recently offered a vigorous challenge to this view, arguing that the rights of the creditor over property pledged as security derived from a praetorian remedy.[54] This protection consisted of a defense, the *exceptio rei pignori datae*, which the creditor could advance when the debtor sought to vindicate ownership of the property in question. Pledge contracts commonly included a clause that the creditor could sell the pledged property in the event of default, and it seems likely that, at least by the Severan period, such a clause was assumed to be part of a credit contract unless some other provision were made.[55] One possibility is an agreement that the creditor would become the owner of the pledged property if the debtor defaulted; this type of agreement is called a *lex commissoria*, and Wacke suggests that such an agreement was relatively common in the third century, during the late classical era of Roman law, when the economy, in his view, was less monetized.[56] But as far as monetization is concerned, the economy in the late third century was not fundamentally different from that of earlier periods, so there must be another explanation for the apparent frequency of agreements of this type. Probably, such agreements, which clearly offered substantial advantages to the creditor, are to be attributed to the power that some creditors exercised over their debtors. Indeed, the government displayed some concern about protecting the interests of economically distressed debtors. Thus the emperor Constantine outlawed the *lex commissoria*, declaring invalid any present and future such agreements (*CTh* 3.2.1; CJ 8.34.3, 320). The possibility for abuse in such agreements is so great that subsequent civilian legal systems, such as the German Bürgerliches Gesetzbuch, have also outlawed them.[57]

The Roman legal authorities as a matter of policy preferred that the creditor satisfy the debtor's obligations through the sale of the pledged property, and that such sales proceed under the watchful eyes of the courts. The creditor was only entitled to make good the debt from the proceeds of the sale, and any funds left over would either be used to pay off other creditors also with a claim to the pledged property or be returned to the debtor. The debtor had the right to sue for any proceeds left over after the sale (*superfluum*) under the *actio pigneraticia* (action on pledge). Clearly, the involvement of the courts might play a critical role in the way legal disputes over debts were resolved. Without the close scrutiny of the courts, for example, creditors might exercise considerable power over weaker debtors, in that the creditors could unilaterally take possession of the pledged property and decide its subsequent disposition. An economically dependent debtor would have no capacity to resist such actions of a creditor.

Examples of such cases can be found in two rescripts, one from Alexander Severus (*CJ* 8.27.5, 231) and a later one from Diocletian (*CJ* 8.27.10, 290). In the first text, a debtor sought relief against a creditor who was going to sell off property that was pledged as security to make good the remainder of a debt, even though the debtor had offered to pay the debt. Alexander Severus ruled that the provincial governor should appoint an arbiter to determine what was owed, and that the refusal of the creditor to submit to this arbitration would not compromise the debtor's rights to his property.[58] The rescript of Diocletian addressed alleged collusion on the part of a creditor to acquire an estate (*praedium*) that a debtor had pledged as security. Diocletian ruled that a creditor could not acquire ownership of the estate by purchasing it through an imaginary person but that, in this circumstance, the debtor could regain the property by offering to pay the principal of the debt with interest.[59] These two cases presuppose that the property pledged as security was likely to be worth a great deal more than the debt so that the creditor might enrich him- or herself at the expense of the debtor by claiming the latter's default and moving against the debtor's property. Creditors with wide latitude in exercising self-help would enjoy substantial economic advantages over debtors and could use lending money at interest to farmers in economic distress as a means of acquiring additional property. Diocletian's ruling sought to protect against predatory actions by creditors who would use the leverage afforded them by the indebtedness to acquire property from economically disadvantaged parties. The government was not in a position to alleviate whatever problems of indebtedness that might have plagued farmers, but it could offer them some protection against their creditors using the institutions of the state to take excessive advantage of the opportunities afforded by debt.

The rulings in these two cases reflect the Roman government's consistent policy to resist this tendency by asserting the exclusive power of the courts to supervise any confiscation of the defaulting tenant's property. This concern dates at least to the reign of Marcus Aurelius, who, in a rescript quoted by the jurist Callistratus, insisted that a creditor use the courts rather than self-help to proceed against a debtor. The emperor regarded the use of force to be any means of compelling a debtor outside of established legal remedies (Callistr. *D.* 48.7.7, 5 *de cognit.*).[60] According to Modestinus, a creditor who seized the property of a debtor without the authority of a judge was held liable under the *lex Iulia de vi privata* (the Julian law on private force). This involved serious sanctions: the offending creditor would lose one-third of his or her property and be deemed *infamis* (infamous, or removed from decent society) (*D.* 48.7.8, 2 *de poenis*).

To be sure, as Alfons Bürge argues, the Roman government allowed creditors to exercise a great deal of self-help in enforcing contractual obligations, and this situation to a large extent was a product of the wide social gap that often existed between the parties to Roman contracts. It seems unlikely that upper-class creditors would have exercised the same restraint in taking legal action against poorer debtors that they often accorded debtors from their same class. This restraint was part of a social code that helped debtors avoid the potential disgrace of adverse court verdicts or foreclosure on their property.[61] Still, the position of the debtor in Roman law was far more favorable than in classical Greek tenancy law, in which the lessor, as creditor, could exercise unilateral action in proceeding against the property of the defaulting tenant.[62]

Beginning at least in the late second century, the Roman legal authorities sought to restrict this exercise of self-help and instead to establish the authority of the courts in settling legal disputes.[63] Thus Septimius Severus ruled that creditors taking possession of pledged property could not be viewed as resorting to force but still must take possession under the authority of the provincial governor (*CJ* 8.13.3, 205). Another rescript of Septimius Severus also seemed aimed at curbing the power that creditors might exercise over debtors (*CJ* 4.24.1, 207). In this text, Septimius Severus ruled that the crops from a property held as security should be reckoned against the debt, and that any crops left over should be returned to the debtor. Somewhat later, Caracalla emphasized that repeated rescripts had upheld the exclusive authority of a judge to alienate property pledged as security (*CJ* 8.22.1, 213). Addressing the same legal issue, Alexander Severus ruled that property awarded to a plaintiff in a judgment should be sold under the authority of the judge, not the plaintiff (*CJ* 8.22.2 pr., 223). Alexander Severus was concerned about preventing chicanery on the part of creditors who might, if left unchecked, acquire debtors' property for themselves at fraudulently low prices. Accordingly, in the same rescript, the emperor ruled that the creditor could only acquire the property if no suitable purchaser had appeared at the auction arranged by the judge. Showing a concern to protect the rights of debtors, this same emperor also ruled on the obligations of the creditor to maintain the property held as security for a debt. The crops that the creditor harvested while holding the property were to count against the debt, and if the creditor allowed the property to deteriorate, he or she could be sued on an action on *pignus* (*CJ* 4.24.3, 222).[64]

Defending the authority of the courts in settling debts was a concern that the Roman government addressed time and again. Thus Gordian once more ruled that property pledged as security when seized under the authority of a judge was to be sold off rather than taken over by the creditor, and only when fraud on the part of the debtor prevented a sale could the property pass to the creditor (*CJ* 8.22.3, 239). Gordian likewise referred a debtor to the protection of the provincial governor for relief against a creditor who sold off an estate pledged as security in contravention of bona fides (*CJ* 8.29.4, 240). To return to Diocletian, that emperor assured a creditor suing debtors for fulfillment of their obligations the right to proceed against the property pledged as security through legal proceedings before the provincial governor (*CJ* 8.13.10, 290).[65] A few years later Diocletian issued a rescript prohibiting a landowner from seeking to make good debts that arose from unpaid rent by seizing the tenants' slaves not included in the *invecta aut illata* (the property brought into the tenancy) (*CJ* 8.14.5, 294).

The government also insisted on the participation of a legitimate court when the property in question was confiscated and sold for the nonpayment of taxes. Thus Diocletian affirmed the rights of a woman who had purchased property (*praedia*) that the people financially responsible for the collection of taxes had confiscated and sold. But the sale was legitimate only if it was carried out under the authority of the provincial governor. Without his permission, the sale was to be rescinded (*CJ* 4.46.2).[66]

In all likelihood, the imperial chancery's practice of interpreting loan arrangements, like lease arrangements, in terms of Roman norms worked to the advantage of debtors. This legal policy seems to have stood behind another rescript of Diocletian, in which that emperor emphasized the illegality of a creditor's seizing a property when the property had not been explicitly pledged as security for a loan of money (*CJ* 7.32.9, 294). This seems to be a straightforward application of Roman legal principles, but it is also likely that in many regions of the empire the status of a debtor's property was not so clear-cut. For example, in Egypt, the creditor in some cases had the right to proceed against all the property of the defaulting debtor.[67] If the case addressed by Diocletian came from a provincial setting, then it seems unlikely that the loan would have been formally contracted as *mutuum* (the Roman form of loan). In this type of loan, any agreement about interest or security had to be made in a separate stipulation.[68] This rigorous application of Roman rules about debt provided the debtor with legal protection against unilateral action by the creditor.

We can glean from this summary of these cases the potential power that creditors could have over debtors, especially at times of economic distress. When a wealthy landowner was claiming a debt from a social inferior, the scope for unilateral action was probably quite large. In reviewing the imperial rescripts on this issue, the policy of the imperial chancery was to balance the interests of creditors and debtors, and it sought to achieve this by insisting that any confiscation and sale of pledged property be carried out strictly under the appropriate judicial authority. To be sure, this does not mean that the imperial government was successful in holding in check the putative power of creditors, but to the extent that it was successful in keeping the courts involved in the settlement of debts, it must have provided some protection to small farmers and tenants. Self-help was not a legally acceptable means to enforce debts.

DISPUTES OVER OWNERSHIP AND POSSESSION

The chancery pursued a policy of asserting the authority of the courts in other legal issues involving the rural economy. It was strictly against the most basic policy of the Roman government to countenance the use of force to settle property disputes. Thus in the second century, the emperor Antoninus Pius wrote to the *koinon* (federation) of Thessaly that when a dispute arose about the use of force and the possession or ownership of property, the alleged use of force should be investigated first (Marcian. *D.* 48.6.5.1, 14 *inst.*). By implication, in the judgment of the emperor, force could not be used even to establish otherwise lawful ownership.[69] The emperor Septimius Severus ruled that the governor had to decide about the possession and the crime of violence when ruling whether a defeated party in a case had a legal right to appeal the verdict (*CJ* 7.62.1, 209). Later, when an individual named Valerius complained to the emperor Diocletian about a person encroaching on his land, the emperor's rescript presupposed that the provincial governor would take steps to defend the rightful possession of the petitioner (*CJ* 7.32.6, 293). Defending rightful possession meant that the imperial government would not recognize the use of force in settling property disputes. To uphold the traditional Roman doctrine of opposing force, Diocletian emphasized that a person losing possession by force but then regaining it lawfully would enjoy the protection of the interdict against forcible eviction (the interdict *unde vi*) indefinitely, instead of for the one-year duration of the interdict (*CJ* 8.35.5, 293). Likewise Diocletian refused to support the efforts of two women to retain possession of property when it emerged that they had gained it by violence (*CJ* 8.4.3, 294).[70] In a similar spirit, Diocletian ruled that a possessor of estates could not lose his or her rights to them if the possessor gave up their cultivation out of fear (*CJ* 7.32.4, 290). In the fourth century, Valens, Gratian, and Valentinian II ruled that a person evicted from possession by force could seek the interdict *unde vi* as well as bring criminal charges against the offending party (*CTh* 9.20.1; *CJ* 9.31.1, 378).[71]

The authority exercised by the courts may have provided provincials some protection against arbitrary or fraudulent decisions by imperial officials. Such protection at least seems to have been available to a woman petitioning Diocletian. She alleged that her adversaries, hoping to acquire her property, had arranged for it to be auctioned by the provincial governor at a low price on the false claim that she owed tax arrears (*CJ* 7.39.1). Diocletian stipulated the procedures under which the provincial governor should adjudicate the case. If the prescribed time for her to bring such an action had not run out, those making a fraudulent purchase would lose the price that they had paid for the property, but the governor could also provide some relief if the conventional time for bringing an action had expired.[72] This case suggests the type of collusion in which a well-placed creditor might engage with a governmental official. At the very least, the existence of this rescript indicates that innocent parties in such situations did have some recourse to the protection of the state to protect their interests, whether or not the woman in this particular instance was successful in prosecuting her case.

In the fourth century, the imperial government's concern about asserting the authority of its courts became more urgent, perhaps in response to the growing influence of locally powerful landowners. To that end Constantine proclaimed that punishments awaited those who took over property by force (*CTh* 2.26.1; *CJ* 8.4.5, 330).[73] This same emperor imposed penalties on a plaintiff who anticipated a judgment over a boundary dispute by taking control of the property in question (*CTh* 2.26.2; *CJ* 3.39.4, 330). Constantine declared that any litigant who lost a case under those circumstances would be punished by losing proportionally the amount of property that the litigant tried to claim for his or her own. The seriousness of the offense that Constantine was seeking to combat is suggested in one of his earlier constitutions, in which he had promised trials and punishments for high-ranking people, including those of senatorial rank, who engaged in various offenses, including rape and boundary incursions (*CTh* 9.1.1; *CJ* 3.24.1, 316).[74] Constantine also sought to protect the rights of those who had been given property by the emperor by declaring that anyone disputing ownership had to make a claim in court (*CTh* 10.8.3, 326). Later, the emperor Valentinian II, in a constitution issued in the West, strengthened the sanctions against those who anticipated court judgments by taking matters into their own hands and invading imperial or private property by force. They would not only lose their cases but also have to pay the value of the property under dispute (*CTh* 4.22.3; *CJ* 8.4.7, 389).[75]

The constitutions discussed here suggest some of the difficulties that the government encountered in defining property rights in the countryside. It is likely that disputes over the ownership of property were often decided at the local level, without recourse to the courts. Certainly it was often advantageous to parties involved in a dispute to resolve them in this way: informal means of resolution might be far less expensive than a case in a Roman court. As Barzel argues, such informal means of settling disputes might be more efficient from the state's point of view because the resolution did not establish a precedent guiding the adjudication of other cases. In such circumstances, the state would have spared itself the costs of using its courts without relinquishing any of its authority.[76] But there was clearly a line that the government would not allow to be crossed, and when disputants resorted to self-help and even force to settle property disputes, such actions compromised the state's delineation of property rights.

The protection against unlawful incursions into property also served the interests of wealthy absentee owners. Thus Constantine issued a constitution requiring provincial governors (*iudices*) to take up the cause of absentee landowners threatened by the loss of possession of their property (*CTh* 4.22.1; *CJ* 8.5.1, 326). Such landowners were at a legal disadvantage when their property was left to the charge of relatives, friends, tenants, freedmen, or any other individuals who, lacking the right of possession in Roman law, were in no position to defend the rights of absentee owners against rival claims of ownership. Constantine afforded relief to such owners by granting the third parties in question the legal capacity to defend property rights on the owners' behalf. Furthermore, absentee owners' rights were not to be compromised by the failure of the third parties to defend them. Thus Constantine granted such landowners the power to sue for restoration of their property, even after the prescribed time limits had run out. For Constantine, the law was to provide aid to landowners against the "violence" of those who took advantage of their absence by taking their property.[77]

This constitution seems to have addressed a situation that must have been fairly commonplace in the countryside, with absentee landowners who rarely set foot on their property facing the loss of such property to intrusions mounted by local farmers. Determining who owned what could be particularly difficult when the land in question sat idle for long periods of time and then was brought under cultivation by new occupiers of the land. As we have seen, Theodosius I responded to this type of situation in a law that established a two-year period for previous owners of unused lands to assert their rights of ownership against new cultivators (discussed earlier in this chapter; *CTh* 5.11.12; *CJ* 11.59.8, 392). Such landowners, to regain their rights, had to compensate the new occupants for any improvements that they had made. If the owners did not lay claim to their land within the two-year period, they would lose any future rights of ownership.

The government's usual insistence on the primacy of the courts is to be contrasted with its indulgence toward veterans when they took over abandoned agricultural land to cultivate themselves (Valentinian I, Valens, and Gratian, *CTh* 7.20.11, 368). Veterans taking this step were to be free from interference by the (former) owners, who would lose their rights entirely, including their rights to a rent. In this case, it is noteworthy that the landlords claiming rent are characterized as people who lie in wait at harvest time after others have sown the land.[78] Taking over land was apparently a special privilege granted to veterans, and it does not seem that, in general, the imperial government sanctioned the unilateral occupation of unused lands.[79] Finally, disputes over property might take a long time to resolve. Valentinian II, in a constitution issued in the West, responded to difficulties arising from prolonged property disputes by imposing substantial penalties, including the loss of the property in general and the payment of all the costs of litigation, on people who delayed legal proceedings in property disputes by failing to appear in court (*CTh* 10.13.1, 386). A litigant in such a dispute was given three chances to appear in court before forfeiting the case.[80]

We can see how such a property dispute might work itself out in the real world by considering a situation that a prominent landowner in fourth-century Hermopolis in Egypt, Aurelius Adelphios, claimed to have encountered. We learn of Adelphios' plight from a petition that he sent to a local official, the *exactor*, at that time the equivalent of the *strategos* (chief administrator of the nome) (*CPR* XVIIA 15, 321); to this petition Adelphios appended an earlier one that he had sent to the provincial governor. Adelphios claimed to own land in two villages, which he had cared for and even sown. But he alleged that a rival landowner named Anysios and a number of villagers had seized the land. In his petition, Adelphios requested that the *exactor* inform the other party of the case and bring that individual to trial.[81] We may see a further step in this dispute in another document (*CPR* XVIIA 18, 321). Here, in an official report from the office of the *exactor*, it is recorded that another of Adelphios' rivals, Theophanes, physically accosted this official at the gate of Hermopolis, seeking to block a suit by Adelphios. Theophanes claimed to have a document recording the sale of the land in question to Anysios' mother and that Adelphios had no rights to the land.

Although it is not possible to judge the merits of either party's claims, this case does suggest how disputes over ownership might arise in the countryside and, absent formal and consistent registration of land, might be very difficult to adjudicate. The constitution of Constantine aimed to protect the rights of owners by maintaining their right to counter actions taken by local landowners or farmers. In the sixth century, Justinian took this effort to protect landowners to its logical conclusion by treating as a brigand (*praedo*) anyone who took possession of land belonging to absent parties without the proper judicial authorization (*CJ* 8.4.11 pr.-2, 532).[82] The case in which Adelphios was involved suggests that it might be difficult to determine when land was unlawfully occupied, but the ideology standing behind Justinian's constitution, that disputes in the countryside could only be resolved through recourse to courts, was consistent with the legal policy that Roman emperors had sought to implement at least from the third century.

These considerations demonstrate the ways in which the Roman government, by asserting the authority of the courts in legal disputes, sought to balance the conflicting rights and interests of parties representing different economic strata. In the rural economy, this effort to discourage self-help and to replace it with formal adjudication surely offered indebted small farmers some protection in their dealings with large landowners. But while the government was obviously concerned with the consistent application of the law, I think that it was also troubled by the economic consequences of allowing people to settle disputes through self-help and other local customs, practices that gave creditors and large landowners disproportionate power over debtors and small farmers. After all, it was in the government's interest to maintain the economic viability of the small farmers who made up a large part of the empire's population, since it was their production that provided the bulk of imperial tax revenues. We can trace this concern in one of Constantine's constitutions, in which he accorded indebted farmers protection against seizure of the property they needed to cultivate their land (*CTh* 2.30.1; *CJ* 8.16.7, 315).[83] Constantine noted that farmers fell into economic peril when, to enforce debts, judicial officials seized as pledged property slaves and livestock used for plowing, which made it impossible for the farmers to continue to cultivate their lands. The result, in Constantine's view, was that imperial tax revenues were threatened. Constantine's response was to impose severe penalties, including capital punishment, on local officials such as village heads and decurions who seized such property from farmers. The concern for tax revenues that Constantine expressed remained central to the imperial government. Thus the emperors Valentinian I and Valens took the same approach for officials who abused their power by requisitioning slaves or livestock from *coloni* for their own use. Such officials were to be punished with the loss of all their property and exile (*CTh* 11.11.1; *CJ* 11.55.2, 368). This judicial orientation of the imperial government, consistent as it was with a traditional policy of protecting the small farmers on whom imperial tax revenues depended, surely offered small farmers some protection in their dealings with larger landowners, and it must have reduced the power that the larger landowners could exercise.

CONCLUSION

This chapter suggests how the imperial government grappled with the problem of maintaining a legal order in an empire with diverse systems of land tenure and a wide range of expectations about the rights and duties of landowners and small farmers. The government was continually engaged in the difficult and messy problem of delineating property rights, but this effort may have enhanced the ability of various parties involved in the rural economy to engage in the private bargaining needed for investment in productive forms of agriculture. In issuing rescripts and constitutions in response to private legal disputes, the primary concern of the legal authorities was not to defend the interests of one group against those of another but to make sure that all legal issues were resolved under the authority of Roman courts. The government's policy certainly helped to establish the property rights of estate owners, but at the same time it also offered legal protection to smaller farmers against unilateral actions by more powerful landowners. We have no reason to believe that this effort was completely successful, and in the later empire it is likely that the authority of the Roman courts to adjudicate agrarian disputes was compromised by the growing influence of locally powerful landowners. But in the early empire, the power of such landowners was not so strong as to render negligible the role of the courts in the rural economy. The emperor, perceived as the ultimate source of justice, was called upon time and again to rule on legal disputes from rural communities. The tendency of the imperial legal authorities to decide these cases whenever possible in terms of Roman private law, albeit gradually influenced by local laws and customs, surely affected the way that governors or their subordinates decided issues in the local courts. The government of course never succeeded in imposing a uniform legal order on the rural Roman Empire, but its assertion of the authority of Roman law and Roman courts over local means of settling disputes must have worked to some extent to the disadvantage of locally powerful landowners and to the advantage of small farmers and farm tenants. This is the case even if many tenure issues were negotiated without considering the conventions of Roman law and resulting disputes were resolved without recourse to the courts. The presence of viable legal institutions always presented both landowners and tenants with an alternative form of dispute resolution that affected their respective bargaining power in traditional, local arrangements.

CHAPTER 5

Late Antique Tax Policy and Incentives for Investment

The reliance of the Roman state and of many private landowners on the continued production of tenants in long-term tenure arrangements created a degree of institutional path dependence with important consequences for the empire's agrarian economy. This institutional path dependence is especially apparent in the fourth century and later. In this period, the difficulty of altering fundamental institutional arrangements imposed serious constraints on the Roman government as it struggled to maintain a fiscal system whose basic principles included the binding of certain categories of farm tenants (*coloni*) to the soil that they cultivated. In this chapter, I focus on the economic implications of late antique fiscal legislation. I do not provide a full account either of agrarian conditions in the later Roman Empire or of the changing legal status of *coloni*. Rather, I am concerned with tracing the likely effects on the incentives for investment that late Roman fiscal policy created, as well as the response of the Roman government to the legal problems engendered by its fiscal policy. Consequently, my focus is primarily on analyzing the legislation itself, especially as it provides a way to discern the capacity of the Roman government to develop laws that promoted growth in the rural economy.

The efforts of the Roman government to restrict the movement of *coloni* had important consequences both for the incentives to invest in agriculture by landowners and tenants and more broadly for the role that law played in defining relationships in the rural economy. The government bound *coloni* to their land to establish a more certain and reliable basis for taxation, and this policy was linked with the tendency in the early empire for many tenants to remain on their estates for long periods of time. The government imposed much of the responsibility to collect taxes and provide revenues to the state on large landowners, and it also undertook to ensure landowners had the means to meet these fiscal obligations by restricting the mobility of the rural workforce. At the same time, restricting the mobility of *coloni* formed part of a broader policy in late antiquity of ensuring the performance of jobs or other functions critical to the state by making them hereditary.[1] The government's interest in *coloni* in the fourth century was chiefly the product of its fiscal policy. For this reason, it perhaps makes more sense to speak of *coloni* bound to the land rather than to use the term *colonate*, since this term suggests the existence of a new class of farmers in a semiservile condition.[2] Still, one must recognize that the Roman government's fiscal policy helped to alter fundamental aspects of the relationship between landowners and tenants, placing many tenants in a more socially dependent relationship than had existed in the early empire.[3] The problem was that the government's fiscal policy ran up against the realities of the late imperial economy: market forces often induced powerful landowners and even some *coloni* to defy this legal order with apparent impunity. Their defiance of this legal order indicates their efforts to bargain around a legal institution that at times hampered potentially more efficient allocations of resources.

This situation had unintended consequences for the role of the state in the rural economy. The need to maintain the empire's tax base compelled the government to intervene in the rural economy repeatedly, and it is likely that the legal policies and institutions of the central government played a greater role in the rural economy in late antiquity than they had in previous centuries. At the same time, the contradiction between the binding of *coloni* to their land and the realities of the agrarian economy drove much of the bargaining beyond the shadow of the law, in that tenure arrangements between landowners and tenants who left their land were not enforceable in Roman courts of law. This circumstance tended to compromise the authority of Roman legal institutions. The government intervened in the rural economy to define the obligations of landowners and *coloni* within the empire's fiscal system in the face of the apparent mobility of many *coloni*, and to check the growing power that landowners exercised, at least in part, as a result of the imperial government's fiscal policies.[4] The distortions in the market surrounding land tenure represented a considerable cost that the late Roman fiscal system imposed on the empire's economy. The government was apparently willing, however, to accept this cost if binding *coloni* to their land helped to ensure more stable revenues for the state. So the government may have had good reasons to maintain its fiscal system, in spite of the cost, if it provided a way to collect revenues vital to the empire's stability. Certainly, the Roman state was not in a position to experiment with other forms of taxation, and it is doubtful that any other system could have been easily devised that would have provided the state the same degree of stability and predictability in its sources of revenues.[5]

THE PROCESS OF BINDING *COLONI*

Let us begin by considering the tax system as it developed in late antiquity. The Roman state traditionally had a vital interest in the productivity of the empire's farmers, since its revenues were based primarily on agriculture. These revenues came from land taxed directly by the imperial government or from the rents and other income from imperial estates. In the early empire, the land tax, termed conventionally the *stipendium* or the *tributum soli*, was assessed on the basis of productive land, although other assets, such as the capital connected with the land, might have been liable to taxation as well. The method of assessment apparently varied from province to province and often derived from the traditional taxing systems that the Romans found when they annexed a given province.[6] In some provinces the taxes on the land were collected in kind, and in others taxes were paid primarily in cash. Under certain circumstances, taxes that in theory were to be paid in kind could be commuted in cash, but with the inflation of the third century the imperial government increasingly resorted to exactions in kind of agricultural products and other commodities to support the military *annona*.[7] We are especially well informed about the tax system in Egypt, where numerous documentary papyri provide a great deal of detailed information about Roman taxing methods. The single most important agricultural tax was the *artabia*, a tax of wheat assessed as a fixed quota (generally one artab per aroura, with some variation) for land cultivated with this crop. Owners of other types of agricultural land paid different types of taxes: for example, owners of vineyards in Egypt were required to pay taxes in cash.[8] It seems likely that, in the grain-producing provinces such as Africa and Egypt, the imperial government as a matter of policy maintained a taxing system that depended on payments of wheat as a means of exercising control over the supply of food for the city of Rome and for the army.

In the later empire, agriculture continued to provide the basis for taxation. The *annona* (the principal tax that the imperial government imposed on the provinces) was assessed in terms of crops, although under certain circumstances, as in the early empire, it could be paid in cash.[9] The late imperial *annona*, administered by the praetorian prefects, developed from ad hoc assessments in kind during the third century into a more comprehensive tax system for agricultural land. The emperor Diocletian (284–305) undertook to make the collection of the *annona* more uniform and equitable throughout the empire, and so he introduced a more systematic method of assessing landowners. At the heart of Diocletian's fiscal system was establishing tax liability on the basis of notional units of productive land, called *iuga*. Under the system of *iugatio*, agricultural lands were assigned values depending on the type of crop cultivated, general agricultural conditions within the province, and quality of the land in question. Thus land cultivated with vineyards would be taxed at a higher rate than grain land, since vineyards produce greater revenue for each unit of land. Similarly, the amount of land that would make up a *iugum* for a given crop was smaller in Egypt, where land was cultivated intensively, than in a province like Africa, where agricultural techniques involved the more extensive cultivation of the land and frequent fallowing. In theory, then, this system of assessing land allowed the imperial government to draw up more equitable tax schedules based on the income that farmers could be expected to achieve from their land rather than on the amount of land that a taxpayer owned. In addition, personnel and livestock under the landowner's control were reckoned in notional units called *capita*. The tax liability represented by an individual *iugum* or *caput* would vary from province to province, but ultimately this system of taxing depended on the imperial government's use of periodic censuses to assess the empire's agricultural resources.

The binding of *coloni* to the land was chiefly a product of the imperial fiscal system. This seems a more likely explanation than the possibility that the Roman government sought to enhance the situation of large landowners by restricting the mobility of the rural labor force, as Jairus Banaji has recently argued.[10] This is not to deny that in some regions of the empire, such as parts of Egypt, large landowners employed numerous wage laborers and labor tenants at the expense of a more independent class of peasant landowners and tenants.[11] In the fiscal system of the later empire, landowners were held liable for the taxes for all the land registered under their names in the census. One could not easily escape this liability, for example, by not cultivating or even abandoning land. Tax liability was not a function of the productivity of the land or the income that the landowner derived from it; instead it was based on the classification of the land. To ensure that taxes would be paid, the imperial government required all cultivators to remain in the village of origin (their *origo* or *idia)* in which they were registered. All land was registered under the name of an individual landowner, and in some areas, particularly in Egypt, a great deal of land might be registered in small parcels under the names of modest landowners.[12] The late imperial fiscal system imposed increasing responsibilities on larger landowners, since the government found it convenient to assign to them much of the responsibility to collect the taxes from the rural population. This process began in the third century, as is indicated by the role played by the large estate of Aurelius Appianus in Egypt in the collection of taxes. The administration of this estate paid the personal taxes for workers on the estate and also organized the performance of liturgies by estate workers and other residents of the villages around which the estate was organized.[13] In the later empire, the government extended the responsibilities of estate owners in the collection of taxes by recognizing estates as the *origo* of *coloni* who were not otherwise registered in the tax rolls as independent landowners. In so doing, the government made the estate owners responsible to pay the capitation taxes for these *coloni* as well as the taxes for the lands that the *coloni* cultivated. The government also provided large landowners with the means of fulfilling these fiscal responsibilities. By restricting the freedom of movement of *coloni*, the Roman government could, in theory, provide landowners with some assurance that they would continue to have the personnel needed to keep their land under cultivation and thereby make it possible for them to meet their fiscal obligations.[14]

The tax system of late antiquity was a product of the institutional arrangements that had developed in previous centuries. Customary arrangements recognized by the government as legally binding frequently involved tenants remaining on their land in open-ended leases and having firmer rights to their land than formally accorded tenants in conventional Roman lease law. In the fourth century, the imperial government took the next logical step and interpreted customary tenure arrangements as permanently binding on landowners and tenants. Thus Constantine ruled that landowners could not raise customary rents, and at the same time this emperor established a process for tenants to seek redress against landowners who had raised their rent in contravention of existing arrangements (CJ 11.50.1; discussed in chap. 4). This constitution certainly presupposes the existence of many long-term tenure arrangements in the empire. A similar conception of long-term tenure arrangements stands behind the ruling of Valentinian I, addressed to the governor of Tripolitania. According to this ruling, landowners had to accept their rents in kind and could not demand cash unless that had been the custom of the estate (*CJ* 11.48.5, 365).[15] Long-term arrangements were necessary components of a tax system based both on the counting of *iuga* and *capita* and on the tenant's registration within the landowner's estate.

Indeed, if Diocletian largely set in place the fiscal system based on *iugatio* and *capitatio*, it is also apparent that the process of formally binding the *coloni* to their land began by the reign of Constantine.[16] Thus a constitution written by Constantine in 319 to Pacatianus, *vicarius* (deputy of the praetorian prefect) of Britain, suggests that by this time *coloni* were already registered for fiscal purposes on the estates owned by decurions (*CTh* 11.7.2).[17] This constitution concerns the fiscal obligations of decurions, and it assumes that farmers termed *coloni* or *tributarii* (tribute payers) might be registered on the land belonging to that group. The situation presupposed in this constitution is in clear contrast to the conventional system of assessing tax liability in the early empire, when, under normal circumstances, the landowner alone bore tax liability and the presence or absence of tenants did not affect this liability. The first text that seems to refer directly to the binding of *coloni* to the land is a constitution of Constantine from the year 332, which established penalties for landowners who harbored *coloni* under the legal authority of another landowner (that is, *coloni iuris alieni*) (*CTh* 5.17.1).[18] The binding of *coloni* to the land, moreover, seems to have been a gradual process. Thus it was apparently only in 371 that this fiscal regime was established in Illyricum (*CJ* 11.53.1).[19] A constitution of ca. 386 established it in Palestine (*CJ* 11.51.1),[20] while a law of 399, issued by Honorius in the West, in addressing the obligations of landowners to acknowledge fiscal liability, distinguishes between provinces in which *coloni* are bound to the land and those in which *coloni* are not (*CTh* 11.1.26).[21] The first of these two constitutions provides a full statement of the obligations of *coloni:* they are not to abandon those lands by whose harvest they are maintained or whose cultivation they have undertaken, and they cannot move about freely but are bound to the owner of the estate. A landowner who takes them in is subject to punishment, while the owner of their estate of origin has the right to recall them.[22]

In defining the obligations of *coloni*, the imperial government applied to this class of cultivators a long-standing policy that considered it the particular duty of the farming population of the empire to cultivate their land and contribute to the empire's revenues. This particular ideology of the Roman state found expression in many places—for example, in the famous edict of Caracalla expelling Egyptians from Alexandria. In Caracalla's formulation, Egyptians were to return to their villages of origin to fulfill their duty toward the state (*Sel.Pap.* II 215, 215 CE).[23] Consequently, farmers who provided revenues to the state by cultivating their land diligently were to be spared imposts or other duties that interfered with their performance of this basic obligation. In accordance with this principle, the emperor Diocletian, in a letter probably addressed to a provincial governor, prohibited the imposition of extra liturgical duties on farmers who contributed to the *annona* through the payment of their capitation taxes (*CJ* 11.55.1).[24] Protecting farmers against fiscal or liturgical demands that interfered with these duties seems to have been a special concern of Constantine. Thus Constantine established sanctions against those who took oxen away from farmers for the use of the *cursus publicus* (public post); in this text, the oxen are characterized as "serving the cultivation of the land" (*CTh* 8.5.1, 315).[25] Likewise, Constantine exempted from *vectigalia* (customs duties) farmers transporting agricultural equipment (*CTh* 4.13.3; cf. *CTh* 4.13.2 and *CJ* 4.61.15, 321). Constantine also ruled that farmers should not be summoned for liturgical duties at the busiest agricultural seasons, such as the sowing and the harvest (*CTh* 11.16.4; *CJ* 11.48.1, 328). Finally, as discussed in the previous chapter, Constantine sought to protect state revenues by outlawing the pledging of crucial resources for farming, including slaves, livestock, and plowing equipment as security for loans (*CTh* 2.30.1; *CJ* 8.16.7, 315).

The late Roman government followed a policy similar to the one that guided the administration of imperial estates under the Principate, in that it sought to reserve the resources of farmers for its own use.[26] So in late antiquity, the government sought to protect farmers against any circumstance that might threaten their capacity to cultivate their land. Again, as discussed in the previous chapter, Valentinian I and Valens imposed severe penalties, including the loss of property and exile, on officials who used the labor, slaves, or draft animals of farmers for their own purposes, as well as similar penalties on those who cooperated with imperial officials for these illegal purposes (*CTh* 11.11.1; *CJ* 11.55.2, 368; for discussion of these texts, see also chap. 4 under "Disputes over Ownership and Possession"). In the formulation of the quaestor of Honorius, *coloni* under no circumstances were to be pulled away from the cultivation of their land because of fiscal debts (*CJ* 11.48.15, 414).[27] The importance that the state placed on the continued cultivation of the land for maintaining tax revenues and the performance of liturgies can be seen from another perspective in a constitution from 423 imposing restrictions on the sale of agricultural property by *curiales* (members of town councils) (*CTh* 12.3.2).[28] This constitution, clarifying an earlier law of 386 of Theodosius I (*CTh* 12.3.1; *CJ*

10.34.1), allowed sales of agricultural or urban property by *curiales* only if the seller could demonstrate legitimate reasons for alienating property to the satisfaction of the provincial governor.[29] To judge by this constitution, the imperial fiscal system was particularly threatened if the members of municipal *curiae* (councils) should lose their financial resources, since they played a substantial role in the collection of taxes and in the performance of other key liturgies. Imperial constitutions against rural patronage (*patrocinium*, see below) make clear that *curiales* constituted a group that might try to avoid these charges by seeking the protection of powerful landowners, to whom they would sell their land. The policy of the government was to protect the financial resources of a social group as a whole and to try to prevent a kind of economic Darwinism, with some landowners becoming wealthy at the expense of others.

It seems likely that, in limiting the mobility of *coloni*, the government recognized that these farmers brought resources to the estates of the large landowners on which they were registered, resources that were crucially important to the ability of these landowners to keep their land productive and thereby meet their fiscal obligations. Thus, in the understanding of the government, the continued access of *coloni* to livestock was crucial to their ability to cultivate their land productively. This understanding is revealed in a constitution issued by Valentinian I about land grants to veterans, who, depending on their rank, would receive differing amounts of land as well as the oxen and seed needed to cultivate it (*CTh* 7.20.8, 364). This constitution modified an earlier policy of Constantine, who provided cash to veterans to buy the equipment needed to cultivate their land, as well as a pair of oxen and one hundred *modii* (one *modius* of wheat = 6.75 kg) of seed (*CTh* 7.20.3, 325).[30]

In the interpretation of the government, the economic value of *coloni* consisted solely of their ability to cultivate the land to which they were bound. Thus the emperor Constantius II ruled that someone selling an estate could not retain the *coloni* under a private agreement to transfer them to other property. Rather, the *coloni* were to remain on the land that was sold (*CTh* 13.10.3; *CJ* 11.48.2, 356).[31] In the wording of the law, "those who believe *coloni* to be useful should either keep them with the property or leave them to profit others, if they themselves lose hope that the property might profit them." Fifteen years later, the emperor Valentinian I issued an edict aimed at curtailing a fraudulent policy whereby, in the wording of the edict, a landowner might separate a small portion of the estate and sell this with all of the estate's *coloni* or slaves, thereby rendering the remaining estate useless for agriculture (*CJ* 11.48.7, 371).[32] Such a sale was a thinly disguised method of transferring to a new owner control over slaves or *coloni* (here called *originarii*). This type of arrangement might benefit the seller and the purchaser, but it would also compromise the state's ability to collect taxes from a large amount of land now depleted of its workforce. In the constitution, a person seeking to acquire slaves or *coloni* in this way had no recourse to regain the purchase price, while the seller could claim back the slaves and their families (*CJ* 11.48.7.2). The illegality of such sales is underscored by the removal of the *longi temporis praescriptio:* no purchaser could benefit from this prescription, because the acquisition of slaves or *coloni* in this way was deemed fundamentally fraudulent (*CJ* 11.48.7.3).[33]

In the conception of the Roman legal authorities, *coloni* were an economic resource to landowners only in a limited sense. Landowners could not freely dispose of their *coloni*, even when doing so might enhance their ability to profit from their estates. In these laws, the *coloni* were bound to the land, and any relationship between them and the landowner was of far less consequence than their relationship to the land. The landowner only exercised power over *coloni* as long as he or she retained control of the land that the *coloni* cultivated; the landowner could not abrogate the obligation of the *coloni* to remain on this land. To be sure, the landowner exercised control over the disposition of the property of the *colonus*, but this control, as Jean-Michel Carrié points out, was like that of a creditor. In this respect not much different from the control that a landlord in a conventional Roman lease exercised over the property of a tenant.[34]

In restricting the mobility of *coloni*, the imperial government was concerned about imposing a legal regime on the countryside, not an economic one. Thus for fiscal purposes it could divide the rural world between landowners and *coloni* working the land of the former group, but this seemingly clear-cut demarcation ignored many of the complexities of the rural economy in the empire. First, it should be recognized that not all tenants on the estates of large landowners were subject to the power of their landlords, although it is impossible to determine what proportion of tenants was subject in this way. Many tenants continued to occupy their land under more conventional lease arrangements, holding their land for limited periods of time with rents that could be negotiated. Such tenants, if they held land of their own, might be registered for tax purposes under their own names and not subject to the authority of a landowner. The persistence of "conventional" tenancy arrangements is suggested by, among other things, the continued importance of Roman lease law for the later empire and for the Byzantine Empire.[35]

To be sure, it should also be recognized that the law surrounding tenancy probably underwent substantial changes in late antiquity. As Ernst Levy argues, Roman legislators showed relatively little interest for the law of classical farm tenancy in the fourth century. This is suggested both by the apparent absence of any treatment of private *locatio-conductio* (lease-hire) from the Theodosian Code and by the fact that the section in the Code of Justinian that treats tenancy (4.65) includes no citation of a text also included in the Theodosian Code.[36] However, this lack of concern on the part of late antique legislators for the classical law of lease does not mean that small-scale tenancy had disappeared. Instead, as can be traced in the vulgar law of the Germanic codes, small-scale tenancy was conceived as a relationship in which a landowner bestowed land on a cultivator, either for a fixed period or even in perpetuity, on the latter's request. The cultivator had to pay a rent, and there might be written documentation of the arrangement. This relationship is described in terms of the classical *precarium*, but in reality it had little to do with the classical institution. Instead, the new language refers to the request for land (*preces*) theoretically made by the cultivator, and so it suggests how, in the West, the relationship between landowner and cultivator was no longer conceived of as equal, as in the early empire, but was now formally hierarchical.[37]

To return to the fiscal concerns of the late antique government, it recognized that the categories of *coloni* and small landowners might be blurred. Thus Valentinian I and Valens required people who owned any land whatsoever to be registered for fiscal purposes under their own names and not under the landowners for whom they might also cultivate land (*CTh* 11.1.14; *CJ* 11.48.4, 371).[38] Clearly the author of this law understood that tenants and small landowners were overlapping groups; the point of this law was to maintain the rigorous distinction between landowners and *coloni* that demarcated liability for fiscal purposes but did not by any means describe how estates were cultivated. Earlier, in keeping with a long-maintained policy of monopolizing the resources of farmers cultivating imperial land, Constantine ruled that *coloni* registered for fiscal purposes on imperial estates, in this case belonging to the *res privata* (property of the emperor), could not be required to perform civic liturgies (*CJ* 11.68.1, 325).[39] In another enactment consistent with this policy Constantine had prohibited imperial *coloni* from engaging in private business arrangements, which probably included leasing land from private owners (*CJ* 11.68.2, 319).[40] But the state's monopoly on the services of imperial *coloni*, based as it was on a strict legal distinction between the cultivators of imperial land and private landowners, proved to be unworkable. Indeed, in Egypt, it had long been common for private landowners at the village level to supplement their holdings by cultivating state land, and the same may have been true in many other parts of the empire.[41]

One danger of this policy was that the state's monopoly on the services of its cultivators might deprive towns of suitable candidates for liturgical duties. We have seen how this situation led to conflicts involving the allocation of taxes and liturgical duties between residents of towns in Asia Minor and tenants of imperial estates (discussed in chap. 2). The emperor Constantius II addressed the problem of potential liturgical candidates hiding behind their service on imperial estates to avoid civic liturgies. Constantius ruled that any imperial tenant who also owned twenty-five *iugera* (about 6 ha) of private land would be subject to serve on municipal councils. Likewise subject to nomination for civic posts were cultivators who owned fewer than twenty-five *iugera* but apparently still had substantial holdings when their imperial land was reckoned in (*CTh* 12.1.33, 342). Penalties were prescribed for those who sought to circumvent the law by fraudulent sales.[42]

ECONOMIC CONSEQUENCES OF RESTRICTING MOBILITY

The late Roman fiscal system imposed substantial costs on the economy, since it engendered economic incentives that were counterproductive to agricultural growth. The interests of agricultural production might have been well served if landowners exercised some freedom to rationalize the use of resources, including both land and farming personnel, but this was not the aim of the imperial administration in restricting the mobility of *coloni*. The government was especially concerned with limiting the mobility of *coloni* who, having substantial resources of their own, would be able to bargain with landowners to gain the most advantageous possible terms of tenure for themselves. But the legal restrictions on their mobility distorted the market for their services. Since severe penalties were imposed both on *coloni* who left their land for a new situation elsewhere and on the landowners who harbored them, those *coloni* willing to run these risks and enlist with new landowners could demand much better terms than would have been available to them in an entirely free labor market. Landowners were likely to have paid a premium for their services and so lost some of the revenues that they might have used to reinvest in more productive forms of agriculture. This distortion surely benefited many *coloni*, but at a cost to society. On the other side of the coin, the binding of *coloni* to the land was a two-way street, and landowners could not easily dismiss *coloni*.[43] As a consequence, landowners had to continue to lease their land to *coloni* even when it was not to their advantage to do so. The capacity of landowners to consolidate or reorganize holdings was constrained by the fiscal demands of the government. The likely consequence was a reduced incentive for landowners to invest in agriculture.

The government's policies were intended to preserve the integrity of its fiscal system by imposing severe sanctions on landowners and *coloni* who flouted imperial laws. This policy was established by Constantine. He required landowners receiving *coloni iuris alieni* (that is, *coloni* registered on another landowner's estate) to restore the *coloni* to their place of origin and at the same time to pay the capitation tax for the time in which the aforesaid *coloni* were away from their *origo* (*CTh* 5.17.1, 332). Constantine also imposed penalties on *coloni* contemplating flight from their *origo*. He stated that they should be bound in chains and so fulfill as slaves the duties that they otherwise would have fulfilled as free persons. This harsh regime became the consistent policy of the imperial administration. Thus Valentinian I imposed similar sanctions in a decree to Germanianus, the praetorian prefect for the Gallic provinces. In this decree, provincial governors were instructed to restore fugitive *coloni* and *inquilini* (*CJ* 11.48.6, 365).[44] This latter term, often translated as "cottagers," seems to refer to laborers who resided on an estate. Around the same time, this same emperor established procedures for discovering fugitive slaves, *coloni* (here called *tributarii*), and *inquilini*, as well as penalties for those harboring them (*CTh* 10.12.2, 368).[45] A few years later the emperors Valentian I, Valens, and Gratian again asserted the principle that *coloni*, in this case *coloni* in Illyricum and in neighboring regions, lacked freedom of movement (*CJ* 11.53.1, 371, discussed in the preceding). *Coloni* or *inquilini* who left their places of origin to take up residence on other estates were to be cast in chains and returned (sec. 1), while landowners receiving them were to provide financial compensation to the places that the *coloni* and *inquilini* abandoned. These landowners were also subject to fines. Later emperors continued to impose similar sanctions. In a constitution addressed to Cynegius, praetorian prefect in the eastern empire, Theodosius I prescribed substantial fines for landowners who accepted *coloni iuris alieni* (*CTh* 5.17.2, 386).[46] Similarly, when it removed capitation as a basis for taxation from the diocese of Thrace, the imperial government reinvoked the obligation of *coloni* to remain on their land, and at the same time it forbade other landowners from harboring *coloni* (*CJ* 11.52.1, 393).[47] Any landowner accepting onto his or her own estate a *colonus* registered on the land of another was to pay the aggrieved landowner a fine of two pounds of gold as well as restore the *colonus* with his property (*peculium*) and family (*agnatio*, sec. 2).

The fiscal liability created by the presence of *coloni* on the land, not the economic interests of landowners, remained the focus of imperial legislation. Thus in describing the tax obligations of landowners in a constitution addressed to the praetorian prefect for the Gallic provinces, the emperor Honorius emphasized that a person acquiring an estate on which *coloni* were registered was required to accept all the fiscal obligations attached to the property in question (*CTh* 11.1.26, 399).[48] A year later the same emperor modified the rule of Constantius II concerning the transfer of *coloni* from one estate to another (*CTh* 13.10.3, discussed in the preceding). In the new law, if an owner of two estates transferred *coloni* from one that had a surfeit of cultivators to another that had a shortage and the estates then passed into the control of new owners, the transfer of *coloni* was recognized as valid, and the offspring (*agnatio*) of the *coloni* transferred also had to be passed to the new estate (*CJ* 11.48.13.1, 400).[49] Although modifying a previously stricter regime, this law still underscores the fundamental attachment of the *colonus* to the land rather than to a landowner. This attachment, of course, created rights for the *coloni*, who could not be dispossessed from their holdings. The scope of the problem that the government confronted is suggested in a law of Theodosius I (*CJ* 11.63.3, 383). According to this law, certain holders of patrimonial estates, that is, estates granted to private possessors from imperial property, had driven off the existing *coloni* and replaced these farmers with their own *coloni* or slaves. Possessors who attempted this in the future would be punished by a loss of their land.[50]

The laws discussed here have important implications for the late imperial agrarian economy. The late imperial fiscal system tended to reduce the possibilities for private bargaining that the state's legal policies under the Principate encouraged. The binding of *coloni* to the land, with the legal prohibitions against raising their rent, diminished the incentives that landowners had to invest in improvements that would make their land more productive. Since landowners could not raise the rent to reflect the enhanced value of their property, they would be less likely to invest and more likely to try to squeeze additional services or charges out of the *coloni*, who were bound as a labor force and whose labor thus represented for landowners a "free attribute," to use the terminology of Yoram Barzel.[51] *Coloni* for their part would have little incentive to cooperate with their landlords, since their rent was established by custom and could not be raised. They had every incentive to cultivate the land in such a way as to suit their own needs in the choice of crops and the efforts applied to them, even when these choices conflicted with the interests of the landlord.

So there was little incentive to engage in mutually advantageous bargaining, with the result that wealth was lost that might otherwise have been generated under a different contract regime. The lack of such incentives was particularly acute when the *coloni* paid a fixed rent in cash or in kind. The one circumstance under which sharing the costs of investment could be mutually advantageous would be if the *coloni* paid a share of their production as rent, since under sharecropping both the landowner and the tenant would each derive a share of any increased output.[52] But the relationship between landlord and tenant was more likely to have been antagonistic, especially when an estate with *coloni* was leased out to large-scale *conductores*, as was apparently common in late antiquity.[53]

The disincentives to cooperative bargaining inherent in such a tenure arrangement can be traced in a letter of Augustine, in which he discusses the purchase of an estate by a bishop of whom he strongly disapproves (*Ep.* 20*.29).[54] Augustine had given this newly installed bishop a *fundus* belonging to the church at Hippo as a means of support. But the bishop in question immediately leased the property out, receiving the full five-year rental in advance. He then used this money to purchase another property for himself. No matter how inappropriate the actions of the bishop might have been, it does not appear that there was anything unconventional in the financial arrangements that he made concerning the *fundus* in question. Accordingly, the way in which he leased this property suggests some of the obstacles that must have stood in the way of any productive bargaining involving the *coloni* actually cultivating the land. The lessee of the property in question in this passage was clearly a middleman leasing the right to collect the rents from the *coloni*, and his function would have been very similar to that of the large-scale lessees on the North African imperial estates. The middleman's primary interest, given the limited term of his lease, would have been to enforce the obligations of the *coloni* to pay their rent. Since he paid the landowner five years' rent up front, he must have demanded a substantial premium for taking on himself all of the trouble of managing the people working the land as well as the risk for the harvest. The landowner in such an arrangement, by contrast, willingly sacrificed a great deal of income that might have been achieved with direct management of the property, but this sacrifice was worth making to gain a guaranteed income. But nothing in this arrangement suggests that either the landowner or the *conductor* had much of an incentive to bargain with the *coloni* or otherwise to invest in the long-term productivity of the property.

The landowner's relationship with the land was at arm's length, and his or her interest consisted solely in gaining a guaranteed income. For his part the middleman, in a lease of limited duration, had limited capacity to bargain with *coloni* who were tied to the property and whose rents could not be raised. Rather, such a middleman would have functioned more as an enforcer of payments if there were *coloni* on the property. This, at least, is the impression that the emperor Justinian had of large-scale *conductores* when he prohibited soldiers from taking up this job (*CJ* 4.65.35). In Justinian's formulation, the soldiers were "not showing ferocity of their arms against the enemy, but turning it against villagers and perhaps against the wretched *coloni* themselves, whose management they have undertaken" (*CJ* 4.65.35 pr.). Soldiers were apparently desired as middlemen because the job involved enforcing contracts rather than managing an agricultural enterprise.[55] Indeed, the job that *conductores* performed gave them an odious reputation. Thus the council of bishops at Carthage in 419 forbade bishops, priests, and deacons from becoming *conductores*, since this was an unsuitable occupation (canon 16).[56]

The deeds of sale in the Albertini Tablets from late fifth-century Africa suggest how the relationship between landowners and *coloni* might have played themselves out in the real world. As discussed in the previous chapter, these documents indicate that people within an estate owned (or held under emphyteutic right) by a certain Flavius Geminius Catullinus could buy and sell the rights to small parcels of land cultivated with fruit trees, in particular olive trees. The cultivators within the estate had perpetual rights to their land, ultimately based on the *lex Manciana* of the early empire, which probably meant that they paid a share of their produce as rent. What role the landowner played in the cultivation of the fruit trees of the individual cultivators is unclear; perhaps the landowner coordinated irrigation within the estate and the maintenance of roads. However, there is no hint in the Albertini Tablets that the owner of the estate engaged in any such activity. Moreover, it seems plausible that many landowners sought to keep their own investment in the estate at a minimum. Landowners would have an incentive to exploit the opportunities created by the specific investments that the *coloni* had made in cultivating their farms—investments that the *coloni* could not easily transfer to a new farm under the ownership of a different landowner—by imposing as many costs as possible on them or by trying to exact additional payments.

RESTRICTIONS ON LANDOWNERS

The weakness of the state's legal institutions was exposed by the government's response to the challenges posed by *coloni* who left the land to which they were legally bound to seek better conditions from other landowners. The response of the Roman government was entirely reactive. It had no capacity to alter this basic situation or to devise a fundamentally different basis for assessing tax liability. So the government repeatedly tried to make the best of a bad situation through a series of enactments that, on the one hand, recognized the de facto mobility of many *coloni* but, on the other hand, sought to redefine the rights and obligations of landowners and *coloni* within a fiscal system so at odds with market forces. But the policy of the government to impose harsh penalties to deter mobility by *coloni* had economic consequences, since it tended to raise the stakes for landowners who took in mobile *coloni* and so exacerbated the distortions in the market resulting from the government's fiscal policy.

One basic concern of the government was to establish a system of rules according to which legal disputes arising from the mobility of *coloni* might be resolved.[57] When a *colonus* abandoned one estate for another, his previous landlord remained liable for the tax obligations based on the *colonus*' services. The same would hold true if the *colonus* was an independent landowner in a village: the village would remain liable for the taxes on the land that the *colonus* had cultivated. Fundamental to the government's legal policy was imposing on landowners the responsibility to account for the juridical status of the tenants whom they employed. We can trace this approach in the constitution of 371 concerned with restricting the mobility of *coloni* and *inquilini* in Illyricum and neighboring provinces (*CJ* 11.53.1, discussed in the preceding). This constitution established severe penalties for *coloni* who abandoned their land and took up residence elsewhere, including returning the offenders in chains. But the constitution also imposed fines on landowners harboring runaway *coloni*, and they could not avoid these penalties by pleading ignorance (sec. 1). Similar penalties were prescribed for landowners who took in slaves or freedmen (sec. 2–3).

In effect, when it imposed the liability for the legal status of the *colonus* on the landowner, the government implicitly recognized the impossibility of controlling the movement of *coloni*. So the continuing task that the government faced was to sort out issues of liability when *coloni* did move from the estate on which they were registered. In assigning liability for *coloni*, a text apparently forming part of the same law distinguished between landowners who knowingly took in *coloni* registered elsewhere and landowners who took in *coloni* who had represented themselves as free (*CJ* 11.48.8).[58] In the first circumstance, the landowners were required to pay the tax obligations for the *coloni*, much as in the other constitutions on this issue. What is interesting is how the legislator determined the intention or knowledge of the landowner concerned. The landowner is assumed to have acted in good faith (i.e., without being aware of the true status of the *coloni* involved) if the *coloni* were paid wages (*merces*) for cultivating land belonging to the landowner (sec. 1). If the *coloni* did not receive wages for the work that they did, then the landowner would be liable for the fiscal obligations attached to the *coloni*, presumably because the individuals in question were assumed to have taken up long-term tenure on the estate in question. The law created an incentive for landowners to employ workers on a shorter-term basis.[59]

The government sought to counter the lure of market forces by creating substantial disincentives for landowners entering into agreements with mobile *coloni*. A good example of this approach is a law of Honorius that imposed harsh penalties on landowners who harbored *coloni* or slaves (*CJ* 11.48.12, 396).[60] These penalties included a fine of twelve pounds of silver to the Fiscus as well as the restoration of the *colonus* or slave to the previous landlord along with another *colonus* or slave of equal value (sec. 2). In this law, as in previous legislation, the burden of proof was imposed on the landowner to ascertain the juridical status of the farmer whom he or she was recruiting. In the reasoning of the legislator, slaves (and presumably *coloni*) would have no incentive to flee their land, because the harsh penalties imposed on landowners would ensure that they would have no place to go. In reality, of course, it must have been difficult for landowners to be sure about the juridical status of farmers who offered their services, and it is also hard to imagine that landowners allowed lands for which they carried tax liability to remain uncultivated when willing farmers showed up. It seems unlikely that laws like the constitutions of 371 and 396 could have had much practical effect in restricting the mobility of *coloni*. What these and similar laws did accomplish was to sort out liability when *coloni* left their land. Now the original landlord had a legal recourse to gain compensation for his or her own tax obligations, since the landowner taking in the *colonus* could be sued.[61]

The government faced a continual challenge in enforcing its fiscal system, as is indicated by the repeated injunctions against *coloni* who left their land and against landowners who harbored them.[62] In promulgating these constitutions that established rights and duties of landowners toward *coloni*, the government was probably responding to petitions and complaints from landowners whose economic interests were threatened by the actual or potential departure of *coloni* from their land.[63] The state's fiscal policy placed a great deal of pressure on landowners, who assumed substantial tax obligations that did not diminish when *coloni* fled. The question is whether penalties imposed on landowners who took in *coloni* discouraged this behavior.[64] The fact that such penalties were imposed again and again with increasing harshness indicates the extent of the concern with which the imperial government viewed the situation, if not that the laws were largely ineffective.[65] Indeed, the fiscal charges that many landowners had to bear for *coloni* were so burdensome that the emperors Constantius II and Constans granted senators a special privilege by releasing them from this liability (*CTh* 11.1.7, 361).[66]

The mobility of *coloni* undermined the integrity of a tax system in part based on the landowner's liability for personnel under his or her control, since the landowner had little capacity to guarantee that such personnel would be consistently available. Assessing taxes on this basis surely led to petitions and complaints and, over time, apparently proved unworkable. As a result, the government modified its system of taxing agriculture by removing the capitation tax in some regions of the empire and instead basing taxes solely on the productive capacity of the land.[67] This policy can be seen in a constitution of 393 abolishing *capitatio* in the diocese of Thrace (*CJ* 11.52.1, discussed in the preceding). In this constitution, the emperors were apparently responding to discontent from landowners about their liability for capitation taxes for their *coloni*. As a result, the emperors announced that tax assessments of this kind would be absolved in perpetuity, with future tax assessments based solely on *iugatio*. Landowners who recruited *coloni* from other landowners' estates were still liable to severe penalties, including fines of two pounds of gold to the aggrieved landowners as well as the obligation to return the *coloni* along with their property (*peculium*) and family (*agnatio*) (sec. 2). But the landowner's interest was now primarily to keep the land cultivated, rather than to exercise direct control over personnel who had previously affected his tax liability.

While the Roman government continually sought to reassert the viability of this tax system, it faced an equally important task of establishing the legal authority of its institutions in the countryside. As it responded to this task, its efforts to adapt its legal definitions of the rural workforce to the realities of the late imperial economy indicate the difficulty of balancing the empire's legal and fiscal policies. We can appreciate the difficulty of this task by considering the steps that the government took in the fifth century to develop a more flexible policy, one that responded to the changing conditions of the late antique economy. The state continued to insist on the obligation of *coloni* to remain on their land and on the landowner's right to their services, but it also sought to balance the interests of the landowner with *coloni* under his or her power against the danger of insisting on a legal order that it had little capacity to enforce. Thus Honorius, in a decree issued at Ravenna, established a thirty-year prescription for lawsuits against *coloni* who had left their land for new estates and against the new landowners who harbored them (*CTh* 5.18.1 pr., 419).[68] Other *coloni* who had abandoned their *origo* within the thirty-year period prior to the promulgation of the constitution were to be returned (sec. 1). This constitution followed a policy evident in an earlier constitution of Honorius issued at Milan (*CTh* 12.19.2; *CJ* 11.66.6, 400). Addressed to the praetorian prefect for Gaul, the earlier constitution established that no action could be heard for the restoration of a *colonus* who had served on a town council, *collegium*, or other corporations for thirty years.[69] The public interest of maintaining the viability of these institutions overrode the rights of the former landowners to whom the *coloni* were bound, whether the land concerned was in private hands or under the administration of the imperial government. The constitution of Honorius from 419, for its part, accepted the fact that the *coloni*, despite all the laws to the contrary, could move from their land and cultivate land elsewhere. In creating a prescription against lawsuits that applied both to the *coloni* and to their new landlords, the government not only defended the interests of small farmers but, more significantly, made a concession to the economic interests of the new landowners, who depended on the production of the *coloni* affected by the law.[70]

The law of Honorius in 419 represented a new direction for dealing with legal issues connected with restricting the mobility of *coloni*, but at all times the government remained committed to maintaining the basic aspects of its fiscal system. Thus later in the fifth century, the emperor Anastasius endeavored to remove an ambiguity about the status of *coloni* who had benefited from the thirty-year prescription (*CJ* 11.48.19). This law repeated the now time-honored insistence that *adscripticii* (that is, *coloni* who had an estate as their *origo*) remained bound with their *peculia* to their landowners. *Coloni* who had leased land elsewhere for thirty years remained free along with their property, but they were now compelled to remain and cultivate the lands of their new landlords.[71] The imperial administration under Justinian modified this regime by abrogating the thirty-year prescription so that henceforth *coloni* would remain tied to the land in perpetuity, no matter what steps they might take to gain their freedom (*CJ*

11.48.23, 531–34). In addition, penalties were established for *coloni* fleeing their estates; like runaway slaves they would be liable to be returned, along with their offspring born off the estate (*CJ* 11.48.23 pr.).[72]

LEGAL INSTITUTIONS AND BARGAINING OUTSIDE THE LAW

The capacity of landowners and tenants to engage in bargaining conducive to greater productivity in agriculture was to some extent a function of the strength of legal institutions, since they provided a setting in which many, but certainly not all, agreements could be enforced. But the lack of success of the government in counteracting the de facto mobility that many *coloni* enjoyed tended to compromise the authority of legal institutions in the rural world. Indeed, the frequent laws prohibiting *patrocinium* (rural patronage) have been seen as signs of the ineffectual efforts of the imperial government to maintain the rule of law in the countryside.[73] The term *patrocinium* refers to the practice of large landowners accepting small landowners, tenants, or even whole villages under their protection. The small farmers seeking the protection of larger landowners characteristically did so to escape fiscal obligations. Often, the small farmers entered into contractual arrangements with their protectors, agreeing to work on their land for long periods under service (*paramone*) contracts.[74] It seems likely that small farmers seeking the protection of large landowners through *patrocinium* included *coloni* bound to their land, but *patrocinium* was threatening to the imperial tax system in a more general way, since it also involved affording protection to small independent landowners who otherwise paid their taxes under their own name. Small landowners who sought *patrocinium* would lose ownership of their land and, as a result, disappear from the tax rolls. The Christian writer Salvian offers a very bleak picture of rural patronage in fifth-century Aquitania, albeit in a period in which Roman rule in the West, and particularly in Gaul, was collapsing. Salvian describes larger landowners adding to their vast holdings at the expense of increasingly pauperized small farmers, who sought the protection of powerful landowners and as a result became their slaves.[75]

This phenomenon of rural patronage was probably a by-product of the role that some large estates, such as that of Aurelius Appianus in third-century Egypt, played in organizing the fulfillment of tax and liturgical duties by the farmers on the estates and from nearby communities (see the preceding). The problem was that this method of organizing public dues potentially threatened the integrity of not only the empire's fiscal system but also the judicial system as well. Landowners responsible for guaranteeing the performance of public functions by local farmers enjoyed a great deal of power, and so the Roman government faced the continuing challenge of holding such landowners accountable to fulfill their own fiscal obligations and those of the farmers under their supervision. Landowners could use their power to allocate public functions to protect farmers from having to perform them and, in extreme cases, offer this protection in exchange for the land owned by the small farmers seeking protection from fiscal burdens. To judge by a series of enactments on this issue by the emperor Arcadius and Honorius, stemming the influence of rural patronage was a particular concern of the Roman government at the end of the fourth and the beginning of the fifth centuries.[76] The continuing efforts of the government to combat rural patronage might suggest that it was losing its control over the countryside.

However, in a recent study Jill Harries argues persuasively that legal institutions in late antiquity were in many respects stronger than under the Principate.[77] Her conclusions invite reappraisal of the traditional view about the strength of legal institutions in the countryside. In what follows, I argue that, despite the increasing power exercised by landowners in late antiquity, legal institutions continued to play a major role in resolving disputes between small farmers and larger landowners. But the very forces that tended to give small farmers greater leverage in the courts undermined the integrity of the Roman legal system by driving some of the economically most important relationships between landowners and tenants outside the control of the law. The capacity of the government to facilitate private bargaining between landowners and tenants to share the costs of investment or to engage in other forms of cooperation was diminished.

It would have been potentially beneficial for both landowners and *coloni* to bargain to reach agreements on such important issues as leaving land fallow to promote soil preservation and greater long-term productivity, choosing the most remunerative mix of crops, or making provision for the replacement of olive trees and vines.[78] But the fiscal definition of the *colonus* as bound to the land created a number of disincentives that stood in the way of such bargaining. *Coloni* were prohibited by law from leaving the land that they cultivated, but at the same time landowners could make no alteration in the traditional terms under which *coloni* cultivated their land or in the form or amount of rent that *coloni* had to pay. The frequent laws restricting mobility of *coloni* and imposing ever-increasing penalties on landowners who took *coloni* in indicate that there was far more flexibility about terms of land tenure than could be recognized within Roman law. As a consequence, any arrangements between landowners and *coloni* formally bound to someone else's land were likely to have been conducted beyond the reach of the law. The only means of enforcement that either party had were informal ones, and it seems likely that locally powerful landowners would enjoy many advantages over *coloni* in the event of disputes.

The power that landowners might exercise over *coloni* who had left their *origo* is nicely illustrated in a letter, probably from the early fifth century, preserved in a manuscript of Orosius.[79] The issue in the letter concerned the status of certain *coloni* and *actores* (possibly slaves managing the estates) on the estate belonging to the author, who, like his correspondent named Salvius, was both a landowner and an advocate. The scene of this conflict was the African town of Matar (modern Mateur, in northern Tunisia). Salvius was preparing to enter a claim over the *coloni* and *actores* in which he asserted that they had left land now belonging to him, where their legal *origo* was situated. The author of the letter was writing Salvius to urge him to give up this legal course and to quit terrifying the "miserable farmers" (*miseros aratores*). Whether or not Salvius had any legitimate claim, this letter suggests the insecurity of *coloni* at the mercy of legal disputes about their status. It helped the farmers in this letter to have an apparently wealthy and well-connected advocate to ward off the harassment by Salvius. But other *coloni*, without a generous protector, were in an inherently weak position when they negotiated tenure arrangements with a new landowner. The *coloni* always faced the possibility of exposure and forced return to their *origo*. Landowners also faced sanctions, but it seems likely that they would have an easier time either paying a fine or using their influence to avoid prosecution than *coloni* would in resisting the efforts of landowners who claimed rights over them.

From a legal perspective, the government's fiscal policy assumed that landowners exercised a certain control over *coloni*. As already suggested, this control was analogous to that of a creditor over a debtor, since the landowner maintained a lien over the property of the *colonus* to ensure that the *colonus* would pay his rent and thereby allow the landowner to fulfill his or her fiscal obligations. The Roman government's understanding of the relationship between landowners and *coloni* finds expression in a constitution of Arcadius addressed to a governor of the province of Asia (*CJ* 11.50.2, 396).[80] Likening the status of the bound *colonus* to a kind of slavery, the emperor found it contrary to social order that *coloni* should be able to sue landowners who otherwise exercised such power over them. Consequently, the emperor excluded *coloni* from bringing suits against their landowners, on the same principle that they did not have the power to alienate property without the permission of the landowner. The earlier constitutions discussed previously that were concerned with the binding of *coloni* to the land also compared *coloni* to slaves. In the constitution from 332, Constantine compared the punishments awaiting *coloni* who fled their land to those customarily imposed on slaves (*CTh* 5.18.1). Valentinian I characterized *coloni* as "slaves of their land" (*CJ* 11.53.1.1, 371, discussed in the preceding). When abolishing capitation as a basis for taxation in Thrace, the imperial government reiterated the obligation of *coloni* to remain on their land, likening them to slaves to the land to which they were born (*CJ* 11.52.1, 393). In prohibiting the practice of landowners assigning certain of their liturgical duties to slaves or *coloni*, the emperor Honorius viewed the *colonus*, like the slave, as a person liable to servitude: "qui sit obnoxius servituti" (*CTh* 8.2.5; *CJ* 10.71.3, 401).[81] The comparison is not to be taken literally, since in this constitution slaves assigned liturgical duties were to be scourged, while no such punishment was prescribed for *coloni*.[82]

But the situation of *coloni* may not have been quite so bleak. Admittedly, a stark social hierarchy allowed landowners to exercise a great deal of influence over many aspects of the lives of their *coloni*.[83] At the same time, this influence was by no means absolute. Indeed, the very law of Arcadius that barred *coloni* from proceeding in court against their landlords in other matters guaranteed their right to bring suit in disputes over increases in the rent (*superexactiones*) (*CJ* 11.50.2.4).[84] This was surely the main area of contention between landowners and their tenants, especially tenants who occupied their land in long-term arrangements. In permitting *coloni* to sue over the rent, the legislator explicitly recognized a right that the state had long granted *coloni*. This right had been recognized as early as Constantine, who prohibited landowners from raising customary rents and further provided that *coloni* whose rents had been raised could seek redress from a judge (*CJ* 11.50.1; discussed in chap. 4 under "Legal Issues Arising from Long-Term Tenancy Arrangements").[85]

The protections that these laws recognized for *coloni* could only be realized if this group actually had access to the courts. In promulgating these laws, the government certainly made this assumption. In fact, at least one constitution on an unrelated matter seems to envision *coloni* as a class with regular access to the courts. In an effort to curb judicial corruption, Theodosius I listed *coloni* along with *honorati* (officeholders), decurions, and landowners as potential victims of corrupt judges (*CTh* 9.27.6; *CJ* 9.27.4, 386).[86] These victims were encouraged to bring charges against the judge under the Julian law on extortion (the *lex Iulia repetundarum*).

The assumption that *coloni* could use the courts to protect their interests is consistent with the prohibitions against *coloni* bringing lawsuits against their landlords. These prohibitions certainly presuppose that such lawsuits might be heard; in prohibiting them, the imperial government emphasized the primacy of the fiscal relationship between landowners and *coloni:* the landowner's chief responsibility in this plan was to meet fiscal obligations, and to accomplish that he or she had to have control over the *colonus*' property. The fiscal relationship that the imperial government maintained between landowners and *coloni* could not take into account the wide array of economic relationships that must have existed in the countryside—for example, the likelihood that at least some *coloni* bound to the land were farmers with substantial resources and that many *domini* were weak absentee landowners with little actual control over what their *coloni* did.[87]

The government provided few formal ways of governing such contractual relationships, and such governance as did exist was usually conducted without the possibility of recourse to courts of law.[88] One deterrent against such opportunism by landowners was the possibility that the *coloni* might eventually leave their land and negotiate more favorable but legally unenforceable terms with another landowner. The best that the government offered was the possibility for the *colonus* to sue the landowner to have the traditional terms of land tenure restored. The role of the government was simply to mitigate the worst effects of antagonism. Indeed, the emperors repeatedly legislated against criminal activity by procurators and *actores* who managed the estates of absentee landowners; these individuals were seen as occupying positions of considerable power. In addition, the Church fathers viewed with great concern the exploitation of *coloni* by managers of estates belonging to absentee landowners.[89]

We can gain a better understanding of the access of *coloni* to the protection of legal institutions by considering the complaints made by the fourth-century orator Libanius about the type of protection that military officials offered to villagers in the region around Antioch, where Libanius was a large landowner.[90] In his forty-seventh oration, Libanius complains bitterly to the emperor Theodosius I about these abuses. Libanius was concerned with the military's offer of protection to two groups: (1) villagers who lived independently of any estate and were registered on the tax rolls as landowners in their own right (Lib., *Or.* 47.4) and (2) villagers who resided within a larger estate belonging to a local landowner. Emboldened by the support of their influential protectors, the independent villagers made inroads against the property of their neighbors, including landowners of Libanius' class, and they did this with seeming impunity, as the courts were powerless to prevent it. The actions taken by the villagers residing within larger estates were even more troubling, since they defied their landlords when they came by to collect the rent (*Or.* 47.11). Both situations compromised the ability of the landowners to meet their fiscal obligations. These landowners, who made up the decurion class financially responsible for the collection of taxes, could neither collect the rent from the land owned by the villagers nor use the rental payments from their own *coloni* to pay the taxes for their own estates. As a result, in Libanius' description, they were forced to sell off their estates, a situation that led to the removal of decurions from the rolls and, ultimately, threatened to cause the collapse of the entire imperial system (*Or.* 47.7, 10).

To set this speech in a broader perspective, the issue that Libanius confronted centered on the exercise of patronage over the farming communities surrounding Antioch. As Peter Brown argues, patronage was an essential element in such communities; the patron would play an important role in settling disputes within the communities as well as in mediating between the farming communities and the city and imperial administration. The exercise of patronage in such communities did not mean that they were becoming less autonomous as part of a process of being subsumed under the control of powerful landowners. Rather, farming communities could often play off one patron against the other to promote their interests. This was the situation that Libanius was confronting, as the growing influence of the military in the region undermined the influence that he and others of his class had traditionally exercised.[91]

For Libanius, the protection that the military officials offered undermined the traditional authority of the landowner. According to his account, Libanius had Jewish tenants who had cultivated his land for four generations (*Or.* 47.13ff.). Although Libanius couches their actions in vague terms, it is apparent that these tenants refused to fulfill what he interpreted to be their traditional obligations. Faced with this situation, Libanius had recourse to the courts, only to be disappointed that the judge, apparently the provincial governor, sided with the tenants, allegedly out of consideration for their military protectors. It is noteworthy that recourse to the courts is something that Libanius presents as a conventional solution to the problems that he experienced with his tenants. What made the result disturbing for Libanius was that he did not achieve the expected result in court—he fully expected that the judge would decide the case in his favor, in view of the social ranks of the parties involved. But the presence of the special protectors changed all this. To be sure, Libanius did not want to deny his *coloni* access to the legal protection of the courts. In his view, however, the *coloni* had violated the traditional relationship between cultivators and landowners by resorting to the protection of a third party instead of first approaching the landowner for a resolution of the problem (*Or.* 47.19):

> Someone will ask me then on behalf of the farmers if it will not be possible to offer them aid. I would say yes as far as aid that is not unjust is concerned, but not at all when the aid is bad. First is the aid that comes from the gods, which is accomplished through prayers and worship; then there is the aid that comes from warding off harmful rain and bringing on rain that will be beneficial. It is possible to make the landlords of estates more kindly disposed toward them, so that they remit what they owe and make gifts, and if they need justice toward one another, to approach him [sc. the landowner], unless they need something more substantial.

Comparing the situation of *coloni* seeking redress to that of a slave petitioning his master, Libanius decries the influence of the peddlers of protection because it destroyed the bond between the landowner and the *colonus*, just as the intervention of a third party would destroy the bond between a master and slave (*Or.* 47.21).[92] As C. Grey and A. Parkin point out, "the interweaving of tenancy arrangements and patronage arrangements" represented a fundamental aspect of the rural economy in late antiquity.[93]

It is striking that Libanius shares the same conception of the relationship between landowners and *coloni* as the imperial legislators in the constitutions we have examined. In the social hierarchy of late antiquity, it might seem inappropriate for a *colonus* to challenge his landowner in a court of law. But the imperial legislation condemning this practice also recognized it as a possibility. So even if Libanius envisioned an ideal of a hierarchical structure on his estates, with the generous landowner responding to the legitimate requests of his or her *coloni*, he nevertheless had to recognize the reality that his *coloni* could and would defend their rights in a court of law. Under this circumstance, we can well imagine what advantages a landowner like Libanius might enjoy in a dispute with his *coloni*. Thus it was disturbing indeed that a state agency, namely, the military, should intervene to tilt the balance in favor of the *coloni*. The corrupt decisions that Libanius saw the courts as making under the influence of these military protectors might simply have been a sign that his and other *coloni* were becoming more successful in defending their rights in court. One may doubt that the *coloni* likewise saw the decisions of the courts as corrupt or as acquired through illegal influence. Ultimately, the type of argument that Libanius made about the dangers posed by this rural patronage to the imperial tax system must have proved persuasive to the imperial government, as can be seen in the repeated legislative attempts to curtail rural *patrocinium*.

CONCLUSION: INCENTIVES FOR INVESTMENT

A property regime involving the binding of the *coloni* to the land had significant implications for the distribution of wealth in the rural economy and for the possibilities for growth. As in the early empire, the urban culture of the late Roman Empire depended on a transfer of wealth from countryside to city. The tax system of the later empire depended primarily on revenues produced in the countryside, and the rural economy bore a disproportionate share of the tax burden in comparison with urban industries and commerce.[94] The efforts of the late Roman government to maintain its tax system indicate that it continued to privilege small-scale cultivation as the surest way of achieving predictable revenues, even as the wealthiest landowners in the empire continued to expand their holdings. The likely losers in this process were those who owned estates on a modest scale, such as the members of town councils and other local elites in Gaul who were the likely owners of the Roman-style *villae* that became widespread in the Gallic countryside during the first and second centuries.[95]

In maintaining this fiscal system, the late antique Roman government had no choice but to build upon the structures inherited from the early empire, but this institutional path dependence created significant disincentives for investment. In the later empire, landowners and tenants did continue to form contractual relationships much as in the early imperial period, an impression confirmed by the records of private farm leases in late Roman Egypt. At the same time, landowners used other means of exploiting their estates, such as wage labor and sharecropping, which the Apiones and other landowners used to a significant degree on their estates in the Oxyrhynchite nome in Egypt during the sixth century.[96] Slavery also remained an important source of labor on estates in many regions of the empire, including Italy.[97] In addition, some regions of the later empire saw significant economic expansion, such as Syria, where olive culture developed.[98] Jairus Banaji's study of the estate of the Apiones indicates that these elite landowners continued to invest in viticulture to meet urban demand.[99] These considerations indicate both that relationships between landowners and tenants were likely to have been more complicated than might be suggested by the late antique legal evidence and that the late

Roman agrarian economy continued to be dynamic and diverse, supporting the demand for foodstuffs of an urban culture that continued to thrive in the later empire.

In terms of distribution of wealth, the late Roman fiscal system offered some advantages to *coloni*. To some extent, *coloni* occupied their land under favorable conditions. Landowners were limited in what they could exact from their *coloni*, who were at the same time protected in their tenure on the land. This situation would have lessened the portion of the surplus produced by the *coloni* that landowners were able to exact and so would have mitigated the transfer of wealth from countryside to the city that was a product of the dominant role played by large landowners in late antique society and the very nature of the imperial fiscal system. *Coloni* enjoyed some advantages when they had perpetual rights of tenure and the support of Roman legal institutions in protecting traditional tenure arrangements. However, the advantages of secure tenure should not be exaggerated. When Roman tax officials were unable to collect a sufficient level of taxes, as lands were abandoned and *coloni* died off, they would naturally have exerted pressures on landowners, who themselves often carried the responsibility not only of paying taxes for their own land but also of collecting taxes from the surrounding area. Some of this pressure must have fallen on *coloni*, which would explain their tendency to seek refuge with powerful protectors in patronage arrangements.

More detrimental is the likelihood that the efforts of the state to enforce its fiscal system tended to push landowners and cultivators into arrangements that undermined the authority of legal institutions. Because many tenure arrangements passed outside the control of Roman law, the state lost much of its capacity to encourage the type of bargains among the parties involved in the rural economy that would lead to more efficient allocations of resources. The main role that the Roman government played in adjudicating disputes arising in the rural economy seems to have involved either establishing the fiscal status of farmers, and thus their tax liability and that of the landowners who employed them, or determining whether landowners were abiding by the traditional land-tenure terms when they exacted rent from their *coloni*. Indeed, the nongovernmental authorities, such as bishops, that resolved disputes were likely to have been concerned with this issue as well.[100]

Clearly, despite the protections accorded to *coloni*, the late Roman fiscal system diminished incentives for investment in agriculture. When the traditional rents were at below-market rates, then landowners had really no inducement to alter the conditions under which land occupied by *coloni* was cultivated, and the *coloni* for their part had no incentive to leave their land. So landowners would be less likely to undertake the kind of investment, say in olive presses or wine presses, that might help them to gain additional revenues from their estates, since they had little capacity to reap the fruits of their investment from *coloni* paying a rent established and protected by tradition. When the traditional rents that *coloni* paid were above the market level, then, to judge by the many laws prohibiting the practice, *coloni* could frequently leave their land and take up residence elsewhere. The traditional rents that landowners were allowed to exact surely established a ceiling for the rents that *coloni* would have to pay, either on land for which they were registered on the census rolls or on land that they occupied by virtue of a formally illegal arrangement with a landowner. But without some possibility of the state's enforcing tenure arrangements, small-scale *coloni* who had left their land would be exposed to opportunism by landowners who might take advantage of the sunk costs that the *coloni* had in their new arrangement to exact additional concessions from them.

In sum, the binding of small farmers to their land in late antiquity, whether or not the *coloni* affected represented a majority of small farmers cultivating their land, would tend to diminish the possibility of growth in the Roman economy. It represented a fact of life with which large landowners had to deal as they sought to extract an income from their estates. To be sure landowners still derived profits from their estates, and they could still invest these profits in other forms of economic activity, but the restrictions on the mobility of *coloni* represented a formal legal institution that tended to impede the investment of profits from agriculture that could promote economic growth. The late antique tax system thus imposed costs on Roman society that the state was willing to bear to maintain the empire's fiscal integrity.

Conclusion

The purpose of this book is to offer an economic analysis of Roman legal policy rather than a comprehensive account of land-tenure arrangements in the Roman Empire. My concern is thus to trace the overarching considerations—legal and economic—that guided the Roman legal authorities in dealing with issues involving land tenure, and then to discuss the likely effects of Roman policy on economic performance, primarily in terms of incentives to invest and distribution of wealth. My primary focus on farm tenancy, both on imperial estates and on private land, seems justified because it offers us a way to evaluate the relationships existing among the state, large landowners, and smaller cultivators in a significant sector of the agrarian economy. Farm tenancy seems to be an especially suitable starting point for examining the economic ramifications of legal institutions, not only because tenancy was important to the Roman economy but also because the law surrounding private tenancy was a continuing concern of the Roman government. This is not to claim that the model for economic relationships emerging from this book entirely explains the empire's agrarian economy, since it does not directly address small-scale private landowners or slave and wage labor. However, it does seem reasonable to hypothesize that the economic relationships arising out of and also influencing institutional arrangements in farm tenancy provide us with insight about the Roman agrarian economy more generally.

The methodologies of the New Institutional Economics are invaluable for such a study because they help us to predict the likely influence of various institutional arrangements on incentives to invest and to engage in the type of bargaining necessary for a dynamic economy oriented toward growth, however modest that growth might be in the aggregate economy of an ancient society. In view of the lack of ancient evidence, such an approach does not allow many quantitative predictions about the degree to which the Roman economy might actually have grown over time, but a better understanding of institutional arrangements helps us to answer some basic questions about the Roman Empire.

One key question is whether Roman rule simply promoted the interests of the political elite, at the expense of the vast majority of the empire's subjects, or it served a broader purpose and fostered conditions amenable to economic growth and to a more equitable distribution of wealth, if only by restraining the power of the elite. There is some evidence for the distribution of land holdings in various parts of the empire, including in Veleia and Ligures Baebiani in Italy, as recorded in the famous alimentary inscriptions, or in Egypt, where in some villages it is possible to gain a relatively complete picture of the patterns of landownership.[1] This evidence, as valuable as it is, tells us relatively little about the economic relationships existing among the people involved in the cultivation of this land, and other sources of evidence are needed to develop some understanding of the role that farm tenancy and other forms of labor may have played in these settings. An analysis of institutions, however, clarifies the role that the state played in the economy.

My analysis of the law and legal institutions of land tenure in the Roman Empire suggests that the state did not simply function to facilitate the efforts of wealthy landowners to exact as great a surplus as possible out of the numerous small farmers cultivating their land. Rather, the state used the law to establish a more even playing field to facilitate the type of investment and cooperation that could lead to economic growth, but its ability to use the law to promote such investment and cooperation was subject to broad constraints imposed by institutional structures that it had little power to alter.

We can appreciate the role that the state played in the economy by considering its policy of privileging small-scale landholding in its administration of imperial properties. This policy had important consequences for the agrarian economy of the Roman Empire. From one perspective, the conflicts recorded in connection with the imperial estates in Asia Minor, discussed in chapter 2, represent the competition between the imperial government and local municipal governments over the resources of the rural labor force. In upholding the traditional tenure rights of imperial tenants, the Roman government was pursuing its own interests, reserving these resources for its own use and minimizing the inroads that towns situated near imperial estates would make on them.

But the policy that the Roman government followed in responding to petitions from imperial estates in Asia Minor represented one aspect of a broadly consistent approach to administering imperial properties. The system of managing the North African imperial estates suggests how the Roman government confronted institutional constraints. To keep its own costs of administration under control, the state instituted two groups with property rights to the land, the small-scale *coloni*, who cultivated the land as permanent leaseholders, and the *conductores*, who were set above the *coloni* as short-term lessees to collect the share rents and other dues from the *coloni*. But the conflicts that inevitably arose as a result of this arrangement were probably useful to the state's interests as long as they did not get out of hand. When conflicts became severe, as they did on the *saltus Burunitanus* under the emperor Commodus, the state had no choice but to intervene to protect the tenure of *coloni*. This intervention to uphold the tenure rights of farmers on imperial estates in North Africa and Asia Minor ruled out other ways of exploiting the estates, but it served to perpetuate a system of agriculture that, once established, would be quite difficult to replace. The Roman government's policy, whatever factors influenced its original development, promoted a distribution of wealth that fostered the continued existence of small farmers, whose production provided crucial revenues. The point is not that the Roman government promoted a particular distribution of resources simply out of concern for justice but rather that a policy designed to promote fiscal goals had distributional consequences.[2] The government was unwilling to alter the terms of tenure of the *coloni*, in spite of the conflicts that resulted, because doing so would have been costly without any sure benefit.

The state also considered the desirability of promoting security of tenure as it developed rules for private farm tenancy, but it again had to deal with the costs of this policy. As it responded to disputes between landowners and tenants, particularly disputes connected with the allocation of the costs of the risks endemic to Mediterranean agriculture, the Roman legal authorities demonstrated a concern to maintain the lease relationship if at all possible. This policy served the interests of large landowners, to the extent they needed to keep productive tenants in place on their land. So the challenge that the legal authorities faced was to adapt the classical law of farm tenancy, which treated the lease as a short-term transaction, in such a way as to encourage the type of bargaining between landowners and tenants that fostered longer-term, mutually beneficial relationships. The problem was that this was easier said than done, and many tenure relationships were characterized less by cooperation than by conflict. Landowners derived their income not so much from cooperative arrangements with their tenants but by skimming a portion of the surplus that they produced. Under these circumstances, the state served to protect both landowners and tenants against opportunism by the other party. So on both imperial estates and on private land, the state functioned mainly to serve as a referee between small-scale *coloni* and landlords or imperial tax officials, and the state's capacity to use the law to promote cooperative forms of investment was limited.

The Roman government faced a constant battle to create a legal order within which economic actors would operate in the face of the realities, and indeed the changing realities, of the empire's agrarian economy. This effort involved asserting Roman law and legal institutions as the authoritative structures to define legal relationships in the agrarian economy, bargaining to be done in the shadow of Roman law, since Roman law would remain the ultimate arbitrator. The government pursued this goal by interpreting diverse tenure arrangements in terms of Roman legal conventions. To some extent this policy resulted from the legal conservatism of the Roman jurists and the other legal authorities, who were much more inclined to interpret legal questions in terms of conventional Roman law rather than to introduce new legal categories that might correspond more closely to the economic realities of the empire. Still, the legal authorities' concern to promote the tenant's continued cultivation of the land led them to be flexible in treating issues connected with land tenure, sticking with traditional legal categories but willing to accommodate within traditional Roman legal categories land-tenure arrangements, arising from local custom, that gave the tenant strong tenure rights, if not de facto possession.

The Roman government's treatment of the legal issues connected with the tenant's tenure rights, however, demonstrates the difficulty that it encountered in imposing a legal order on the empire's rural economy. The government always had to strike a balance between recognizing these rights and infringing on those of landowners. To be sure, the government could not impose a uniform system of land tenure on the diverse regions of the empire, but its effort to treat legal issues connected with the rural economy in a more consistent manner surely had important implications for the relationships between elite landowners and tenants. Undoubtedly, the Roman legal authorities, in their persistent effort to recognize property rights, did much to strengthen the hand of large landowners. But in the process of interpreting property rights more uniformly throughout the empire, the courts' authority in settling disputes was also strengthened, thus checking some of the power that large landowners could exercise by virtue of their economic and social status. Although it is difficult to determine whether this policy enhanced production in the rural economy, it is consistent with the Roman government's broader policy of protecting small farmers against excessive inroads by wealthy oppressors.

Certainly the capacity of legal policy to influence land-tenure arrangements was limited, and the Roman government developed its legal policies in response to what it found. The limited capacity of the government to impose any sort of tenure regime is best illustrated in its efforts to enforce its fiscal system in late antiquity. The creation of this institution arose out of the government's efforts to establish a more reliable basis for collecting taxes from land. It was imposed on a rural economy in which tenants tended to remain on estates for long periods of time. The practice of many landowners of securing their incomes by exacting a portion of the surplus produced by tenants who shouldered most of the costs of maintaining their farms represented a fundamental institutional arrangement that the Roman government had no power to alter. Instead, it took the next logical step to ensure that landowners would be able to meet their fiscal responsibilities by taking the same tenants who occupied their land under customary arrangements that gave them security of tenure and making them bound to the land. The binding of *coloni* then, was a product of the same institutional path dependence that constrained both the state and private landowners under the Principate in their capacity to exploit their lands. But the fiscal system of late antiquity imposed costs on the economy, as it created distortions in landowners' and tenants' incentives to invest. At the same time, it drove much of the bargaining between landowners and tenants outside the control of the law, since private arrangements between these parties would be in violation of imperial laws.

The experience of the Roman government's effort to maintain this fiscal system in late antiquity helps to put the role of law and legal institutions in the rural economy under the Principate in a clearer perspective. In the Principate, the legal policies of the Roman government did promote productivity in agriculture, but within broader economic constraints to which the legal authorities had to adapt. All told, in examining the ways in which it interpreted laws and local customs to settle disputes between tenants and landowners, we see that the imperial chancery was careful to maintain a delicate balance of many competing rights and interests. While the imperial government often sought to protect the property rights of landowners, it also helped to make it possible for small farmers to make efficient use of the resources available to them.

In broader terms, the Roman government's legal policies concerning land tenure had far-reaching consequences for the relationships between the urban and rural economies. The growth of the urban economy in the early empire depended on the elite's ability to exact surpluses from their agricultural holdings and to spend these revenues in the cities. This transfer of wealth benefited the cities but deprived the countryside of resources and spending power.

The policies of the Roman government worked to limit the effects of this transfer of wealth to some degree, but at a significant cost. To be sure, the revenues that the Roman government itself collected from imperial estates represented a loss to the countryside in much the same way as the revenues exacted by private landowners. However, the protection of tenure rights helped to foster the continued existence of a viable peasantry both on imperial estates and on private land in the Roman Empire throughout antiquity. The strength of the peasantry in the Roman Empire is perhaps suggested by the situation in the sixth-century Oxyrhynchite nome in Egypt, when the Flavii Apiones and other aristocratic houses had created large estates, on a scale never seen before in Egypt, that contributed to their status as members of the wealthiest class in the Roman Empire. Even in this circumstance, when large landowners combined political power, the responsibility to collect taxes, and the ownership of estates comprising thousands of arouras, the villages in the Oxyrhynchite nome continued to have small owner cultivators and tenants who had substantial resources and could enter into contracts with the estates owned by the aristocratic houses.[3] In earlier periods, it seems very likely that the power of locally influential landowners was never so great as to overshadow completely the resources of a large class of small owners and tenants, who in many regions of the empire, in particular Egypt, overlapped to a large extent.[4]

The purchasing power of the peasantry—maintained in part thanks to the protection, as limited and imperfect as it was, that the state offered against exploitation by larger landowners—was surely a factor in the widespread development of small-scale industries, such as ceramic production, in rural locations.[5] To some extent, the relationship between tenants on imperial estates and the Roman government may be illuminated by Kent Deng's analysis of the rural economy in imperial China, beginning in ancient times. In Deng's account, governments in imperial China depended on a symbiosis with a huge class of peasant cultivators. The state constantly supported the interests of the rural population by protecting its tenure rights, and when the state failed to do so, it risked violent opposition from farmers seeking to maintain their traditional rights. In Deng's view, urbanization in China was largely a function of the production of a food surplus from the countryside, but the urban commercial class was limited in its influence, particularly over the rural economy.[6] In the Roman Empire, elite, urban-based landowners stood between the rural labor force and the state, and they were responsible for much of the transfer of wealth from the countryside on which the empire's cities depended. Still, the Roman state's relationship with farmers on imperial estates helped to check some of the power that these elite landowners exercised. The state's efforts to protect private tenants against the worst effects of opportunism on the part of their landowners served this same purpose. In its wisdom, the Roman government saw the need to prevent large landowners from monopolizing resources to the point of threatening the productive capacity of the rural economy, since that would ultimately threaten the fiscal stability of the empire as a whole.

But if the Roman government's policy promoted the welfare of a broad class of farmers, it also suggests some of the contradictions in the Roman agrarian economy. The lack of capital and infrastructure for commerce made many landowners in the early empire dependent for their incomes on their ability to exact a portion of the surplus production of small-scale tenants who took upon themselves many of the costs of investment in agriculture. The government recognized this aspect of the economy and so developed a legal policy that accommodated tenure arrangements that were, in origin, foreign to Roman law. However, a legal policy that fostered such tenure arrangements to some extent inhibited the type of investment that could result in growth. Without any prospect to reinvest profits in farms that could be leased out for higher rents, many landowners had to content themselves with skimming off a portion of the surplus production of large numbers of tenants rather than pursuing a proactive strategy of investing to meet an urban demand for particular crops. Perhaps the major disincentive to upper-class investment was the lack of a sufficient market to absorb the products of commercial agriculture.[7] Much of the investment in agriculture came from small-scale farmers rather than from their landowners. The delicate task that the Roman government faced was to balance protecting the interests of these small farmers against those of larger landowners and the state, whose revenues ultimately depended on the continued production of the small farmers. The production of small farmers represented the core of the Roman economy, and the state was always aware of this situation as it adjudicated disputes involving the rural world.

Notes

INTRODUCTION

1. For the link between population and economic growth, see especially Scheidel 2001, 181–250; 2002; and Zelener 2003. For population and agrarian development, see Lo Cascio 1991b, 707–16. For the role of technology, see Greene 2000 and Zelener 2003, 112–42.

2. For basic discussions of the Roman economy, see especially Morris, Saller, and Scheidel, forthcoming. See also Garnsey and Saller 1987, 43–103; Lo Cascio 1991a; and Drexhage, Konen, and Ruffing 2002. For the stratification in landownership in the Roman Empire, see Goldsmith 1987 and, from a different perspective, Jongman 1988, 187–203.

3. See Banaji 2001, and the discussion in the conclusion to chap. 5.

4. See North 1990, as well as North 1981 and North and Thomas 1973.

5. For application of the law and economics approach to the ancient world, see Frier and Kehoe, forthcoming.

6. See Saller 2005, 234 (2002, 263), on the possibility of elite control and declines in agricultural productivity.

7. See Furubotn and Richter 2005, 117.

8. See Tollison 1998. This approach is criticized by economists in the Institutional Economics tradition, in whose view this approach privileges certain market forces that are themselves the product of institutional arrangements: see Medema, Mercuro, and Samuels 2000, 442–43.

9. For this view of the relationship between ancient landowners and tenants, see Andreau and Maucourant 1999.

10. Verboven 2002, especially 287–329.

11. For a broad introduction to the economic analysis of legal rules, see Shavell 2004.

12. For an introduction to this literature, see Mercuro and Medema 1997, especially 130–56; P. G. Klein 2000; as well as Furubotn and Richter 2005 and Eggertsson 1990.

13. P. G. Klein 2000, 456.

14. For discussion of the importance of HNIE to legal history and of the interaction between economic and legal history, see R. Harris 2003.

15. For discussion of the complexities in understanding decision-making in economic matters, see North 2005.

16. See Hopkins 2002 (a reprint of Hopkins 1995/96) and Pleket 1990. Lo Cascio 2000 argues that the Roman state promoted "the basic mechanisms of growth: in the nexus between urbanization, shift towards the market and monetization, and specialization in production" (80). Temin 2004 judges that Roman financial institutions compared favorably with those of eighteenth-century Europe. Hitchner 2005 argues in favor of sustained growth in the Roman economy, but for the limited extent of the economic growth possible, see Saller 2005, a reprint of Saller 2002).

17. See Frier 2000 and Scheidel, forthcoming. For discussion of the debate about Roman population numbers and arguments against higher estimates for the overall population of the empire, see Scheidel 2004.

18. For the consumer city model, see Erdkamp 2001; Jongman 1988, 15–62; Morley 1996, 13–32; and Scheidel, forthcoming. For a somewhat different interpretation of the relationship between city and countryside, see Engels 1990.

19. The dependence of landowners on capturing the surplus from the countryside is an implicit theme in Horden and Purcell 2000, 175–297 (see especially 206 and 218). For this view of the relationship between ancient landowners and tenants, see also Andreau and Maucourant 1999 and, earlier, de Ste. Croix 1981, 213.

20. Scheidel, forthcoming.

21. This is a theme of the *Cambridge Economic History of the Greco-Roman World*.

22. See Mattingly 1993 and Mattingly and Hitchner 1993.

23. See Wilson 2002.

24. Scheidel, forthcoming.

25. See Boserup 1965.

26. Scheidel, forthcoming.

27. E. L. Jones 1988.

28. On this issue, see Field 2000, 737, 742.

29. See P. G. Klein 2000, 458.

30. P. G. Klein 2000, 458, citing O. E. Williamson.

31. See North 1990.

32. P. G. Klein 2000, 461.

33. Field 2000, 742.

34. Medema, Mercuro, and Samuels 2000, 440. For discussion of the relationship between NIE and the old Institutional Economics (OIE), see Rutherford 1994.

35. Medema, Mercuro, and Samuels 2000, 437–39.

36. Field 1991. For the possible uneven distribution of the benefits of economic growth in the ancient world, see Millett 2001.

37. E. L. Jones 1988, 49, 62–63.

38. Barzel 2002.

39. The Theodosian Code, in fact, provides the source for the texts of the imperial decrees from this period that are preserved in the Code of Justinian. For the process by which the Theodosian Code was compiled and edited, see Matthews 2000 and Honoré 1998, 12–53.

40. For this view, see Watson 1995.

41. For urban leasing, see Frier 1980; for private farm tenancy, see Frier 1979, 1989–90; for the building industry, see Martin 1989; for the law surrounding transportation, see Martin 2002; and for adultery and prostitution, see McGinn 1998.

42. See Kehoe 1997, chaps. 3–4.

43. For a very pessimistic assessment of the strength of legal institutions in the Roman countryside, see Garnsey 1998, 91–106.

44. For the view that, in the law of tenancy, legal remedies were mostly available only to the wealthiest tenants (i.e., those able to make use of the law courts on an equal basis with their landlords), see Frier 1980, 39–47. For the related argument that the Roman law of tenancy concerned primarily the "upper stratum" of tenants, cf. the reviews in Frier 1983, 674 and n. 34; 1985, 566—an argument accepted by Zimmermann 1990, 348–50, although Prof. Frier has subsequently modified his views. Cf. Scheidel 1994, which argues the view that the juristic sources offer evidence only for the wealthy stratum of tenants; I challenge this view in Kehoe 1996; see also Kehoe 1997, chap. 3.

45. For a contrasting view about the status of Roman farm tenants, see De Neeve 1990, 383–88. De Neeve argues that Pliny's tenants were "substantial" farmers (387). Capogrossi Colognesi 1995, 225–37; (1992–93, 210–16), emphasizes that Roman tenants represented a wide range of economic status. Cf. the useful discussion by de Ste. Croix 1981, 210–14, on the range of resources of peasant cultivators.

46. On dependent labor, see Garnsey 1980b.

47. See Millar 1981.

48. Peachin 1996, 10–91. For the view that the increased size of the government in the later empire increased the scope for influence and venality, see MacMullen 1988, 122–70. For a more nuanced interpretation, see C. Kelly 2004, 114–85.

49. Hobson 1993.

50. J. M. Kelly 1966; Garnsey 1970, especially 181–218; and Saller 1982, especially 145–94, which focuses on Africa to analyze the complex role that patronage played in the power relations in Roman provinces. For this situation in late antiquity, see Krause 1987, 34–50. For a broad discussion of the power relations in the Roman Empire, which seem to have become more hierarchical in late antiquity, see MacMullen 1988, 58–121.

51. Bürge 1980.

52. On the rural economy of early-modern Madrid, see Morley 1996, 24–27.

53. See Harries 1999, 47–53, on *suggestio* (legislating at the prompting of petitions from individuals).

54. Whittaker 1980b.

55. Capogrossi Colognesi 1986 and Lo Cascio 1993.

56. Jongman 1988, 97–154.

57. De Ste. Croix 1981, 205–75.

58. See Brenner 1976. Brenner argues that class structures, rather than demographic change or the development of commerce, were the crucial factors in shaping the economic history of medieval Europe. Brenner's thesis has met with a strong reaction, which he addresses in Brenner 1982.

59. For this issue in connection with ninth-century China, see E. L. Jones 1988, 77.

60. Peachin 1996. As Burton 1993 suggests, imperial procurators in public provinces may have gradually taken over judicial functions as well as other administrative

duties not tied with the imperial properties to meet the increasing press of court business.

61. On the purposes of rescripts and the process of their publication, see Nörr 1981; Turpin 1991; Corcoran 1996, 43–73, 95–122; Coriat 1997, 283–456; Hauken 1998, 296–317; and Ando 2000, 376–81.

62. Corcoran 1996, 25–42.

63. Coriat 1997, 283–456, especially 329–68.

64. Wacke 1980. Chastagnol 1982, 269, points out that the principle by which lawsuits would be heard where the defendant was domiciled offered some protection against lawsuits to senators who had property in the provinces, since they were officially domiciled in Rome.

65. Bürge 1995.

66. On these texts, see Frakes 2001, 157, and, earlier, Wacke 1980, 582–83, and MacMullen 1988, 259 n. 102. Keeping the courts fair was also an issue for the late Roman government. Thus in 422 Honorius and Theodosius II issued a constitution aimed at curbing similar practices (*CTh* 2.14.1; *CJ* 2.14.1, 400; *CTh* 2.13.1; *CJ* 2.13.2, 422; Wacke 1980, 582–83).

67. For general discussion of this office, see Frakes 2001. For this passage, see Frakes 2001, 112, and, on the general issue of access to courts for the poor, Krause 1996, 44–45 and n. 3.

68. For the bishops' courts, see Harries 1999, 172–211, and Frakes 2001, 195–229. For Constantine's legislation (*CTh* 1.27.1), see Frakes 2001, 198–206, with discussion of the date. Constantine's law was greatly modified in the late fourth and early fifth centuries: see Frakes 2001, 206–11.

69. C. Kelly 2004, 138–45. The *Ordo salutationis: CIL* VIII 17896; *FIRA* I 64. For the imposition of court costs on litigants, see Kaser and Hackl 1996, 557–58.

70. For the jurisdiction of municipal courts, see Kaser and Hackl 1996, 175–83; for late antiquity, see 545–47.

71. For detailed discussion of the procedures at the municipal level focusing on the *lex Irnitana,* see Metzger 1997, with bibliography.

72. On the administration of Roman Egypt, see Bowman and Rathbone 1992. But there were substantial differences between the administration of justice in Egypt and that of the rest of the empire, such as the lack of the formulary system and a hearing process not based on *cognitio extraordinaria* (a hearing presided over by a magistrate): see Hackl 1997.

73. On the judicial functions of the prefect of Egypt, see Haensch 1997a; 1994. For the *conventus* (a meeting to hear cases) as a basic duty of Roman governors, see Haensch 1997b, 28–34.

74. For discussion of the significance of this document for the administration of justice, see Ando 2000, 376–77; see also Foti Talamanca 1974, 179–84, which dates it to 209, and Foti Talamanca 1979, 115–24.

75. See Kehoe 1995.

76. Rowlandson 1994, 497, sees the detailed terms of farm leases as evidence that tenants could enforce their rights in courts of law. Cf. also Rowlandson 1996, 272–79, for the differences in social status between lessors and tenants in Roman Oxyrhynchus.

77. Ando 2000, especially 73–130. For the role played by Roman legal forms in establishing the legitimacy of Roman rule, see Meyer 2004.

78. See Peachin 1996, 10–13, as well as Ando 2000, 79–80.

79. See Weßel 2003, 21–25.

80. See Cotton 1993, as well as Nörr 1998 and Meyer 2004, 191–93. For the annexation of the kingdom and the adoption of Roman law, see Bowersock 1983, 75–89. For the complex relationship process of assimilating provincial legal practices with Roman practices, see Meyer 2004, 169–215.

81. This document is published by Feissel and Gascou 1989, and republished by Feissel and Gascou 1995, with discussion, 67–83. Priscus would subsequently hold an extraordinary command over the eastern part of the Roman Empire; see Feissel and Gascou 1995, 80–83, and Peachin 1996, 170, 174–79. For discussion of the process of petitioning in this document, see Ando 2000, 73–80.

82. The village is characterized as a *kyriake kome* (imperial village) near Appadana (lines 4–5). For the following interpretation of the petitioners' request, cf. Haensch 1997b, 254–55 n. 139.

83. See Millar 1993, 155–56.

84. According to Feissel and Gascou 1995, 73–74, the imperial constitutions to which the petitioners refer may have included the one of Marcus Aurelius concerning a creditor who unilaterally took possession of the debtor's property (Callistr. *D*. 48.7.7, 5 *de cognit*.); Ulpian indicates that there were other rescripts as well on this issue (*D*. 43.16.1.2, 69 *ad ed*.). The petitioners likewise may have been seeking application of the interdicts *unde vi* (on force) (*D*. 43.16) and *uti possidetis* (on possession) (*D*. 43.17). The former was aimed at protecting possessors of immovable property against forceful eviction (Ulp. *D*. 43.16.1.3). On these protections, see Kaser 1971, 396–400, and Berger 1953, s.v. "interdictum de vi" and "interdictum uti possidetis." For further discussion of force in property disputes, see chap. 4 under "Disputes over Ownership and Possession."

85. For the ideology of late Roman emperors in protecting small farmers against the powerful and influential, see Krause 1987, 179–80.

86. Crook 1995.

87. Crook 1995, 72, no. 3.

88. Crook 1995, 98–99, no. 29.

89. Crook 1995, 102–3, no. 33.

90. Crook 1995, 104–7, no. 35; for discussion, see also Frakes 2001, 50–51. On the *praescriptio longissimi temporis*, see Berger 1953, s.v. "Praescriptio quadraginta annorum."

91. Crook 1995, 112; the latest document is dated to 237.

92. This is the explanation of Crook 1995, 91–95, no. 25. For analysis of the legal situation, see Kunkel 1974, especially 258–59 on the advocates; for the theory of the rhetorical entertainment, see Williams 1974; see also Peachin 1996, 83. Perhaps the plaintiffs in this case were trying to maintain privileges for their temple in much the same way as the managers of a temple at Baetocaece in Syria, who petitioned the emperor Valerian to safeguard privileges that they had originally received in the Hellenistic period: see *IGLSyr*. VII 4028, with the commentary of J.-P. Rey-Coquais; cf. on this inscription Ando 2000, 107.

CHAPTER 1

1. See P. G. Klein 2000.

2. See Finley 1999 (first published 1973), especially 95–122 for the agrarian economy, and the challenging review by Frederiksen 1975.

3. For a bibliography on the New Institutional Economics and discussion of Institutional Economics (OIE), see n. 12 of the introduction.

4. North 2005.

5. See Cheung 1992, with the comments by Becker 1992 and Coase 1992. From a different perspective, Demsetz 1967, 348, argues that defining property rights serves "to achieve a greater internalization of externalities," in that the costs of economic activity are reckoned in the bargaining process.

6. Cheung 1992, 62.

7. Becker 1992, 67.

8. See Coase 1990, 95–156, a reprint of Coase 1960. For discussion of the literature on the Coase Theorem, see Field 2000, especially 737–38, and Medema and Zerbe 2000.

9. See Eggertsson 1990, 19, 39–40. For a discussion and critique of the basic assumptions of neoclassical economic theory, see Furubotn and Richter 2005, 1–45.

10. Coase 1990, 114, a reprint of Coase 1960.

11. For discussion of the substantial literature on this topic, see Allen 2000. Two important contributions in this literature for analyzing contracts are those of Williamson 1979 and Dahlman 1979, which links the presence of externalities with transaction costs impeding bargaining.

12. Barzel 2002, 15; cf. Allen 2000, 898, which defines property rights as "the ability to freely exercise a choice over a good or service." Shavell 2004, 9–26, distinguishes between "possessory rights," which "allow individuals to use things and to prevent others from using them" (1) and "the right to transfer a possessory right" (18).

13. Allen 2000, 898.

14. Allen 2000, 899.

15. Allen 2000, 900.

16. Allen 2000, 901.

17. Allen 2000, 902.

18. See Medema and Zerbe 2000, 876.

19. Medema and Zerbe 2000, 877.

20. Cooter 1982.

21. Cooter 1982, 28.

22. Cooter 1982, 17.

23. Cooter 1982, 28. For a broad discussion of the issues raised by the Coase Theorem for the effects of legal rules on the allocation of resources, see Shavell 2004, 77–109.

24. See Mercuro and Medema 1997, chap. 1, for discussion of the concept of Pareto efficiency. Many economists recognize that this concept is not always a meaningful criterion for analyzing the economic performance of institutions: see Rutherford 1994, 152–55.

25. Alchian 1950. Williamson 1985, 46–47, terms Alchian's approach "process or organic rationality," linking it with an "evolutionary" approach to economic change.

26. Simon 1986, excerpted in Katz 1998, 288–303, on 300, as well as Simon 1983, 84–85. For additional discussion of bounded rationality, see Williamson 1985, 45–46.

27. For the centrality of the assumption of bounded rationality to analysis in NIE, see Williamson 1996, passim, especially 36–37, 55–57. For the difficulty in NIE, as well as in Institutional Economics (OIE), of reconciling rational behavior with compliance with socially imposed norms, see Rutherford 1994, 51–80.

28. For discussion of the problems in applying rational choice theory, see Ulen 2000.

29. See Furubotn and Richter 1997, 164–65, 171; cf. 2005, 109–10.

30. See the discussion of Rutherford 1994, 129–72, on the efficiency of institutions, and, 81–128, on the fundamental question whether institutional change is the result of active planning or the "invisible hand" of market forces.

31. See Rathbone 1991; 2005. For development of Rathbone's thesis, see Carrié 2005. For the limits on what could be accomplished with ancient accounting methods, see Minaud 2005. For the limits on the rationality practiced by Appianus, see Tchernia 2005.

32. Andreau and Maucourant 1999.

33. Cf. the analysis of the late Republican credit market in Verboven 2002, 116–82, which discusses the importance of personal relationships in the credit exchanges but also argues that a real market existed for credit. In my view, personal relationships are likely to have played such a large role in the credit market because of the absence of commercial credit institutions and legal institutions to enforce credit transactions. The absence of such commercial institutions was itself at least in part a by-product of the likely relatively small savings accumulated by the Roman upper classes, with the result that commerce accounted for a small portion of upper-class wealth. For discussion of these issues, see Zelener 2003, 166–200.

34. Also published as *P.Giss.* 40 col. ii.23–24; *W.Chr.* 22. Earlier, in a letter to a procurator inscribed at Epiphania in Syria, the emperor Domitian, in an effort to curtail abuses of officials of their authority to requisition draft animals, pointed out that such abuses lead to a disruption of agriculture (Oliver 1989, no. 40, earlier published as *SEG* XVII 755; *IGLSyr.* V 1998). Cf. Kolb 2000, 120 n. 9, and Drexhage, Konen, and Ruffing 2002, 83.

35. On the distribution programs in Rome, and later Constantinople, see Rickman 1980 and Sirks 1991. For the basic aspects of Roman alimentary foundations, see Duncan-Jones 1982, 288–319, 333–42.

36. For discussion of the law of tutorship, see Kaser 1971, 85–86, 352–54, as well as Sachers 1948. For general discussion of the institution, see Saller 1994, 181–203; Crook 1986; and Krause 1995, 85–112.

37. See Kehoe 1997, 22–76. For additional discussion of investment goals by Roman landowners, see Pleket 1993, especially 332–42; Andreau 2004; and, earlier, Veyne 1979.

38. See Saller 1994, 181–203, and Crook 1975.

39. Millar 1977.

40. Saller 1982.

41. See Peachin 1996.

42. Lendon 1997, especially 24–27, 176–236.

43. For broad remarks on basic agency problems, see Furubotn and Richter 2005, 27–28.

44. See Harries 1999, e.g., 54, referring to the decree of Valentinian I on the duty of the *defensor civitatis* to act in the interests of "innocens et quieta rusticitas" (*CTh* 1.29.5, 370, discussed in the introd.). On the late imperial government's concern for protecting the small farmer against the influence of the rich and powerful, cf. Krause 1987, 75, 149–50, 180.

45. Harries 1999, 58–64, and, more generally on the circumstances surrounding the publication of the Theodosian Code, Matthews 2000, 1–54, 168–99.

46. On this point, for legislation in late antiquity, see Harries 1999, 77–98.

47. See Galanter 1981.

48. For general discussion of this concept as it applied to the choice of technologies, see Liebowitz and Margolis 2000.

49. North 1990.

50. See Hodgson 1999, 199–219; this chapter is a revised version of Hodgson 1993.

51. See Hopkins 2002 (a reprint of Hopkins 1995/1996).

52. See Woolf 1998, 148–68, as well as Pleket 1990, 90–91, and Drexhage, Konen, and Ruffing 2002, 79–80.

53. For the increased production of olive oil as an indicator of economic growth, see Mattingly 1988a, 1988b, and 1988c and Hitchner 1993, reprinted in Scheidel and von Reden 2002, 71–83.

54. Haley 2003; cf., earlier, Mattingly 1988a, 48–54.

55. For the sources of wealth of the elite in the Greek provinces of the East, see Pleket 1984.

56. Mitchell 1993, 143–64; cf. Drexhage, Konen, and Ruffing 2002, 80–81.

57. On Appianus, see Rathbone 1991; for the development of a municipal structure in Roman Egypt, see Bowman and Rathbone 1992.

58. Safrai 1994, 322–64.

59. See Vera 1995a, 1995b.

60. See, e.g., Mattingly 1993.

61. Andreau and Maucourant 1999, especially 66–67.

62. See Barzel 2002 for the "rule-of-law" state and the "tyrannical" state, also discussed in the introduction.

63. For a survey of imperial estates, see Crawford 1976. For the share of the state in the Roman economy, cf. W. V. Harris 1993, 17. For imperial estates in North Africa, see Kolendo 1991, Weber 1983, and Kehoe 1988a.

64. For the development of the general fiscal responsibilities of the Fiscus and the blurring of the distinction between property belonging to the emperor and to the state in the early empire, see Brunt 1966; for a different interpretation, see Millar 1963, which emphasizes the role of the Fiscus in administering the emperor's property. Alpers 1995 insists that in the first century CE the Fiscus is to be understood as exclusively referring to the private property of the emperor.

65. See Rowlandson 1996, 70–101. Cf. the analysis of landowning patterns in the village of Philadelphia in the Fayum by Schubert 2001. Schubert 2001, 15–16, presents a chart of six comparable villages from the Fayum during the second or early third centuries. In these villages, privately held land accounts for between 32 percent

and 48 percent of the total area, which leaves a great deal of room for state-owned land.

66. For a broad discussion of the limitations on the free market for grain in the Roman Empire, see Erdkamp 2005, especially 206–57. For problems of securing adequate food supply, see also Garnsey 1988; 1999, 22–42. The Roman government's policy in this regard should be seen alongside its effort to promote the private importation of foodstuffs into the city of Rome by offering shippers serving the *annona* substantial incentives. On these incentives, see Rickman 1980 and Sirks 1991.

67. Rathbone 1991, 15–17; Andreau and Maucourant 1999, 61.

68. For the auctioning off of treasures, see Duncan-Jones 1994, 10. The imperial government followed the same practice in the later empire and in the Byzantine period, selling treasures but not productive land in fiscal emergencies: see Hendy 1985, 228–42. The one exception may have occurred under the emperor Valens, who, as Lenski 2002, 306, argues, citing Hesychius of Miletus, fr. 6 (*FHG* 4.155), tried to raise revenue by selling imperial properties at very low prices. But the description by Hesychius does not provide enough specific details to reveal a policy.

69. Sharp 1999.

70. See Rathbone 1991. For the development of estates in Egypt in the period ca. 200–400, see Banaji 2001, 101–33. The growth of estates beginning around 200, as Roger Bagnall has observed (oral communication), was linked to the development of city councils in Egypt under Septimius Severus.

71. See Bowman and Rathbone 1992.

72. On this, see Kehoe 1988a, 205–15; see also Banaji 2001, 6–22.

73. For the impact of confiscations of property by the state, see Duncan-Jones 1994, 5–7.

74. See Hodgson 1999, 207–9.

75. Barzel 2002, 170.

76. Barzel 2002, 171–73.

CHAPTER 2

1. For the concept of economic rights, see the discussion in chap. 1 in the text accompanying n. 11.

2. I argue this position in Kehoe 1988a; for a similar view, see Erdkamp 2005, 222–37.

3. For discussion of the difficulties in securing supplies of food, see the discussion in chap. 1 in the text accompanying n. 66. For the significance of frequent localized drought and crop failures on agricultural techniques in the Mediterranean area, see Horden and Purcell 2000, 175–230.

4. For the significance of a long-term perspective, which reduces the constraints on a state in its efforts to exact revenues, see Levi 1988, 13.

5. For this understanding of the role of legal institutions in creating economic rights, see Medema, Mercuro, and Samuels 2000, especially 441.

6. On institutional path dependence, see the discussion in chap. 1 under "Legal Institutions and the Enforcement of Policy."

7. Banaji 2001.

8. For a survey of North African culture based on archaeology, see Mattingly and Hitchner 1995; see also Mattingly 1994, 138–59, for the development of the economy

of Roman Tripolitania. For general discussion of Africa under Roman rule, see Whittaker 1996 and 2000.

9. Mattingly and Hitchner 1995, 195, 198–204; cf. Mattingly 1994, 138.

10. For discussion of these documents, see Kehoe 1988a, as well as Weber 1983, 309–43; Kolendo 1991; De Ligt 1998–99; Weßel 2003, 89–123; and, more generally, Whittaker 2000, 531–34. For the text, see also Flach 1978.

11. The likeliest candidate for this accomplishment is a senator named T. Curtilius Mancia, who was consul under Nero and proconsul of Africa: see Kehoe 1984 and, from a different perspective, Pleket 1990, 92–93, and Whittaker 2000, 531–34.

12. On this point, see De Ligt 1998–99.

13. Weßel 2003, 107, regards the *lex Manciana* as establishing rights on private land, which explains its survival on estates in Africa in late antiquity (see the following text). For a tentative endorsement of this view, see Whittaker 2000, 534.

14. For discussion of the documents in this inscription, see Kehoe 1988a, 55–63.

15. There is a preliminary publication of this inscription, which consists of two fragments of a base, in De Vos 2001. The inscription does not include the petition in the AD inscription, but it preserves large fragments of the *sermo procuratorum*. It adds a few details to what has been reconstructed of this document based on the AD and AW inscriptions.

16. For the most recent discussion of this issue, see Hauken 1998, 20–21, and De Ligt 1998–99.

17. AD 2.4ff.; AW 2.1ff. (with words present in the version of the *sermo* in the AW inscription in italics): "*sermo procurato[rum* im] / p(eratoris) <C>aes(aris) Hadriani Aug(usti):*quia Cae[sar n(oster) pro] / infatigabili cura sua per qu[am adsi]/due humanis utili<ta>tibus excu[bat om]/nes partes agrorum, quae tam oleis* au[t] vineis quam frumentis aptae sunt, e[x]/coli iubet, i<d>circo permissu{m} prov[id/en]tiae eius potestas fit omnibus eas partes occupandi . . . [*-nec a conductoribus exer/centur; <i>isque qui occupaverint pos/sidendi ac fru<en>di{i} eredique su/o reliquendi id ius datur, / quod e<s>t lege Ha<drian>a compre/hensum de rudibus agris / et iis qui per X an<n>os conti/nuos inculti sunt* . . .]."

18. The rent-free seasons were only offered to *coloni* cultivating vineyards in the place of existing ones: HM 2.24–30.

19. Such lessees had to pay the rent to maintain their rights: Ulp. *D.* 6.3.2 (17 *ad Sab.*). For these rights, see Kaser 1971, 455. For a broad discussion of the economic advantages and disadvantages of various forms of ownership in land, see Ellickson 1993.

20. See Weßel 2003, as well as the discussion in chap. 4 under "Legal Order and Traditional Tenure Arrangements."

21. For a different interpretation, see Whittaker 2000, 533–34, which interprets the AW inscription as evidence that the *lex Manciana* was only gradually promulgated.

22. See also Weber 1983, nos. 80–81.

23. This section is based on Rowlandson 1996, 70–101.

24. For the *ousiai*, see Parássoglou, 1978; for their cultivation, see Kehoe 1992, 16–57.

25. See Rowlandson 1996, 294–304, table 5.

26. Rowlandson 1996, 72. For discussion of grain taxes, including rents for state land, in Egypt, see also Duncan-Jones 1994, 47–50.

27. For discussion of yields, see Rathbone 1991, 242–43, 465; for more generous estimates, see Erdkamp 2005, 44–45.

28. Rowlandson 1996, 86.

29. Rowlandson 1996, 88–92.

30. See Knoeber 2000.

31. On the incentives in agency, see Furubotn and Richter 2005, 162–70.

32. What follows is based on Eggertsson 1990, 204, which cites S. Fenoaltea's study of slavery. Columella (*De re rust*. 1.7.3) views vines as requiring greater care than wheat.

33. Cf. n. 9, chap. 2.

34. See Banerjee, Gertler, and Ghatak 2002.

35. See Cheung 1969.

36. For the economic issues surrounding sharecropping on the imperial estates, see Kehoe 1988a, chap. 5. According to Alston, Datta, and Nugent 1984, sharecropping may help landowners to reduce the costs of enforcement (over wage labor) when landowners supply substantial inputs. This does not seem to have been the case on the North African imperial estates.

37. On this aspect of sharecropping, see Barzel 1989, 33–38.

38. For investment in olive presses in North Africa, see Mattingly 1988a, 1988b, 1988c.

39. On this lever-press, see Mattingly and Hitchner 1993.

40. On seasonal labor, see Mattingly 1994, 143–44.

41. See De Vos 2001, 22–29.

42. For these terms see Katz 1998, 189–90.

43. See Katz 1998, 207 n. 10, and 189–90; Schwartz 1992a, 290–91; as well as the discussion in chap. 3 under "The Allocation of Risk." For detailed discussion of the circumstances under which breach of contract will be economically efficient, in the sense of allocating resources to the highest-valued use, see Shavell 2004, 338–85.

44. For discussion of the Roman law of tenancy law, see chap. 3.

45. For the various protections to entitlements discussed in the text, see Calabresi and Melamed 1972, excerpted in Katz 1998, 103–15; for discussion of the relative merits of liability and property rules, see Kaplow and Shavell 1996.

46. For "incentives for private transactions," see Katz 1990, excerpted in Katz 1998, 189–97.

47. Katz 1998, 41–42.

48. On opportunistic behavior, see Williamson 1979; 1985, 30.

49. This is called the "lock-in effect," when a party to a contract has committed substantial investment and so is vulnerable to actions by the other party: see Furubotn and Richter 2005, 150.

50. For the most recent discussion of this inscription, see Hauken 1998, 2–28.

51. SK 3.13ff.: "I<d>que sine ulla contro/versia sit, utpote cum in aere incis<um> et ab / omnib(us) omnino undiq(ue) versum vicinis nostr[is] / perpetua in hodiernum forma praestitu[m], / tum et proc(uratorum) litteris, quas supra scripsimus, / ita conf[ir]matum."

52. For the influence that the *conductores* exercised with the imperial procurators, see Saller 1982, 166–67.

53. SK 4.4–8: "proc(uratores) contemplatione dis/cipulinae et instituti mei—'ne plus / quam ter binas operas'—curabunt / ne qui<d> per iniuriam contra perpe/tuam formam a vobis exigatur." The phrase concerning the *operae* is likely to have been

added by the *coloni*. For this and discussion of the possible disappointment of the *coloni* in the emperor's response, see Hauken 1998, 26.

54. Meyer 2004, 91–120; cf. Ando 2000, 89, for the methods used in publishing the SK inscription to accord it the greatest authority possible, and 381, for the importance to the petitioners of publishing the petition and response. For discussion of the authority that the Roman government attributed to published documents, see Ando 2000, 96–117.

55. SK 2.3–4: "contra fas atq(ue) in perniciem / rationum tuarum . . ."

56. GM A.6: "[—ut domum? re]vertamur ubi libere morari possimu[s-]." For discussion of this inscription, see Hauken 1998, 29–34.

57. On the credibility of threats to abandon imperial estates, see Hauken 1998, 56–57, as well as Mitchell 1993, 185, for the Aga Bey estate. For more general treatments of this theme, see Whittaker 1976, 149, and Krause 1987, 177–79.

58. Again, the analysis of the medieval rural economy by Robert Brenner is instructive. In his view, the relative strength of peasant communal structures had a direct effect in countering the ability of landlords to exercise power over the peasants and, in some instances, to impose or maintain a feudal system of land tenure: Brenner 1976, 51–52.

59. See Kehoe 1988a, chap. 6.

60. On one imperial estate, the *fundus Turris Rutundae*, the *coloni* cooperated to restore a temple, under the leadership of a *magister* and a priest (*ILTun*. 1568; *CIL* VIII 16411).

61. See Kehoe 1988a, 205–15.

62. Cf. Mattingly and Hitchner 1995, 195.

63. Shaw 1981.

64. For this way of looking at entitlements, see Calabresi and Melamed 1972, excerpted in Katz 1998, 103–15. Kaplow and Shavell 1996, 744–45, are skeptical that rules of this sort represent an efficient way to achieve a just distribution of income; they prefer transfers of wealth through an income tax, which was not an option in the Roman world.

65. See Hauken 1998 for new additions of the inscriptions with full commentary.

66. Mitchell 1993, 143–64. Cf. also Pleket 1984 and the discussion in chap. 1 in the text accompanying n. 55.

67. Mitchell 1993, 163–64.

68. See Mitchell 1993, 227–40.

69. Aga Bey: Hauken 1998, 35–57; Abbott and Johnson 1926, no. 142 (Philip). Güllüköy: Hauken 1998, 251–56 (fragmentary). Aragua: Hauken 1998, 140–61; Abbott and Johnson 1926, no. 141 (Philip). Takina: Hauken 1998, 217–43, and, on the status of the village, Mitchell 1993, 180.

70. See Hauken 1998, 117–18.

71. Mitchell 1976; for efforts to regulate the use of the *cursus publicus* (public post), see Kolb 2000, 49–122.

72. See Burton 2000.

73. Hauken 1998, 264–68, discussing the exordia to petitions.

74. For commentary on this document, see J. C. Shelton, ad loc. (1971), and for a similar document, see *P.Lugd.Bat.* XVI 34, 35 (144 CE).

75. For interpretation of the document, see H. Maehler, *BGU* XI.1, 89.

76. For Aquila's activity as judge during his *conventus* in the Arsinoite nome, see *P.Yale* I 61 (ca. 208–10 CE), discussed in the introduction under "The Economic Significance of Roman Legal Institutions."

77. For the detailed discussion of the archive of Adelphios in general, see Worp 1991.

78. Hauken 1998, 226.

79. For full discussion of the inscription from Skaptopara, see Hauken 1998, 74–139; the new text of Hallof 1994 supplants previous texts.

80. Cf. the complaints from the town of Tabala (Hauken 1998, 203–14) in Asia Minor to the emperor Pertinax about the abuses by soldiers departing from the public roads, as well as a similar petition from the town of Euhippe in Caria to Caracalla (215–16). Hauken also discusses the very fragmentary proconsular edict from Demerci, a village in Lydia, about illegal requisitions (244–46).

81. Hauken 1998, 35–57.

82. For discussion of this inscription and the likely duties of the tax officials, see Mitchell 1993, 229, 233.

83. Aurelius Marcianus is styled as the *epitropos tes taxeos*, which is probably the equivalent of *procurator regionis* (procurator of a region); see Hauken 1998, 48–49.

84. For the text and commentary, see now Campbell 2000, 42, 35–51; the text is quoted by Agennius Urbicus, but it apparently derives from Frontinus (333).

85. See Parássoglou 1978 and Kehoe 1992, chap. 2.

86. Pap. Iust. *D.* 50.1.38.1: "Item rescripserunt colonos praediorum fisci muneribus fungi sine damno fisci oportere, idque excutere praesidem adhibito procuratore debere."

87. Callistr. *D.* 50.6.6.11: "Coloni quoque Caesaris a muneribus liberantur, ut idoniores praediis fiscalibus habeantur." For discussion of these passages, see Rosafio 2002, 137–57, which traces the controversy into late antiquity.

88. See Oliver 1989, nos. 164–66; the texts are also published as *W.Chr.* 26.

89. See Hauken 1998, 36.

90. It is possible that no formal document existed establishing the terms of cultivation, but that the claims of the Aga Bey farmers were based on customary practice. Servitudes in Roman law were legally enforceable even if their origin lay so far in the past that no one could remember it: see Kaser 1971, 445, as well as Nörr 1969, 46–63.

91. A very fragmentary inscription from a site called Güllüköy in ancient Lydia (Hauken 1998, 251–56) may indicate a similar conflict between villagers on an imperial estate and the town of Philadelphia over liturgies and other obligations.

92. Hauken 1998, 140–61; Abbott and Johnson 1926, no. 141; see also, for additional discussion, Mitchell 1993, 230.

93. See Hauken 1998, 154–55, for discussion of the possibilities.

94. Aragua, lines 3–4: "proco[n]sule v(ir) c(larissimus) perspecta fide eorum quae [adlegastis si] / quid iniuriose geratur, ad sollicitudinem suam revocabit."

95. On rural social relationships, see MacMullen 1974, 1–27; cf. MacMullen 1988, 84–86.

96. The text of this inscription is in Hauken 1998, 188–202.

97. The governor in question was the father-in-law of the emperor Pertinax and was city prefect in 193: Hauken 1998, 192–93.

98. On the *sacrae litterae*, see the discussion of Mitchell 1993, 134 n. 108, 230, as well as that of C. P. Jones 1984. For the text, of which there are multiple copies in both Latin and Greek, see C. P. Jones 1984, 94–95, and Hauken 1998, 230 n. 12.

99. Mitchell 1993, 253–55.

100. For the importance to economic growth of investment in public goods in preindustrial economies, see E. L. Jones 1988, 78.

CHAPTER 3

1. For discussion of formal and informal institutions and their effect on economic performance, see North 1990.

2. The most important recent literature on Roman farm tenancy includes De Neeve 1984, 1990; Scheidel 1994; the collection of essays in Lo Cascio 1997a; Capogrossi Colognesi 1995, 143–301 (also published as Capogrossi Colognesi 1992–93); and Vera 1995a, 1995b.

3. For this aspect of tenancy in Roman Egypt, see Bagnall 1993b, 133–34, and Rowlandson 1996 202–79; cf., for a more general discussion of the role of tenancy in villages in Roman Egypt, Rowlandson 1999.

4. For example, tenancy has been seen as fulfilling this function on the third-century estate of Aurelius Appianus, the management of which is recorded in the Heroninos archive: see Rathbone 1991, 176, 183–88; 1994, 435. Rathbone emphasizes that landowners might lease out land to avoid risk.

5. See Kehoe 1997, chap. 4, and, for Roman Egypt, Kehoe 1992, chap. 4.

6. For further discussion of the Roman legal authorities' understanding of the Roman economy, see Kehoe 1997, especially 2–3, 12–13, 23–25.

7. As Zelener 2003 emphasizes, upper-class Romans had no choice but to invest much of their wealth in agriculture, whose share of the economy dwarfed that of commerce.

8. In this respect, the government's policy was quite different from the one it implemented on imperial estates, where it protected the tenure of *coloni* and inhibited bargaining.

9. For the formal elements of the Roman farm lease, see Kehoe 1997, chap. 3, especially 147–49, as well as Köhn 1983 and Frier 1979. See also Kaser 1971, 565–68; Mayer-Maly 1956, for a thorough critique of the ancient texts; and Zimmermann 1990, 338–83, for the development of lease law in the civilian tradition. For the difficulty of determining the prevalence of forms of land tenure from the juristic treatment of legal problems involving farm tenancy, see Capogrossi Colognesi 1997.

10. For ancient concern with the problem of monitoring tenants, see Carlsen 1997.

11. See Shavell 2004, 379.

12. For discussion of the endowment effect and the controversies surrounding it, see Curran 2000.

13. The shortage of tenants with adequate resources was a problem that Pliny confronted; see Kehoe 1988b, as well as Garnsey 2000, 704.

14. See Macneil 1974, 1978; Goetz and Scott 1981; and Furubotn and Richter 2005, 154–61, 173–90, 291–92. For an overview of recent literature, see Hviid 2000 and, for general discussion of various approaches to contract theory, Masten 2000, especially 32–34 on relational contracting. For the economic principles underlying contract law, see Shavell 2004, 289–385.

15. Goetz and Scott 1981, 1091.

16. See Macneil 1978, 856–62.

17. Goetz and Scott 1981, 1089–90; quotation from 1090.

18. Macneil 1978, 875. Cf. also Goldberg 1976 for a treatment of modern commercial contracts that views the notion of the discrete transaction as inadequate.

19. On the duration of Egyptian farm leases, see Rowlandson 1996, 252–57.

20. For the role that social dependence might play in tenancy relationships, see especially Foxhall 1990 and Capogrossi Colognesi 1995, 194–97 (= 1992–93, 191–93).

21. Bürge 1980, especially 139–54.

22. This, at least, is what the Egyptian evidence tends to tell us: most of the legal disputes surrounding farm tenancy that are preserved in the papyrological record arose when one party, usually the tenant, sought to withdraw from the lease. See Kehoe 1995, and for additional discussion, see the following in this chapter.

23. I discuss this text in greater detail in Kehoe 1997, 203–6. For a different interpretation, see du Plessis 2003, 41–42. Ulpian cites two rescripts in this passage, including one, ascribed to the emperor Antoninus, on a request for a rescript on the basis of the poor crop, and the rescript discussed here. Du Plessis does not attribute this latter rescript to Antoninus Pius.

24. Schwartz 1992a, 273. Cf. Ayres and Gernter 1989, which emphasizes that parties may withhold information when negotiating a contract to gain for themselves a larger share of the reduced proceeds from the contract. This may benefit the party pursuing "strategic incompleteness," but it is not economically efficient.

25. For discussion of the issues surrounding default rules and the difficulties of establishing economically efficient ones, see Ayres and Gertner 1989, especially 92–93, 115–17; Katz 1990, 217; Schwartz 1992a, 272–73; as well as Craswell 2000, which characterizes efficient default rules, sometimes called *market-mimicking default rules*, as the "rules that the parties themselves would have chosen, if they had taken the time to agree explicitly on a rule to govern their relationship" (3).

26. Schwartz 1992a, 1992b.

27. Schwartz 1992a, 282.

28. See Craswell 2000, 9–10. Still less did the Roman courts adopt default rules that required the better-informed party to disclose information to the less-informed party, termed "'information-forcing' or 'penalty' default rules" (5–7).

29. Cf. De Neeve 1983, 312–13, and n. 56, which argues that the tenant could only be entitled to a remission of rent if there had been no failure on his part, that is, if he had not failed to make adequate provision for the renewal of the vines.

30. See Ayres and Gertner 1989.

31. Ellickson 1991 and, more generally, Panther 2000.

32. Mnookin and Kornhauser 1979; cf. also Cooter, Marks, and Mnookin 1982. For discussion of this concept, see Ellickson 1991, 52 and n. 44, as well as Galanter 1981, 8 n. 9, which points out that the phrase was originally coined by Tocqueville. To be sure, Ellickson does not argue that formal legal rules shaped the bargaining among ranchers and farmers in Shasta County; indeed, in arguing against "legal centrism," he sees these groups as bargaining "beyond" the shadow of the law (48). However, Ellickson's own analysis suggests that residents of Shasta County would resort to formal legal remedies when the monetary stakes were high (98–100).

33. Mnookin and Kornhauser 1979, 968.

34. Mnookin and Kornhauser 1979, 997.

35. Cf. Galanter 1981.

36. Galanter 1981, 34.

37. Galanter 1981, 12, 23–24.

38. For full discussion of Columella's prescriptions about farm tenancy, see Scheidel 1994, 84–117.

39. For Columella's aversion to the city tenant, see Scheidel 1994, 112–15, and Garnsey 2000, 705.

40. Kehoe 1988b. For other discussions, see especially De Neeve 1990 and Rosafio 1993.

41. Pliny, *Ep.* 10.8.5: "Agroroum enim, quos in eadem regione possideo, locatio, cum alioqui CCCC excedat, adeo non potest differri, ut proximam putationem novus colonus facere debeat." The term *novus colonus* collectively refers to the various tenants on the estate; see Kehoe 1997, 177–78 n. 93; for different views, see De Neeve 1990, 379–83, 392–93; Scheidel 1994, 65; and Garnsey 2000, 704.

42. For the role of landowners in settling disputes involving their *coloni*, see Krause 1987, 117–18.

43. For the concept of social remissions, see Frier 1989–90, 245–46, and Sitzia 1978, 351–55, on the evidence of Columella and Pliny.

44. On the risks involved in Mediterranean agriculture, see Horden and Purcell 2000, e.g., 178–79, as well as Garnsey 2000, 686–87, and Drexhage, Konen, and Ruffing 2002, 96–100.

45. For the treatment of risk in Roman lease law, see especially Frier 1989–90; Capogrossi Colognesi 1995, 143–99, also published in Capogrossi Colognesi 1992–93, 163–94; De Neeve 1983; and Sitzia 1978, as well as Mayer-Maly 1956, 140–47; Zimmermann 1990, 377–83; and most recently Müller 2002, especially 19–58; and du Plessis 2003, especially 7–47.

46. See Katz 1998, 41–42, and Dahlman 1979. Dahlman defines an externality as "a divergence between private and social cost. We interpret this to mean that when all voluntary contractual arrangements have been entered into by market transactors, there still remain some interactions that ought to be internalized but which the market forces left to themselves cannot cope with" (141). Dahlman critiques the market-failure approach to understanding externalities and argues instead that externalities arise when transaction costs prevent bargaining between parties. To apply this approach to the problem of risk in Roman tenancy, the costs of bargaining, including of acquiring adequate information, represented an impediment to landowners and tenants negotiating an agreement that accounted for the full range of risk that they faced. For discussion of the controversies surrounding the interpretation of externalities, see also Eggertsson 1990, 19, with discussion of the work of A. C. Pigou (*The Economics of Welfare*, 4th ed. [London, 1932]) and other critics of the free market system: "Production and exchange often confer benefits and impose costs upon individuals without involving them in voluntary exchange. If such spillover costs and benefits are ignored, the allocation of resources is suboptimal by the neoclassical criterion." But if transactions costs disappear with zero transaction costs, the problem of externalities also disappears: "No matter how the rights to the various resources are distributed initially, the resources will always end up in their highest valued use, and rational agents will always take spillover costs and benefits into account. The problem of social cost disappears" (Eggertsson 1990,

19). For discussion of various approaches to dealing with externalities, in particular, the challenges posed by the Coase Theorem, see Shavell 2004, 77–109.

47. For risk-reducing strategies in Mediterranean farming, see Horden and Purcell 2000, 175–230, and Gallant 1991, 34–59.

48. See Scott 1990.

49. Posner and Rosenfield 1977, 85–86; cf. the discussion of "efficient breach" in chap. 2 under "Incentives to Cooperate and Resolve Conflicts."

50. Posner and Rosenfield 1977, 89. For another argument in favor of efficiency considerations in judging contract disputes, see Bruce 1982.

51. See Posner and Rosenfield 1977, 87.

52. See especially Schwartz 1992a and 1992b. For additional discussion of the policy issues raised by incomplete contracts, see Schwartz 1998.

53. Posner and Rosenfield 1977, 90–91. For application of this approach to *remissio mercedis* (remission of rent) in Roman law, see Frier 1989–90, 266–67.

54. Horden and Purcell 2000, 197–200.

55. For the legal norms of Egyptian farm leases, see Herrmann 1958; for the grounds to seek a rent abatement, see 161–62.

56. Kaser 1975, 311 n. 28. On emphyteusis, see the discussion in chap. 4 in the text accompanying n. 35.

57. For the Greek law of leasing, see Schultheß 1932 and, for broader discussion, Osborne 1988. I wish to thank Prof. Christian Habicht for references to the Greek texts discussed in this section.

58. This is the case in a lease by the Prasiae deme (*SEG* XXI 644, lines 11–16) and in the lease from the deme of Aixone (*IG* II^2 2492, lines 12–14), a forty-year lease. For leasing by Attic demes, see Whitehead 1986, 152–58.

59. For discussion of this text, see Wilhelm 1935, 189–200.

60. See Frier 1989–90, 259–60, and Müller 2002, 47–58.

61. For this discussion of observable and verifiable information, see Schwartz 1992a, 279–82, 286–87.

62. On this text, see Müller 2002, 57.

63. See Müller 2002, 103–4.

64. I discuss the jurists' treatment of the obligations of landowners and tenants when remissions of rent were granted in Kehoe 1997, 221–34.

65. Papin. apud Ulp. *D.* 19.2.15.4: "Papinianus libro quarto responsorum ait, si uno anno remissionem quis colono dederit ob sterilitatem, deinde sequentibus annis contigit uber[i]tas, nihil obesse domino remissionem, sed integram pensionem etiam eius anni quo remisit exigendam. hoc idem et in vectigalis damno respondit. sed et si verbo donationis dominus ob sterilitatem anni remiserit, idem erit dicendum, quasi non sit donatio, sed transactio. quod tamen, si novissimus erat annus sterilis, in quo ei remiserit? verius dicetur et si superiores uberes fuerunt et scit locator, non deberi eum ad computationem vocari." Frier 1989–90, 253–54 and n. 74, citing additional literature, argues that "someone" (*quis*) refers to an imperial official rather than to a landowner. For discussion of the issues raised in this text, see du Plessis 2003, 36–40.

66. Alexander Severus, *CJ* 4.65.8, to Sabinianus Hyginus: "Licet certis annuis quantitatibus fundum conduxeris, si tamen expressum non est in locatione aut [aut VC cum Graecis, ut PR] mos regionis postulat, ut, si qua labe tempestatis vel alio caeli vitio damna accidissent, ad onus tuum pertinerent, et quae evenerunt sterilitates ubertate

aliorum annorum repensatae non probabuntur, rationem tui iuxta bonam fidem haberi recte postulabis, eamque formam qui ex appellatione cognoscet sequetur." For the most recent treatment of this text, see Müller 2002, 51–53; and du Plessis 2003, 44–46.

67. These two conditions, in fact, may be regarded as tautological, since transaction costs will be zero if property rights are perfectly specified; see the discussion in chap. 1 in the text accompanying n. 8.

68. Schwartz 1992b, 98–99.

69. Cf. Schwartz 1992b, 83–84.

70. For the significance of tenant indebtedness in exacerbating their economic dependence, see Finley 1976b, 115–17, and, for late antiquity, Vera 1997, 214–17.

71. Coriat 1997, 378–79, sees the imperial chancery, especially beginning with the Severans, as working to adapt local legal institutions within the broader conventions of Roman law as it increasingly faced the task of responding to the needs of people in the provinces through the rescript process. Cf. also Kehoe 1997, chap. 4. Vera 1997, 197, argues that the classical contract of *locatio-conductio* (lease-hire) continued to play a role in farm tenancy throughout late antiquity, particularly for the wealthiest class of farm tenants.

72. *CJ* 4.65.8, quoted in n. 66 of this chapter.

73. *CJ* 4.65.18: "With the exception of the time in which the flaw of a poor harvest entered in because of a devouring plague of locusts, the governor of the province will order that the crops of the following period be given to you that it is established were owed to you in accordance with past custom." (Excepto tempore, quo edaci lucustarum pernicie sterilitatis vitium incessit, sequentis temporis fructus, quos tibi iuxta praeteritam consuetudinem deberi constiterit, reddi tibi praeses provinciae iubebit.)

74. On the purposes to which litigants put rescripts, see the discussion in the introduction, in the text accompanying n. 61.

75. *CJ* 4.65.19: "Circa locationes atque conductiones maxime fides contractus servanda est, si nihil specialiter exprimatur contra consuetudinem regionis. quod si alii remiserunt contra legem contractus atque regionis consuetudinem pensiones, hoc aliis praeiudicium non possit adferre." The author of this rescript is likely to be Hermoginianus, Honoré 1994, no. 20.

76. See Furubotn and Richter 2005, 173–88.

77. See Parisi 2000, 607–11.

78. See Williamson 1996, 57, referring to Galanter 1981.

79. If the Roman government sought to foster relational contracts in farm tenancy, however, it did not always succeed, and as we will see, the chancery often had to deal with conflicts arising from tenure arrangements that were adversarial rather than relational.

80. See n. 22 of this chapter. A dispute over back rents resulting from the death of a tenant is recorded in *CJ* 4.65.24, 293. In this case, a lessee had died, but his wife took over the lease. The lessor, who petitioned about the back rents, was instructed to seek these from the heirs of the lessee, and not from the wife, except for that period in which the wife actually held the lease.

81. For the tenant's lack of possession rights, see Köhn 1983, 191–95, as well as Mayer-Maly 1956, 42–60. For the rights of possession of tenants in the later civilian tradition, see Zimmermann 1990, 377–83.

82. *CJ* 4.65.9: "Emptori quidem necesse non est stare [sinere *suppl. Mommsen*] colonum cui prior dominus locavit, nisi ea lege emit. verum si probetur aliquo pacto consensisse, ut in eadem conductione maneat, quamvis sine scripto, bonae fidei iudicio ei quod placuit parere cogitur."

83. Vera 1986, 288 and n. 11, argues that *CJ* 4.65.10 and 4.65.11 refer to large-scale leasing rather than to small-scale tenancy. De Martino 1993, 813 and n. 128, argues that the rescript of Philip suggests the efforts of landowners in the third century to keep tenants against their will, since it refers to previous rescripts on the same issue, "saepe rescriptum est."

84. On *relocatio tacita*, see Ulp. *D.* 19.2.13.11, 32 *ad ed.*; *D.* 19.2.14, 71 *ad ed.*; and Zimmermann 1990, 356–57. I discuss this principle in more detail in Kehoe 1997, 206–9.

85. Valerian, Gallienus, *CJ* 4.65.16: "Legem quidem conductionis servari oportet nec pensionum nomine amplius quam convenit reposci. sin autem tempus, in quo locatus fundus fuerat, sit exactum et in eadem locatione conductor permanserit, tacito consensu eandem locationem una cum vinculo pignoris renovare videtur." The likely author of this rescript is no. 15. (129) in Honoré 1994, who was the secretary for Gallienus in the West. For the process by which local practice might be interpreted in terms of Roman private law, cf. Vera 1997, 197–98 n. 35.

86. Cf. the discussion of Schwartz 1992a, 291–92.

87. See Barzel 2002, 170. This situation is expressed somewhat differently in Schwartz 1992a, 78, which suggests that incomplete contracts impose costs on the state because they lead to disputes and frequently must be adjudicated. In Schwartz's formulation, "the state could increase welfare by supplying solutions to recurrent contracting problems."

88. This principle is developed in Nerat. apud Ulp. *D.* 19.2.19.2, 32 *ad ed.*, on which see Frier 1979.

89. Cf., however, the argument in Jolls 1997, which presents a very different perspective on the relational contract debates. Jolls argues that the parties to a contract may actually benefit from strict enforcement of contract rules, a practice that would rule out future renegotiation. Under conventional doctrine, forced modification of a contract is not allowed, but she argues that strict enforcement of original contract provisions promotes "bilateral commitment," as opposed to individual commitment. Similarly, Baird 1990 argues that a legal obligation to renegotiate in long-term contracts can enable one party to use the courts to take advantage of the other.

90. Williamson 1979. Williamson (234 n.3) defines *opportunism* as follows: "Opportunism is a variety of self-interest seeking but extends self-interest seeking to include self-interest seeking with guile." See also Williamson 1985, 30. For a critique of Williamson's conception of opportunism, see B. Klein 1992.

91. See B. Klein, Crawford, and Alchian 1978, 298, and Furubotn and Richter 2005, 345–46, on the public regulation of contracts.

92. Williamson 1979, 246–47.

93. See B. Klein 1992, with comments by Meckling 1992 and Moore 1992. For detailed discussion of "nonlegal sanctions" in enforcing a variety of legal relationships, see Panther 2000.

94. B. Klein 1992, 155–59.

CHAPTER 4

1. This is one of the chief themes of Lo Cascio 1997a and Rosafio 2002.

2. *CJ* 11.50.1 (addressed to Maximus, Vicarius Orientis): "Quisquis colonus plus a domino exigitur, quam ante consueverat et quam in anterioribus temporibus exactus est, adeat iudicem, cuius primum poterit habere praesentiam, et facinus comprobet, ut ille, qui convicitur amplius postulare, quam accipere consueverat, hoc facere in posterum prohibeatur, prius reddito quod superexactione perpetrata noscitur extorsisse." The interpretation of the term *superexactiones* as referring to rents, as suggested by Goffart 1974, 68–69, and Vera 1997, 205 n. 66, seems much more likely than the alternative that it refers to fiscal imposts. For discussion of the possibilities, see Rosafio 2002, 169–71. For the date, see Seeck 1919, 175.

3. Schwartz 1992a, also discussed in chap. 3 under "Roman Legal Policy and the Relational Contract."

4. Goffart 1974, 68–69 and n. 6.

5. Levy 1951, 5–10. Cf. also Panitschek 1990. Panitschek sees the imperial legislation concerning the colonate as an effort to incorporate within Roman legal norms traditional peregrine systems of land tenure. For the development of vulgar law, see also Kaser 1967, especially 1294–95 on the change from Diocletian to Constantine.

6. *CJ* 11.48.5: "Domini praediorum id quod terra praestat accipiant, pecuniam non requirant, quam rustici optare non audent, nisi consuetudo praedii hoc exigat." For discussion, see Vera 1997, 206 and n. 71; for the date and promulgation, Seeck 1919, 226.

7. For discussion of the limited ability of a sovereign to control contract norms arising from society, see Macneil 1983.

8. On the *longi temporis praescriptio*, see Kaser 1971, 424–25; Schulz 1951, 359–60; and Berger 1953, s.v. "praescriptio longi temporis." The decrees of Septimius Severus and Caracalla first documenting this principle is printed in Oliver 1989, no. 223 A, B (199–200 CE): See also M.*Chr.* 374; *FIRA* I 84, 85; *Sel.Pap.* II 214; Diocletian, *CJ* 7.35.7; and [Paul.] *Sent.* 5.2.3–5. For the circumstances under which this principle was developed, see Nörr 1969 and Coriat 1997, 381–93 (with additional bibliography), which emphasizes the influence of the local Greek practice on the chancery in developing this principle. The term used in the legal sources to describe lawful acquisition is *iustum initium*. For the development of prescriptions in later Roman law, see Levy 1951, 176–94.

9. Nörr 1969, 74–79. For the likelihood of widespread economic effects of the plague across the empire, see Duncan-Jones 1996; Duncan-Jones' assessment is questioned by Greenberg 2003 and Bruun 2003. Scheidel 2002 applies Duncan-Jones' findings and other evidence to argue that the plague fundamentally altered the economy of Egypt and, by implication, of other provinces as well; for this view see also Zelener 2003. Scheidel's interpretation of the evidence from Egypt is questioned by Bagnall 2002; cf. earlier Bagnall 2000.

10. Nörr 1969, 82–84, and Coriat 1997, 328, referring to rescripts of Caracalla cited by Marcian. *D.* 44.3.9, 5 *regul.*, that applied the prescription to movables. Cf. also Hamza 1999, 200–201.

11. Coriat 1997, 382–93.

12. *CJ* 7.36.1: "Diuturnum silentium longi temporis praescriptione corrobatum creditoribus pignus persequentibus inefficacem actionem constituit, praeterquam si

debitores vel qui in iura eorum successerunt obligatae rei possessioni incumbant. ubi autem creditori a possessore longi temporis praescriptio obicitur, personalis actio adversum debitorem salva ei competit." For the authorship of this rescript, see Honoré 1994, no. 12.

13. For tenancy in vulgar Roman law, see Levy 1956, 249–75; cf. Levy 1951, 19–99, for the transformation of Roman principles of ownership in vulgar law.

14. *CJ* 7.30.1: "Qui ex conducto possidet, quamvis corporaliter teneat, non tamen sibi, sed domino rei creditur possidere. neque enim colono vel conductori praediorum longae possessionis praescriptio quaeritur." This text is attributed to Modestinus by Honoré 1994, no. 8.

15. *CJ* 7.32.5 (Diocl., Max., n.d.): "Cum nemo causam sibi possessionis mutare possit proponasque colonum nulla extrinsecus accedente causa ex colendi occasione ad iniquae venditionis vitium esse prolapsum, praeses provinciae inquisita fide veri dominii tui ius convelli non sinet." The date is after Aug. 1, 290, and the author is identified as Arcadius Charisius by Honoré 1994, no. 19, 156–62.

16. For the promulgation of the law, see Seeck 1919, 224.

17. *CJ* 7.39.2 pr.: ". . . eos autem possessores non convenit appellari, qui ita tenent, ut ob hoc ipsum solitam debeant praestare mercedem." For the treatment of *precarii* in this text, see Levy 1956, 259–60, and the discussion in chap. 5. Chastagnol 1982, 317, views the *precarii* as landowners who have turned their land over to powerful protectors, but this interpretation seems at odds with the conflict addressed by the law. On this point see Krause 1987, 260. It is possible that the term *precario possidentes* is simply a general term for people who did not have full possession rights in the law.

18. See *CIL* 8.25902, 4.2–9, discussed in chap. 2 under "Property Rights on North African Imperial Estates" (HM 4.2–9). On the inheritance rights deriving from the *lex Manciana*, see Weßel 2003, 96–97, 115–16.

19. For full discussion of the estate and the documents, see Weßel 2003. This treatment supplants the earlier comprehensive study, Courtois et al. 1952.

20. Mattingly 1989.

21. Weßel 2003, 120; for the strong possibility that Flavius Geminius Catullinus was an emphyteutic possessor of the *fundus Tuletianos*, see 109–13. For the assimilation in late Roman vulgar law of hereditary tenure rights with ownership rights, see Levy 1951, 90–94. For the transfer of rights among such cultivators of land in the Byzantine period, cf. Patlagean 1977, 263–64.

22. *CTh* 5.19.1, 365: "Non dubium est colonis arva, quae subigunt, usque adeo alienandi ius non esse, ut, et si qua propria habeant, inconsultis atque ignorantibus patronis in alteros transferre non liceat."

23. On this point, see Carrié 1983, 233. Cf. also Vera 1997, 203 and n. 60, referring also to *CJ* 1.3.16, 409 (for the author, see Honoré 1998, E18), and *CJ* 1.3.36, 484; *Nov. Val.* 35.3, 6, 452, (452), according to which a *colonus* could not take religious orders without the permission of the landlord. See also the discussion in chap. 5 in the text accompanying n. 34.

24. *CJ* 7.38.2, issued at Constantinople: "Universas terras, quae a colonis dominicis iuris rei publicae vel iuris templorum in qualibet provincia venditae vel ullo alio pacto alienatae sunt, ab his, qui perperam atque contra leges eas detinent, nulla longi temporis praescriptione officiente iubemus restitui, ita ut nec pretium quidem iniquis comparatoribus reposcere liceat." For the authorship, see Honoré 1998, 55–56, E7.

25. For the date, see Seeck 1919, 346. For the authorship, see Honoré 1998, 23–47, W14.

26. For the authorship, see Honoré 1998, 110–12, E22.

27. For the date, see Seeck 1919, 261. For the authorship, see Honoré 1998, 47–48, E3.

28. For the date and authorship, see Honoré 1998, 73–76, E11; Seeck 1919, 279, dates the text to 391.

29. For the authorship, see Honoré 1998, 81–92, E13.

30. "Invaders of other people's property" (possessionis alienae invasores) (*CJ* 8.4.10 pr.). In more general terms, Zeno established a forty-year prescription for claims against the right to possess certain categories of land donated to individuals by the state (*CJ* 11.62.14, 491). On efforts to curtail the forceful takeover of land, see the discussion later this chapter.

31. In the sixth century, Justinian addressed legal issues arising from the customary claims of landowners to collect rents from *coloni,* who for their part might resist such claims and view themselves as landowners in their own right (*CJ* 11.48.20, 529). In another constitution, Justinian excluded emphyteutic possessors, *conductores,* and procurators from any possibility of establishing full rights of ownership over land on the basis of any prescription (*CJ* 7.39.7.7, 525).

32. For the relationship between reducing transaction costs and promoting private ordering, see Williamson 1985, 29.

33. On the "governance" needed to guide private ordering, see Williamson 1985, 30–35. For the contrast between the informal rules that groups use to settle disputes and the formal rules imposed by the courts, see Galanter 1981.

34. Barzel 2002, 186; for the notion of economic rights, see the discussion in chap. 1 in the text accompanying n. 11. For discussion of the Roman law of servitudes for water in agriculture, see Bannon 2001.

35. For a full discussion of this constitution, see Vera 1988, 967–92. Many scholars have seen the *coloni* in the constitutions as occupying their land under the *lex Manciana:* see most recently De Ligt 1998–99, 229–31, and Weßel 2003, 111–13.

36. *CJ* 11.63.1 pr.: "Emphyteuticarios gravant coloni agros praeter consuetudinem usurpantes, quos nullis culturis erudierunt, cum sollemnitas id eos attractare permittat, quod eorum labore vel olivetis est obsitum vel vinetis. sed et inriguas fontium aquas usurpare conantur, quarum fructus solis emphyteuticariis debentur."

37. *CJ* 11.63.1.1–2: "Ideoque placuit, ut deinceps aquarum ius potestasque penes emphyteuticarios permaneant, tantumque ex eis colonis impertiatur, quantum culturis eorum agrorum sufficere manifestum est, quos ipsi colunt. Pro modo autem supefluae inrigationis, quam ultra culturas suas usurpaverint, emphyteuticariis possessoribus pensiones accessionesque praebeant."

38. On the Lamasba inscription, see Shaw 1982.

39. On the gains from "internalizing externalities," see Medema and Zerbe 2000, as well as Allen 2000.

40. *CJ* 4.10.11: "You have been overcome by excessive credulity because you believed that you could demand back from the owner of the property what you have given as a loan to the tenants for their own property; nor does the presence of his [the owner's] business managers help you to obligate him." (Nimia credulitate circumventa

es, quia, quod colonis in rem suam mutuo dedisti, a domino praedii postulare posse credidisti: nec ad eum obligandum actorum ipsius adiuvat te praesentia.)

41. *CJ* 4.65.27: "Si tibi quae pro colonis conducti praedii prorogasti dominus fundi stipulanti dare spopondit, competens iudex reddi tibi iubebit. nam si conventio placiti fine stetit, ex nudo pacto perspicis actionem iure nostro nasci non potuisse."

42. For the *actio quod iussu*, see Kaser 1971, 608, as well as Berger 1953, s.v. "iussum." For the authorship, see Honoré 1998, 243–47, W14.

43. *CJ* 11.57.1: "Grave est et non solum legibus, verum etiam aequitati naturali contrarium, pro alienis debitis alios molestari. idcirco huiusmodi iniquitates contra omnes vicanos perpetrari modis omnibus prohibemus."

44. On mutual sureties, see Mirković 1997, 79–84.

45. On credit for small farmers, see Bagnall 1993a, 73–77.

46. See Finley 1976b.

47. On the use of self-help by creditors in enforcing debts, see Bürge 1980.

48. For the imprisonment of debtors, see Krause 1996, 152–69; for the policy of the Roman government to discourage private prisons, see 59–63.

49. Bagnall 1993a, 73.

50. On these, see Bagnall 1993a, 73; Jördens 1990; and Erdkamp 2005, 120–23.

51. For a basic introduction, with further literature, see Rupprecht 1994, 127.

52. On *pignus*, see Kaser 1971, 457–73; for the *interdictum Salvianum* and the *actio Serviana*, see 472–73. For the postclassical developments, see Kaser 1975, 312–21. Comparable to the pledge, or *pignus*, was another type of real security, called *fiducia cum creditore*. This involved a transfer of ownership to the creditor, although the debtor could continue to hold the property, and the sale of the property in the event of a default on the loan, but this form of pledge had passed out of use by the time of the compilation of the Digest of Justinian. See Kaser 1971, 46–63; 1975, 313; Berger 1953, s.v. "fiducia cum creditore"; and Noordraven 1999, 1–11, 64–65.

53. For discussion of the issues, see Wacke 1998, which critiques M. Kaser, *Studien zum römischen Pfandrecht* (Naples, 1982).

54. Wacke 1998.

55. Kaser 1971, 460–61, 470–71; Wacke 1998, 182–83.

56. Wacke 1998, 201. On these agreements, see also Berger 1953, s.v. "commissoria lex."

57. Wacke 1998, 177, 179, and, earlier, Kaser 1975, 320. For the date, see Seeck 1919, 169.

58. Cf. the appointment of arbitrators (*logothetai*) in a dispute about debts owed in connection with a lease of land belonging to the wealthy Claudia Isidora in Egypt (*P.Oxy.* XIV 1630, lines 11–14, ca. 222); on the texts associated with this woman, see Thomas 2004. Gordian likewise ruled that a creditor could not sell property pledged as security when the debtor offered to make good the debt (*CJ* 8.27.8, 239).

59. The creditor could acquire the property if the debtor sold it as long as there was no deceit (*dolus*) or compulsion (*metus*) (*CJ* 8.27.10.1).

60. Callistr. *D.* 48.7.7, also excerpted in *D.* 4.2.13: ". . . Caesar said: 'Do you think it is only force, if people are injured? Force also exists then, whenever someone demands back what he thinks is owed him without recourse to a judge' . . ." For this text and other efforts of the Roman government to suppress the use of force by landowners

in property disputes, see Krause 1987, 142. For the types of dispute encompassed by this decree, see Bürge 1980, 108–10, and Frier 1980, 83–92, which emphasizes the important role that self-help continued to play in urban tenancy, despite the efforts of the legal authorities to limit its scope.

61. See Ioannatou 2004, for the application of this code in the late Republic.

62. Schultheß 1932, 2126; cf. Todd 1993, 282–83, and, earlier, Lipsius 1966, 947–52.

63. Bürge 1980. At the same time, the Roman government established measures to make sure that sales of property confiscated by the Fiscus to satisfy fiscal debts should be conducted in a lawful and orderly fashion, without graft: see Sirks 1995.

64. *CJ* 4.24.3: "*pigneraticia actione obligatur*" (is obligated by the action on pledge), on which, see the preceding text.

65. Cf. Diocletian's ruling in *CJ* 8.13.11, 293, that a *nominator* needed the governor's authority to exercise the right of *pignus* over the debtor's property.

66. A law of Constantius II also required the sale of property confiscated for fiscal debts to be carried out under the authority of a judge (*CTh* 11.9.2; *CJ* 4.46.3, 337, addressed to the governor of Baetica). For the pledging of property for taxes, cf. Goffart 1974, 34, 43.

67. See Rupprecht 1994, 143–53, for the procedures in Egypt to make a claim against the property of a debtor. In a farm lease, the lessor was allowed to proceed against all of the property of the defaulting tenant, and not just the property that the tenant had brought onto the farm held under lease: see Herrmann 1958, 139–53.

68. Kaser 1971, 530–32.

69. This rescript is also cited in Callistr. *D.* 5.1.37, 5 *cognit.*, where it is ascribed to Hadrian. On this text, see also Krause 1987, 142.

70. Diocletian did allow a just possessor to use force to repel a violent attack on his property (*CJ* 8.4.1, 290). This same principle stands behind a later ruling of Valentinian II, Theodosius, and Arcadius, who granted the right to defend property against illegal incursions by soldiers, who were to be treated as bandits (*CTh* 9.14.2; *CJ* 3.27.1; 3.27.1, 391, issued at Trier).

71. On the interdict *unde vi*, see Kaser 1971, 399; the criminal accusation could be made under the *lex Iulia de vi publica et privata* (the Julian law on public and private force) (222).

72. This case may have some similarities to the efforts of villagers in Egypt to avoid tax liabilities for properties that they claimed two sisters owned: Crook 1995, no. 35, discussed in the introduction in the text accompanying n. 90.

73. The *CTh* version refers to the punishment established by the edict (*poena edicti*), while the *CJ* refers to "statutory punishment" (*poena legitima*). The part of this same law including prescriptions as to how boundary disputes are to be resolved by an *agrimensor* (surveyor) is recorded in *CJ* 3.39.3. The use of compulsion by powerful landowners to take over the land of the less fortunate was a frequent topic of concern for the Church fathers. For discussion of this theme and the efforts of the government to prevent this, see Krause 1987, 295–301, which also cites *Nov. Val.* 8 (440, Ravenna).

74. The constitution was issued to the *comes Hispaniarum* (the governor of the provinces of Spain).

75. For the authorship, see Honoré 1998, 15–87, W2. In the *CJ* version of this law, even the rightful owner who took possession of property by force would lose ownership of the property in dispute, whereas the nonowner who took this step would not only lose the property but also have to pay the value of it. Cf. the constitution of the emperor Zeno (*CJ* 8.4.9, 477), in which the emperor outlined a protocol for determining what the purveyor of *vis* would have to make good if the use of force were detected by a court.

76. Barzel 2002, 175–76. Cf., for the importance of informal means to resolve contract disputes, B. Klein 1992, also discussed in chap. 3 under "Roman Legal Policy and the Relational Contract."

77. *CTh* 4.22.1: "iudicio reservato iustis legitimisque personis, cum valde sufficiat possessionem tenentibus absentium nomine contra praesentium violentiam subveniri."

78. *CTh* 7.20.11: "nihilque illis, qui messium tempus adsolent aucupari, agratici nomine deferatur." For the date, see Seeck 1919, 230.

79. On the second-century North Africa estates, *coloni* would lose their rights to their land if they left it uncultivated for two years, but a formal process involving witnesses was required for the land to be taken over by other cultivators (HM 4.9–22); discussed in chap. 2 in the text accompanying n. 35.

80. On Valentinian II's legislation, see Honoré 1998, 180–83. Cf. the more general principle formulated by Constantine, whereby defendants (it is not clear in what kind of cases) who failed to appear in court within a year would forfeit all their property to the Fiscus—even if they could prove their innocence, they would still forfeit their property (*CTh* 9.1.2; *CJ* 9.40.2, 319).

81. This same dispute may be the subject of two other documents from the archive of Aurelius Adelphios. *CPR* XVIIA 16, 321, concerns unauthorized grazing initiated by Anysios. For the archive of Aurelius Adelphios, see the commentary of Worp 1991.

82. For another ruling on boundary disputes, see Constantine, *CJ* 3.38.4, 330.

83. *CJ* 8.16.7 pr. also mentions equipment used for plowing. In 414, a constitution stated that no equipment used for agriculture could be pledged as security (*CJ* 8.16.8; for the authorship, see Honoré 1998, 237–41, W12). See Kaser 1975, 315 n. 2. The constitution attributed to Constantine may have been issued by Licinius: see Corcoran 1996, 287, no. 5.

CHAPTER 5

1. On this aspect of the late imperial tax system, see especially Carrié 1983, 1997; as well as Vera 1997, 185–86; Whittaker 1997, 296; and Giardina 1997, 322. For a survey of the late Roman rural economy, see Whittaker and Garnsey 1998, as well as A. H. M. Jones 1964, II: 767–823; Marcone 1993; and, for the fifth century and later, Ward-Perkins 2000a, 2000b.

2. On this point, see especially Carrié 1997, 85–96, with discussion of the generally prevailing view of the colonate as a class of farmers. Cf. also Goffart 1974 for a similar conception that the binding of a *colonus* represented a legal rather than an economic status. Gascou 1985, 20–27, emphasizes the public aspect of the obligations of bound *coloni*. For the difficulty of ascertaining the continuity between farm tenants in the early empire and *coloni* in late antique fiscal legislation, see Lo Cascio 1997b, as well as the review by Scheidel 2000 of Lo Cascio 1997a. For discussion of the evolving

situation of farm tenants in late antiquity and the degree to which their situation approximated that of slaves, see Whittaker 1987 and de Ste. Croix 1981, 249–59. Recent studies emphasizing the continuity between the bound colonate and conditions in the early empire include Giliberti 1999 and Rosafio 2002; cf. also the reviews of recent approaches by Marcone 1997 and Giardina 1997.

3. On this question, see, among other works, De Martino 1993, 789–822, and, for the Byzantine Empire, Patlagean 1977, 236–340, especially 271–301.

4. The repeated implementation of laws about *coloni* does not necessarily mean that such laws were ineffective or ignored; rather, it may indicate the imperial government's concern with a particular situation, often in response to requests for intervention from interested parties, including affected landowners; see Harries 1999, 82–88. For a very different view, see MacMullen 1964.

5. Duncan-Jones 1994, 57–59, suggests that tax revenues declined in late antiquity, in part at least because of excessive taxation, which tended to drive marginal lands out of cultivation. It is certainly an important question how large a portion of tax revenue those collecting it, whether private contractors or state officials, kept for themselves. For additional discussion of the late antique tax burden, see Krause 1987, 308–31, especially 308–15, and Carrié 1993b, 767–70. Both authors are skeptical that the tax burden imposed on farmers in late antiquity was substantially higher than in the early empire. For the difficulties in assessing this tax burden, cf. Whittaker 1980a and Bowman 1980. According to MacMullen 1988, 41–42, the problem was a redistribution of the tax burden onto the less wealthy, as the result of the increasingly chaotic and corrupt collection of taxes; cf. MacMullen 1987.

6. See Neesen 1980; Brunt 1990; and Duncan-Jones 1990, 187–98. For a broad survey of Roman taxation and state expenditures, see also Duncan-Jones 1994, 3–63. For taxation in kind, see Erdkamp 2005, 219–25. For the methods used to collect taxes in the Roman Empire, cf. Aubert 1994, 325–47.

7. See Howgego 1992, 22–24.

8. Wallace 1938, 11–30, 47–76. Grain land was also subject to some additional payments in kind and in cash.

9. For the development of the late imperial fiscal system, see especially A. H. M. Jones 1964, I: 411–69; Carrié 1993a, especially 292–301; 1993b. For discussion of the *iugum* and the difficulties involved in imposing a uniform standard of taxation in the empire, see Duncan-Jones 1990, 199–210. For a recent treatment, especially of fiscal issues involving Egypt, see Bagnall 1993a, 153–60. See also Whittaker and Garnsey 1998, 281–85, and, earlier, Krause 1987, 171–72, on the tax liability of landowners.

10. See Banaji 2001, 190–212; 1997. For a somewhat different perspective, see Whittaker and Garnsey 1998, 287–94, which argues that the Roman government as a matter of policy strengthened the position of large landowners against their labor force. In Banaji's view, the late antique legislators were concerned largely with wage laborers rather than with farm tenants, as late antique landowners increasingly exploited this former group as the labor force on their estates. For a similar view, see Sirks 1993. For a very different assessment of the likely reaction of landowners to imperial fiscal legislation, see Goffart 1974, 85–86.

11. Banaji 1999.

12. For the binding of farmers in Egypt to their village of origin in the early empire, see Krause 1987, 157–58.

13. On the tax collectivities on the estate of Appianus, see Rathbone 1991, 121–25, 404–7. See also Aubert 1997 and Sirks 1997 for discussion of the role of landowners in organizing the performance of liturgies.

14. For this interpretation, see Carrié 1997, 104–18. Rosafio 2002, 177–214, argues that the *origo* of the *coloni* established their fiscal obligations.

15. See the discussion in chap. 4 under "Legal Issues Arising from Long-Term Tenancy Arrangements."

16. See, e.g., Carrié 1983. Goffart 1974 argues that the binding of *coloni* began later in the fourth century, as the method of assessing taxation on the basis of *capita* as notional tax units was discarded and replaced by a tax liability entirely based on the land.

17. For discussion of the controversies surrounding the interpretation of this constitution, see Rosafio 2002, 159–60; cf. Safrai 1994, 328.

18. As Krause 1987, 168 n. 65, argues, with discussion of other literature, this passage does refer to bound *coloni*; for a different view see Goffart 1974, 70–75, which argues that the *colonus* was envisioned as remaining free of any tie to a landlord but was not free to leave his *origo* (village of origin), where he continued to have tax liability. But this conclusion is based on an unconvincing interpretation of the term *iuris alieni*, which he views as referring to an ordinary contractual relationship with another landowner.

19. For the law and its date, see Seeck 1919, 240.

20. *CJ* 11.48.8 (discussed later in the chapter) was issued at the same time to the praetorian prefect Probus, and *CJ* 6.3.13 is from the same law: see Seeck 1919, 240. For the date of *CJ* 11.51.1, see Seeck 1919, 271; for the authorship, see Honoré 1998, 54–55, E6. *CJ* 11.59.7 seems to be from the same law; see *CJ* app. crit. ad loc.

21. For identification of the author, see Honoré 1998, 221–25, W5.

22. On the laws discussed in this paragraph and their connection with the binding of *coloni* as a phenomenon of the later fourth century, see Goffart 1974, 84–90. The process of binding *coloni* can also be seen in the imperial government's policy of confiscating land from certain defeated tribes and making the tribesmen *coloni* of new Roman landowners (*CTh* 5.6.3, 409). The newly established *coloni* would remain bound to the land. On this constitution, see Rosafio 2002, 166–67, 205–6.

23. For additional discussion of this text, see the discussion in chap. 1 in the text accompanying n. 34.

24. *CJ* 11.55.1 is addressed as a letter to a Charisius. *CJ* 9.41.9, 290, is addressed to Charisius as governor of Syria. On this text, cf. Goffart 1974, 47–48, which argues that the *plebs rustica* (rural common people) was being offered an incentive to register for taxes to avoid extra public liturgies.

25. *CTh* 8.5.1: ". . . culturae terrae inservientes." This measure was one of many aimed at curbing abuse of the *cursus publicus*: see Kolb 2000, 117–22. For the concern of the late imperial government for protecting weaker parties against the stronger in courts of law, see Harries 1999, 44–45, and, more generally, Frakes 2001, as well as Lenski 2002, 272–86, on the efforts of the emperor Valens to eliminate corruption.

26. In general on the efforts of emperors in the later Roman Empire to maintain a fair tax system and to protect smaller farmers against depredations by governmental officials and influential landowners, see Krause 1987, 315–27, and MacMullen 1987.

27. For identification of the author, see Honoré 1998, 237–41, W12. *CTh* 7.8.1 and *CJ* 11.59.13 apparently belong to the same law: see Seeck 1919, 326. Cf. also *CJ*

8.16.8, 422, in which Honorius deemed unlawful the seizure of any movable property used in agriculture (also discussed in chap. 4).

28. The author of this constitution was Sallustius (E21), according to Honoré 1998, 106–10.

29. Consistent with this principle, the constitution rescinded sales of property by *curiales* in the province of Osroene and provided for the return of the purchase price with consideration for expenses that the purchaser may have encountered in interest payments or in improvements to the property. On the capacity of *curiales* to alienate property, see Horstkotte 1988, 102–4, and, earlier, Wacke 1980, 580–81. For the authorship of *CTh* 12.3.1, see Honoré 1998, 54–55, E6.

30. For the date, see Seeck 1919, 175.

31. For the date, see Seeck 1919, 202.

32. For the law, see Seeck 1919, 240. For discussion of the restrictions imposed by these two laws, see Goffart 1974, 77–80. For a modest loosening of these restrictions, see the following in this chapter.

33. On the *longi temporis praescriptio*, see chap. 4 under "Legal Order and Traditional Tenure Arrangements."

34. See the discussion in chap. 4 in the text accompanying n. 23.

35. On conventional tenancy in the later Roman Empire, see Vera 1997 and, earlier, Kaser 1975, 308–9, 400–408: classical short-term leasing declined in importance in the later empire, especially in the West, but it survived in the East, particularly in Egypt. On Egypt, cf. Carrié 1983, 231–32, and Kaser 1975, 406. It seems likely that short-term leasing represented one system of exploiting the estate documented in the fourth-century account book from Kellis in the Dakhleh Oasis (Egypt): see Bagnall et al. 1997 and Kehoe 1999.

36. Levy 1956, 251–52.

37. Levy 1956, 249–75; Kaser 1975, 407; and Steinwenter 1954, 1821–25.

38. For the date, see Seeck 1919, 241. For discussion, see Carrié 1997, 100–101, and on this text, see Vera 1997, 212–13 and n. 101, with additional bibliography; cf. Rosafio 2002, 183 n. 13.

39. For the date, see Seeck 1919, 175.

40. For the date, see Seeck 1919, 167.

41. On the cultivators of public land (*ge demosie*) in Roman Egypt, see the discussion in chap. 2 under "The Cultivation of Public Land in Egypt."

42. For discussion of this text, see Rosafio 2002, 148–49.

43. Carrié 1983, 231–33, seeks to refute the time-honored supposition that the binding of *coloni* involved fixed tenure. But even if the laws attaching *coloni* to the land did not guarantee their right to remain there, the recognition of customary rents as legally enforceable indicates that bound *coloni* retained rights to the land they cultivated.

44. The term *adscripticii*, modifying *coloni* in the text and referring to *coloni* and householders contractually bound to a landowner, is likely to be interpolated, since this term was used only in the East: see Rosafio 2002, 182, with other discussions. For the date, see Seeck 1919, 226. *CJ* 10.32.29, concerning the status of children with mothers who are *inquilinae* on imperial property and with decurion fathers, seems to be from the same law.

45. See Rosafio 2002, 186–88, and for the law and the date, see Seeck 1919, 232; the years 370 and 373 are also possible.

46. See Rosafio 2002, 197–98. The fines were six ounces of gold if the *colonus* was private and one pound of gold if the *colonus* came from an imperial estate. Cf., for the same law but applied only to imperial *coloni* *CJ* 11.64.2. For other texts connected with this law, see Seeck 1919, 271; for discussion of the authorship, see Honoré 1998, 54–55, E6.

47. For the date, see Seeck 1919, 281. Honoré 1998, 73 n. 174, dates it to 393–95; for the authorship, see Honoré 1998, 73–76, E11. Settlement in Thrace was apparently organized around autonomous villages: Giliberti 1999, 105.

48. For the authorship, see Honoré 1998, 221–25, W5.

49. For discussion of the authorship, see Honoré 1998 225–27, W6. As Goffart 1974, 79 n. 40, points out, referring also to *Nov. Val.* 35.18 (452; for the authorship, see Honoré 1998, 271–74, W19), the government was compelled to reassure landowners that they could transfer *coloni* within their own estates; see also Krause 1987, 266–67 and n. 173.

50. On the likely terms under which the *coloni* in this constitution cultivated their land, see Vera 1997, 210. For the date, see Seeck 1919, 133; cf. Honoré 1998, 52 n. 237, which views the date uncertain. The likely author is Honoré's E5, 52–53.

51. See Barzel 1989, 33–38.

52. Barzel 1989, 33–38. For the conditions under which sharecropping can involve cooperative investment, see Cheung 1969 and Kehoe 1988a, chap. 5. For the likelihood that sharecropping was a widespread tenancy arrangement in late antiquity, see Vera 1997, 213–15, 220–23.

53. See Whittaker 1997, 305–7, as well as Vera 1997, 200.

54. This letter is in the collection published by Divjak 1981.

55. See Patlagean 1977, 314, for the concern of the Byzantine government about such abuses by soldiers.

56. *PL* 56, 868B: "clerics should not seek their livelihood in any disgraceful and dishonest business" (nec ullo turpi negotio et inhonesto victum quaerant). The same prohibition is expressed in canon 3 of the Council of Chalcedon in 488 (*PL* 84, 166D–67A). Similarly, in canon 5 (*PL* 56, 865B–C), clerics are prohibited from accepting interest. On the prohibition to become *conductores*, see Levy 1956, 254 and n. 494, and Kaser 1975, 402 and n. 13.

57. On the efforts of the Roman government to inhibit the movement of *coloni*, see Krause 1987, 167–83.

58. On the author of this law, the quaestor Felix, see Honoré 1998, 219–20, W4.

59. For discussion of the presumed activities of the *coloni* in this law, see Carrié 1997, 132–33; Rosafio 2002, 189–92; and, earlier, Goffart 1974, 79–80.

60. This constitution was issued at Milan in 396: Seeck 1919, 288.

61. The law did recognize the rights of the landowner who took in *coloni* (*CTh* 4.23.1; *CJ* 11.48.14, 400). To address disputes between a landowner who is defined a good-faith possessor of the *coloni* in question and another party asserting rights over the *coloni*, the emperors Honorius and Arcadius provided the former landowner with the legal protection of possession before the status of the *coloni* was adjudicated. A good-faith possessor enjoyed possession over the property in question, but his or her title to the property might be defective: see Nicholas 1962, 125. Cf. Kaser 1971, 384–400, on possession, and 422–23, on *bona fides*.

62. On this problem, see Whittaker 1987, 102.

63. On imperial legislation in response to petitions from concerned landowners, see Harries 1999, 47–53. This was a practice that the senatorial aristocracy in principle opposed; thus when presented with the Theodosian Code, the senate requested that the emperor not legislate in response to *preces*, which tended to threaten the security of landowners (66).

64. As Krause 1987, 165–66, suggests, in connection with efforts to restrict the movements of slaves, the capacity of the state to accomplish this purpose was limited, and only wealthier landowners were likely to have had the resources to track down fugitive slaves.

65. See Harries 1999, 82–88, and n. 4 of this chapter.

66. For this interpretation, see Carrié 1997, 108; for discussion of this law, see also Goffart 1974, 75–76.

67. This modification in the assessment of taxes took place ca. 370–400; see Carrié 1983, 220–25.

68. For discussion of the authorship of this law, see Honoré 1998, 243–47, W14.

69. This law appears to be part of the same constitution addressed to Vincentius, praetorian prefect of Gaul, in *CJ* 11.48.13, discussed in the preceding text: see Seeck 1919, 300, and Honoré 1998, 225 n. 178. For its authorship, see Honoré 1998, 225–27, W6.

70. For discussion of this law, see Krause 1987, 182–83. The emperor Valentinian III extended the principle of the thirty-year period to *coloni* and other groups on imperial estates: *Nov. Val.* 27.4, 449, discussed by Krause 1987, 183. This same emperor also confronted the problem of establishing which landowners could exercise rights over *coloni* who shifted their residence frequently to avoid becoming attached to the land: *Nov. Val.* 31, 451, discussed by Krause 1987, 178, 277. For the authorship of these laws, see Honoré 1998, 271–74, W10.

71. The law of Anastasius is also quoted by Justinian: *CJ* 11.48.23.1. For the laws of Anastasius and Justinian, see Carrié 1997, 121–28. For the controversies surrounding the meaning of the term *adscripticii* and the distinction between these people and other *coloni*, see De Martino 1993, 798–803.

72. On this law, see Vera 1997, 205. In a previous constitution, Justinian had ruled that the sons of *coloni* who remained on the land cultivating it could not establish their freedom under the thirty-year prescription (*CJ* 11.48.22.3–5, 531).

73. For this concern of the imperial government, cf. Whittaker and Garnsey 1998, 291, 300, 309–11, as well as Harries 1999, 78 and n. 5, and Patlagean 1977, 288–92. For efforts to control *patrocinium*, see also Sirks 1997; Carrié 1997, 118–29; Giliberti 1999, 123–29; and Grey and Parkin 2003. Frakes 2001, 156–62, discusses the connection between this practice and the evolution of the office of the *defensor civitatis*.

74. In general on *patrocinium*, see especially Krause 1987. Krause is skeptical that in late antiquity landowners were able to extend their holdings substantially through the recruitment of small farmers and thereby to threaten imperial tax revenues. See also Whittaker and Garnsey 1998, 309–11, and, for the relative advantages offered to peasant cultivators from this institution, de Ste. Croix 1981, 224–25. On *paramone* contracts, see Jördens 1990, 284–95; cf. Kaser 1975, 405.

75. Salv., *De Gub. Dei* V 38: ". . . [pauperes] tradunt se ad tuendum protegendumque maioribus, dedicitios se divitum faciunt et quasi in ius eorum dicionemque trascendunt . . ." This passage is quoted by Ruggini 1995, 27 n. 37. For full discussion

of Salvian and the relevance of his writing for late antique agrarian conditions, see Krause 1987, 233–331, as well as Carrié 1997, 93. The pauperization of farmers at the hands of wealthy landowners was a common theme among bishops: see Marcone 1993, especially 829–36.

76. These constitutions include *CTh* 12.1.146, 395 (Milan); *CTh* 11.24.3, 395 (applying to Egypt); *CTh* 11.24.4; *CTh* 11.24.5, 399; *CTh* 11.24.6, 415—and, earlier, *CTh* 11.24.1, 360, and *CTh* 11.24.2, 368—as well as *CJ* 11.54.1, 468; *CJ* 11.56.1, 468; and *CJ* 10.19.8. All but the first were promulgated in the East. The last three texts are all from the same law: Seeck 1919, 415; cf. Krause 1987, 250–52.

77. Harries 1999 and Brown 1992, 11, on the greater availability of courts resulting from Diocletian's subdivision of the provinces into smaller administrative units. Krause 1987, 34–50, discusses the widespread perception in late antiquity that the rich and powerful enjoyed a dominant advantage in court cases. But in Krause's view such perceptions should not lead to the conclusion that the courts did not dispense justice in accordance with the law. Indeed, the integrity of the courts was bolstered by closely enforced procedural rules and a system of appointing advocates (49, citing other literature).

78. For the difficulties in maintaining productivity with *coloni* bound to the land, cf. De Martino 1993, 814–19, which describes a "black market" for *coloni* (814).

79. For full discussion of the text, see Lepelley 1989, 240–51; cf. also Rosafio 2002, 208–11.

80. On this text and its implications for the relationships between landowners and *coloni*, see Vera 1997, 202–3, as well as Carrié 1997, 144–46. For the date, see Seeck 1919, 291; cf. *CTh* 5.19.2. For the authorship, see Honoré 1998, 81–92, E13, which dates the law between Mar. 25, 396, and Jan. 9, 397 (86 n. 102).

81. For the author, Honoré's W6, see n. 49 of this chapter.

82. See Carrié 1997, 85–96, for the metaphorical use of slave terms in these texts, which should not be taken to imply that being a bound *colonus* created a specific personal status. Cf. also de Ste. Croix 1981, 222–24, 252, which argues that the use of "slave" terminology indicates the abasement of the peasant population in the Roman Empire. Goffart 1974, 80–84, argues that the *coloni* envisioned in this law occupied a much less free status than they had earlier in the fourth century: Goffart sees this law as indicating the development of the bound colonate.

83. For the social influence of landowners over *coloni* and its limits, see Krause 1987, 88–155.

84. *Coloni* were likewise able to bring criminal charges against their landlords (*CJ* 11.50.2.4): "Sed ut in causis civilibus huiusmodi hominum generi adversus dominos vel patronos et aditum intercludimus et vocem negamus exceptis superexactionibus, in quibus retro principes facultatem eis super hoc interpellandi praebuerunt, ita in criminum accusatione quae publica est non adimitur eis propter suam suorumque iniuriam experiendi licentia."

85. Much later, in several constitutions, Justinian maintained the rights of *coloni* to sue their landowners over the rent (*CJ* 11.48.23.2, 531–34; discussed in the text accompanying n. 72 of this chapter) and to dispute the right of landowners to collect rent in the first place (*CJ* 11.48.20, 529). See also Krause 1987, 95–96, 110–11, and Vera 1997, 202–3, 205, on the capacity of *coloni* to proceed in court against their landowners.

86. For the authorship, see Honoré 1998, 54–55, E6.

87. For discussion of the idea that widespread absentee landownership contributed to a decline in late antique agriculture, see Krause 1987, 152–55.

88. For the problem of protecting tenants against exploitation by their landowners when they had made "specific investments" in their farms, see the discussion in chap. 3 under "Security of Tenure and Roman Legal Policy." Williamson 1985, 85–130, discusses the need to create governance structures to manage specific investments as a factor influencing vertical integration of firms. This can be applied to agriculture in the Roman Empire: landowners might be led to consolidate holdings farmed by tenants and integrate a farming operation if doing so lessened the costs of overseeing and enforcing the investments that the tenants made in their farms. Such large estates as that of Appianus in the third-century Fayum in Egypt or that of the house of the Apiones in sixth-century Oxyrhynchus were able to integrate production among numerous small parcels because the scale of ownership presented the landowners with options to control costs not available to smaller landowners.

89. On the concern of the imperial authorities and Church fathers about checking the power of estate managers, see Krause 1987, 149–51. In particular on Ambrose of Milan's concern, see Ruggini 1995, especially 96–98.

90. On this speech and the judicial activities of the Roman military in Syria, see Liebeschuetz 1972, 192–208; Pollard 2000, 86–96; as well as Krause 1987, 83–89, 112. For economic conditions in fourth-century Antioch, see Liebeschuetz 1972, 40–100, especially 43–48 for Libanius' own finances, and 61–73 on the likely conditions under which the farmers mentioned in this oration cultivated their land. For the possibility that *curiales* profited from collecting taxes in the way that Libanius describes, see Corbier 1991, with discussion of this speech on 232.

91. See Brown 1982, 115–30, 153–65, republications of Brown 1971, 1976.

92. For a similar assessment, see C. Kelly 2004, 169–71. As Krause 1987, 88–89, suggests, Libanius saw serving as his tenants' patron as part of his role as landowner; cf. MacMullen 1988, 169.

93. Grey and Parkin 2003, 296.

94. On the imbalance of the tax system, see A. H. M. Jones 1964, I: 464–65: the only major tax collected on trades and industries in late antiquity was the *collatio lustralis* (the five-year collection), assessed on the persons (including slaves and family members) and capital of *negotiatores* (business people) and paid to the *sacrae largitiones* (the office of imperial largerse) every five years in the fourth century and apparently every four years in the fifth century (discussed by A. H. M. Jones 1964, I: 431–32). This tax may have been burdensome on many of those required to pay it: de Ste. Croix 1981, 272.

95. See Woolf 1998, 148–68.

96. The use of wage labor in late antiquity is one of the principal emphases of Banaji 2001. Tenancy also played a significant role in the financial affairs of the Apiones: see Hickey 2001, 75–136. For wage contracts from late antique Egypt, see Jördens 1990.

97. Vera 1992–93. Cf. de Ste. Croix 1981, 226–39; Whittaker 1982; 1987.

98. For the expansion of olive culture in late antique Syria, see Tchalenko 1953, 377–438, discussed in Pollard 2000, 201–3, 232–37, with additional bibliography.

Whittaker 1976 is justified in its skepticism that the third and fourth centuries were characterized by widespread abandonment of land and a collapse of agriculture.

99. Banaji 2001. The funds that these landowners invested were gained partly through the profits of collecting taxes. It is not clear that this transfer of wealth promoted economic growth: see Kehoe 2003.

100. On informal means of settling disputes in late antiquity and the role of bishops as judges, see the discussion in the introduction, in the text accompanying n. 68. For the economic significance of arbitration over formal means of settling disputes in court, see Barzel 2002, 171–76.

CONCLUSION

1. For discussion of the distribution of land in the Roman Empire based on the alimentary inscriptions and other sources, see Duncan-Jones 1990, 121–42; for land distribution at the village level in Egypt, see n. 4 of this conclusion.

2. For the importance of distributional considerations when moving toward seemingly more efficient allocations of resources, see Calabresi 1991.

3. See Banaji 2001, 146–47, 192–94, and Kehoe 2003.

4. Bagnall 1992, 137–39, estimates that villagers owned roughly two-thirds of the arable land in the fourth-century Hermopolite nome. For the Oxyrhynchite nome during the Principate, Rowlandson 1996, 124, without having comparable figures, judges that metropolitans owned a substantial portion of village land; cf. Sharp 1999, 172, for the village of Theadelphia in the Fayum during the second century, where most households owned at least some land. In sixth-century Aphrodito in Egypt, Keenan 2000, 635, emphasizes that there was a "core" of small landowners. For discussion of other evidence for the distribution of land in Roman Egypt, see Bagnall 1993a, 148–53; 1995, 75–80.

5. For the role that favorable terms of land tenure might play in keeping wealth in the hands of peasant cultivators, cf. Engels 1990. For rural industries, see Whittaker 1990, reprinted in Whittaker 1993. Poblome 2004, 501, emphasizes the importance of agricultural prosperity for the production of textiles and ceramics. For the role played by rural labor in the manufacturer of ceramics and other products, see Erdkamp 2005, 81–86, 318–21. De Ste. Croix 1981, 259–69, argues that the maintenance of a viable peasantry could promote military security by facilitating the recruitment of soldiers.

6. Deng 2003.

7. Cf. E. L. Jones 1988, 62–63.

Bibliography

Abbreviated titles of classics journals

ANRW	*Aufstieg und Niedergang der römischen Welt*	JESHO	*Journal of the Economic and Social History of the Orient*
AntAfr	*Antiquités africaines*	JRA	*Journal of Roman Archaeology*
APF	*Archiv für Papyrusforschung*	JRS	*Journal of Roman Studies*
ARID	*Analecta Romana Instituti Danici*	MBAH	*Münsterische Beiträge zur antiken Handelsgeschichte*
BAR	*British Archaeological Reports*		
BASP	*Bulletin of the American Society of Papyrologists*	PTA	*Papyrologische Texte und Abhandlungen*
BCH	*Bulletin de correspondence hellénique*	RE	*Realencyclopädie der Altertumswissenschaft*
BEFAR	*Bibliographie de l'École Française d' Athènes et de Rome*	REA	*Revue des études anciennes*
		ZPE	*Zeitschrift für Papyrologie und Epigraphik*
BIDR	*Bulletino dell'Istituto di Diritto romano*	ZRG	*Zeitschrift der Savigny-Stiftung für Rechtsgeschichte (Romanistiche Abteilung)*
CRAI	*Comptes rendus de l'Académie des Inscriptions et Belles Lettres*		

Abbott, F. F., and A. C. Johnson. 1926. *Municipal Administration in the Roman Empire*. Princeton.

Alchian, A. A. 1950. Uncertainty, Evolution, and Economic Theory. *Journal of Political Economy* 58 (3): 211–21.

Allen, D. W. 2000. Transaction Costs. In Bouckaert and De Geest 2000, I: 893–926.

Alpers, M. 1995. *Das nachrepublikanische Finanzsystem: Fiscus und Fisci in der frühen Kaiserzeit*. Untersuchungen zur antiken Literatur und Geschichte 45. Berlin and New York.

Alston, L. J., S. K. Datta, and J. B. Nugent. 1984. Tenancy Choice in a Competitive Framework with Transaction Costs. *Journal of Political Economy* 92 (6): 1121–33.

Amouretti, M.-C., and J.-P. Brun, eds. 1993. *La production du vin et de l'huile en Méditerrannée*. BCH Suppl. 26. Paris.
Ando, C. 2000. *Imperial Ideology and Provincial Loyalty in the Roman Empire*. Berkeley and Los Angeles.
Andreau, J. 2004. Sur les choix économiques des notables romains. In Andreau et al. 2004, 71–85.
———. 2005. La modernité du domaine d'Appianus. *Topoi Orient-Occident* 12–13: 305–9.
Andreau, J., J. France, and S. Pittia, eds. 2004. *Mentalités et choix économiques des Romains*. Ausonius Éditions, Scripta Antiqua 7. Paris and Bordeaux.
Andreau, J., and J. Maucourant. 1999. À propos de la "rationalité économique" dans l'antiquité gréco-romaine: Une interprétation des thèses de D. Rathbone [1991]. *Topoi orient-occident* 9 (1): 48–102.
Aubert, J.-J. 1994. *Business Managers in Ancient Rome: A Social and Economic Study of Institores, 200 B.C.–A.D. 250*. Leiden.
———. 1997. Liturgie, lavoro coatto e colonato nell'Egitto tardoromano. In Lo Cascio 1997a, 281–94.
Ayres, I., and R. Gertner. 1989. Filling Gaps in Incomplete Contracts: An Economic Theory of Default Rules. *Yale Law Journal* 99 (1): 87–130.
Bagnall, R. S. 1992. Landholding in Late Roman Egypt: The Distribution of Wealth. *JRS* 82: 128–49.
———. 1993a. *Egypt in Late Antiquity*. Princeton.
———. 1993b. Managing Estates in Roman Egypt: A Review Article. *BASP* 30: 127–35.
———. 1995. *Reading Papyri, Writing Ancient History*. London and New York.
———. 2000. *P.Oxy.* 4527 and the Antonine Plague in Egypt: Death or Flight? *JRA* 13: 288–92.
———. 2002. The Effects of Plague: Model and Evidence. *JRA* 15: 114–20.
Bagnall, R. S., with contributions from C. A. Hope, R. G. Jenkins, A. J. Mills, J. L. Sharpe III, U. Thanheiser, and G. Wagner. 1997. *The Kellis Agricultural Account Book (P.Kell. IV Gr. 96)*. Oxford.
Baird, D. G. 1990. Self-Interest and Cooperation in Long-Term Contracts. *Journal of Legal Studies* 19: 583–96.
Banaji, J. 1997. Lavoratori liberi e residenza coatta: il colonato romano in prospettiva storica. In Lo Cascio 1997a, 253–80.
———. 1999. Agrarian History and the Labour Organisation of Byzantine Large Estates. In Bowman and Rogan 1999, 193–216.
———. 2000. State and Aristocracy from the Late Empire to Byzantium. In Lo Cascio and Rathbone 2000, 92–99.
———. 2001. *Agrarian Change in Late Antiquity: Gold, Labour and Aristocratic Dominance*. Oxford.
Banerjee, A. V., P. J. Gertler, and M. Ghatak. 2002. Empowerment and Efficiency: Tenancy Reform in West Bengal. *Journal of Political Economy* 110 (2): 239–80.
Bannnon, C. J. 2001. Servitudes for Water Use in the Roman Suburbium. *Historia* 50: 34–52.
Barzel, Y. 1989. *Economic Analysis of Property Rights*. Cambridge.

———. 2002. *A Theory of the State: Economic Rights, Legal Rights, and the Scope of the State*. Cambridge.

Becker, G. S. 1992. Comments. In Werin and Wijkander 1992, 66–71.

Berger, A. 1953. *An Encyclopedic Dictionary of Roman Law*. Transactions of the American Philosophical Society, n.s. vol. XLIII, pt. 2. Philadelphia. Repr., 1980.

Boserup, E. 1965. *The Conditions of Agricultural Growth: The Economics of Agrarian Change under Population Pressure*. Chicago.

Bouckaert, B., and G. De Geest, eds. 2000. *Encyclopedia of Law and Economics*. 5 vols. Cheltenham, UK, and Northampton, MA. On-line edition (1999): http://users.ugent.be/~gdegeest/.

Bowersock, G. W. 1983. *Roman Arabia*. Cambridge, MA.

Bowman, A. K. 1980. The Economy of Egypt in the Earlier Fourth Century. In King 1980, 23–40.

Bowman, A. K., P. Garnsey, and D. Rathbone, eds. 2000. *The Cambridge Ancient History*. 2d ed. Vol. XI, *The High Empire, A.D. 70–192*. Cambridge.

Bowman, A. K., and D. Rathbone. 1992. Cities and Administration in Roman Egypt. *JRS* 82: 107–27.

Bowman, A. K., and E. Rogan, eds. 1999. *Agriculture in Egypt from Pharaonic to Modern Times*. Proceedings of the British Academy 96. Oxford.

Brenner, R. 1976. Agrarian Class Structure and Economic Development in Pre-industrial Europe. *Past and Present* 70: 30–75.

———. 1982. The Agrarian Roots of European Capitalism. *Past and Present* 97: 16–113.

Brown, P. 1982. *Society and the Holy in Late Antiquity*. Berkeley and Los Angeles. Including republications of P. Brown, The Rise and Function of the Holy Man in Late Antiquity, *JRS* 71 (1971): 80–101, and P. Brown, Town, Village and the Holy Man: The Case of Syria, in *Assimilation et résistance à la culture gréco-romaine dans le monde ancien*, ed. D. M. Pippidi, 213–20 (Bucharest, 1976).

———. 1992. *Power and Persuasion in Late Antiquity: Towards a Christian Empire*. Madison.

Bruce, C. J. 1982. An Economic Analysis of the Impossibility Doctrine. *Journal of Legal Studies* 11: 311–32.

Brunt, P. A. 1966. The "Fiscus" and Its Development. *JRS* 56: 75–91.

———. 1990/1981. The Revenues of Rome (review of Neesen 1980). In *Imperial Themes*, 326–53, 531–39. Oxford. Revised version of *JRS* 71 (1981): 161–72.

Bruun, C. 2003. The Antonine Plague in Rome and Ostia. *JRA* 16: 426–34.

Bürge, A. 1980. Vertrag und personale Abhängigkeiten im Rom der späten Republik und der frühen Kaiserzeit. *ZRG* 97: 105–56.

———. 1995. Zum Edikt de edendo: Ein Beitrag zur Struktur des römischen Zivilprozesses. *ZRG* 112: 1–50.

Burton, G. P. 1993. Provincial Procurators and Public Provinces. *Chiron* 23: 13–28.

———. 2000. The Resolution of Territorial Disputes in the Provinces of the Roman Empire. *Chiron* 30: 195–215.

Calabresi, G. 1991. The Pointlessness of Pareto: Carrying Coase Further. *Yale Law Journal* 100: 1211–37.

Calabresi, G., and A. D. Melamed. 1972. Property Rules, Liability Rules, and Inalienability: One View of the Cathedral. *Harvard Law Review* 85 (6): 1089–1128. Excerpted in Katz 1998, 103–15.

Cameron, A., B. Ward-Perkins, and M. Whitby, eds. 2000. *The Cambridge Ancient History*. 2d ed. Vol. XIV, *Late Antiquity: Empire and Successors, A.D. 425–600*. Cambridge.

Campbell, B. 2000. *The Writings of the Roman Land Surveyors: Introduction, Text, Translation and Commentary*. Journal of Roman Studies Monograph 9. London.

Capogrossi Colognesi, L. 1986. Grandi proprietari, contadini e coloni nell'Italia Romana (I–II d.C.). In Giardina 1986, 326–65, 703–23.

———. 1992–93. Il regime degli affitti agrari. *Scienze dell'antichità, Storia, Archeologia, Antropologia* 6–7: 163–253.

———. 1995. *Ai margini della proprietà fondiaria*. Rome.

———. 1997. Lavoro agricolo e struture fondiarie. In Lo Cascio 1997a, 27–46.

Carlsen, J. 1997. I sovrintendenti degli affituari durante il Principato. In Lo Cascio 1997a, 47–60.

Carrié, J.-M. 1983. Un roman des origines: les généalogies du "colonat du bas-empire." *Opus* 2: 205–51.

———. 1993a. Le riforme economiche da Aureliano a Constantino. In *Storia di Roma*, ed. A. Schiavone, vol. III, pt. 1, 283–322. Turin.

———. 1993b. L'economie e le finanze. In *Storia di Roma*, ed. A. Schiavone, vol. III, pt. 1, 751–87. Turin.

———. 1997. "Colonato del Basso Impero": la resistenza del mito. In Lo Cascio 1997a, 75–150.

———. 2005. Une rationalité quand même? *Topoi Orient-Occident* 12–13: 293–303.

Chastagnol, A. 1982. *L'évolution politique, sociale et économique du monde romain de Dioclétien à Julien: La mise en place du régime du Bas-Empire (284–363)*. Paris.

Cheung, S. N. S. 1969. *The Theory of Share Tenancy*. Chicago.

———. 1992. On the New Institutional Economics. In Werin and Wijkander 1992, 48–65.

Coase, R. H. 1960. The Problem of Social Cost. *Journal of Law and Economics* 3: 1–44. Reprinted in R. H. Coase, *The Firm, the Market, and the Law*. Chicago, 1990, 95–156. Excerpted in Katz 1998, 68–79.

———. 1992. Comments. In Werin and Wijkander 1992, 72–75.

Cooter, R. 1982. The Cost of Coase. *Journal of Legal Studies* 11: 1–33. Excerpted in Katz 1998, 170–76.

Cooter, R., S. Marks, and R. Mnookin. 1982. Bargaining in the Shadow of the Law: A Testable Model of Strategic Behavior. *Journal of Legal Studies* 11: 225–51.

Corbier, M. 1991. City, Territory and Tax. In *City and Country in the Ancient World*, ed. J. Rich and A. Wallace-Hadrill, 211–39. London and New York.

Corcoran, S. 1996. *The Empire of the Tetrarchs: Imperial Pronouncements and Government A.D. 284–324*. Oxford.

Coriat, J.-P. 1997. *Le prince législateur: La technique législative des Sévères et les méthodes de création du droit imperial à la fin du principat*. BEFAR 224. Rome.

Cotton, H. 1993. The Guardianship of Jesus Son of Babatha: Roman and Local Law in the Province of Arabia. *JRS* 83: 94–108.

Courtois, C., L. Leschi, C. Perrat, and C. Saumagne. 1952. *Les Tablettes Albertini: Actes privés de l'époque Vandale (fin du Ve siècle)*. Paris.
Craswell, R. 2000. Contract Law: General Theories. In Bouckaert and De Geest 2000, III: 1–24.
Crawford, D. 1976. Imperial Estates. In Finley 1976a, 35–70.
Crook, J. A. 1976. Classical Roman Law and the Sale of Land. In Finley 1976a, 71–83.
———. 1986. Women in Roman Succession. In *The Family in Ancient Rome: New Perspectives*, ed. B. Rawson, 58–82. London and Ithaca.
———. 1995. *Legal Advocacy in the Roman World*. Ithaca.
Curran, C. 2000. The Endowment Effect. In Bouckaert and De Geest 2000, I: 819–35.
Dahlman, C. J. 1979. The Problem of Externality. *Journal of Law and Economics* 22: 141–62.
De Ligt, L. 1998–99. Studies in Legal and Agrarian History I: The Inscription from Henchir-Mettich and the *Lex Manciana*. *Ancient Society* 29: 219–39.
De Martino, F. 1993. Il colonato fra economia e diritto. In *Storia di Roma*, ed. A. Schiavone, vol. III, pt. 1, 789–822. Turin.
Demsetz, H. 1967. Toward a Theory of Property Rights. *American Economic Review* 57 (2): 347–59. Excerpted in Katz 1998, 93–102.
De Neeve, P. W. 1983. Remissio mercedis. *ZRG* 100: 296–339.
———. 1984. *Colonus: Private Farm-Tenancy in Italy during the Republic and the Early Principate*. Amsterdam.
———. 1990. A Roman Landowner and His Estates: Pliny the Younger. *Athenaeum* 78: 363–402.
Deng, K. G. 2003. Development and Its Deadlock in Imperial China, 221B.C.–1840 A.D. *Economic Development and Cultural Change* 51 (2): 479–522.
de Ste. Croix, G. E. M. 1981. *The Class Struggle in the Ancient Greek World: From the Archaic Age to the Arab Conquest*. Ithaca.
de Vos, M., ed. 2001. *Rus Africum: Terra acqua olio nell'Africa settentrionale. Scavo e recognizione nei dintorini di Dougga (Alto Tell tunisino)*. Trento.
Divjak, J. 1981. *Sancti Aureli Augustini Opera, Epistolae ex Duobus Codicibus Nuper in Lucem Prolatae*. CSEL 88, sect. II, par. VI. Vienna.
Drexhage, H.-J., H. Konen, and K. Ruffing. 2002. *Die Wirtschaft des Römischen Reiches (1.–3. Jahrhundert): Eine Einführung*. Studienbücher, Geschichte und Kultur der Alten Welt. Berlin.
Duncan-Jones, R. P. 1982. *The Economy of the Roman Empire*. 2d ed. Cambridge.
———. 1990. *Structure and Scale in the Roman Economy*. Cambridge.
———. 1994. *Money and Government in the Roman Empire*. Cambridge.
———. 1996. The Impact of the Antonine Plague. *JRA* 9: 108–36.
du Plessis, P. J. 2003. *A History of Remissio Mercedis and Related Legal Institutions*. Diss. Erasmus University Rotterdam.
Eggertsson, T. 1990. *Economic Behavior and Institutions*. Cambridge Surveys in Economic Literature. Cambridge.
Ellickson, R. C. 1991. *Order without Law: How Neighbors Settle Disputes*. Cambridge, MA.
———. 1993. Property in Land. *Yale Law Journal* 102 (6): 1315–1400.

Engels, D. 1990. *Roman Corinth: An Alternative Model for the Classical City*. Chicago.

Erdkamp, P. 2001. Beyond the Limits of the "Consumer City": A Model of the Urban and Rural Economy in the Roman World. *Historia* 50 (3): 332–56.

———. 2005. *The Grain Market in the Roman Empire: A Social, Political and Economic Study*. Cambridge.

Feissel, D., and J. Gascou. 1989. Documents d'archive romain inédits du moyen Euphrate (IIIe siècle après J.-C). *CRAI*, 535–61.

———. 1995. Documents d'archives romains inédits du moyen Euphrate (IIIe s. après J.-C.). *Journal des savants*, 65–119.

Field, A. J. 1991. Do Legal Systems Matter? *Explorations in Economic History* 28: 1–35.

———. 2000. New Economic History and Law and Economics. In Bouckaert and De Geest 2000, I: 728–53.

Finley, M. I., ed. 1976a. *Studies in Roman Property*. Cambridge.

———. 1976b. Private Farm Tenancy in Italy before Diocletian. In Finley 1976a, 103–21.

———. 1999. *The Ancient Economy*. Updated edition, with a forward by I. Morris. Berkeley and Los Angeles.

Flach, D. 1978. Inschriftenuntersuchungen zum römischen Kolonat in Nordafrika. *Chiron* 8: 441–92.

Foti Talamanca, G. 1974. *Ricerche sul processo nell'Egitto greco-Romano*. Vol. I, *L'orginazzazione del "conventus" del "Praefectus Aegypti."* Milan.

———. 1979. *Ricerche sul processo nell'Egitto greco-Romano*. Vol. II, *L'introduzione del Giudizio*. Milan.

Foxhall L. 1990. The Dependent Tenant: Land Leasing and Labour in Italy and Greece. *JRS* 80: 97–114.

Frakes, R. M. 2001. *Contra Potentium Iniurias: The Defensor Civitatis and Late Roman Justice*. Münch. Beitr. 90. Munich.

Frederiksen, M. W. 1975. Theory, Evidence and the Ancient Economy. *JRS* 65: 164–71.

Frier, B. W. 1979. Law, Technology, and Social Change: The Equipping of Italian Farm Tenancies. *ZRG* 96: 204–28.

———. 1980. *Landlords and Tenants in Imperial Rome*. Princeton.

———. 1983. Review of *Servus Quasi Colonus: Forme non Tradizionali di Organizzazione del Lavoro nella Società Romana*, by G. Giliberti, and *Colonus: Privégrondpacht in Romeins Italie tijdens de Republiek en het vroege Principaat*, by P.W. de Neeve. *ZRG* 100: 667–76.

———. 1985. Review of *Die Kolonen in Italien und den westlichen Provinzen des Römischen Reiches: Eine Untersuchung der literarischen, juristischen und epigraphischen Quellen vom 2. Jahrhundert v.u.z. bis zu den Severern*, by K.-P. Johne, J. Köhn, and V. Weber. *ZRG* 102: 564–69.

———. 1989–90. Law, Economics, and Disasters down on the Farm: "Remissio Mercedis" Revisited. *BIDR*, 3d ser., 31–32: 237–70.

———. 2000. Demography. In Bowman, Garnsey, and Rathbone 2000, 787–816.

Frier, B. W., and D. P. Kehoe. Forthcoming. Law and Economic Institutions. In Morris, Saller, and Scheidel, forthcoming.

Furubotn, E. G., and R. Richter. 2005 *Institutions and Economic Theory: The Contribution of New Institutional Economics*. Ann Arbor. First edition, 1997.

Galanter, M. 1981. Justice in Many Rooms: Courts, Private Ordering, and Indigenous Law. *Journal of Legal Pluralism* 19: 1–47.
Gallant, T. 1991. *Risk and Survival in Ancient Greece: Reconstructing the Rural Domestic Economy*. Stanford.
Garnsey, P. 1970. *Social Status and Legal Privilege in the Roman Empire*. Oxford.
———, ed. 1980a. *Non-Slave Labour in the Greco-Roman World*, Cambridge Phil. Soc. Suppl. vol. 6. Cambridge.
———. 1980b. Non-Slave Labour in the Roman World. In Garnsey 1980a, 34–47.
———. 1988. *Famine and Food Supply in the Graeco-Roman World: Responses to Risk and Crisis*. Cambridge.
———. 1998. *Cities, Peasants and Food in Classical Antiquity: Essays in Social and Economic History*. Ed. and addenda, W. Scheidel. Cambridge.
———. 1999. *Food and Society in Classical Antiquity*. Cambridge.
———. 2000. The Land. In Bowman, Garnsey, and Rathbone 2000, 679–709.
Garnsey, P., and R. Saller. 1987. *The Roman Empire: Economy, Society and Culture*. Berkeley and Los Angeles.
Gascou, J. 1985. *Les Grands Domaines, La Cité et l'État en Égypte Byzantine*. Collège de France, Centre de Recherchre d'Histoire et Civilisation de byzance, Travaux et Mémoires 9. Paris.
Giardina, A., ed. 1986. *Società romana e impero tardo-antico*. Vol. I, *Istituzioni, ceti, economie*. Rome and Bari, 1986.
———. 1997. Gli schiavi, i coloni e i problemi di una transizione. In Lo Cascio 1997a, 311–23.
Giliberti, G. 1999. *Servi della terra: Ricerche per una storia del colonato*. Turin.
Goetz, C. J., and R. E. Scott. 1981. Principles of Relational Contracts. *Virginia Law Review* 67 (6): 1089–1150.
Goffart, W. 1974. *Caput and Colonate: Towards a History of Late Roman Taxation*. Phoenix Suppl. 12. Toronto.
Goldberg, V. P. 1976. Regulation and Administered Contracts. *Bell Journal of Economics* 7 (2): 426–48.
Goldsmith, R. W. 1987. *Premodern Financial Systems: A Historical Comparative Study*. Cambridge.
Greenberg, J. 2003. Plagued by Doubt: Reconsidering the Impact of a Mortality Crisis in the 2nd C. A.D. *JRA* 16: 413–25.
Greene, K. 2000. Technological Innovation and Economic Progress in the Ancient World: M.I. Finley Re-considered. *Economic History Review* 53 (1): 29–59.
Grey, C., and A. Parkin. 2003. Controlling the Urban Mob: The *Colonatus perpetuus* of *CTh* 14.18.1. *Phoenix* 57.3–4: 284–99.
Hackl, K. 1997. Der Zivilprozeß des frühen Prinzipats in den Provinzen. *ZRG* 114: 141–59.
Haensch, R. 1994. Die Bearbeitungsweisen von Petitionen in der Provinz Aegyptus. *ZPE* 100: 487–546.
———. 1997a. Zur Konventusordnung in Aegyptus und den übrigen Provinzen des römischen Reiches. In Kramer et al. 1997, I: 320–91.
———. 1997b. *Capita provinciarum: Statthaltersitze und Provinzialverwaltung in der römischen Kaiserzeit*. Kölner Forschungen. Mainz.

Haley, E. W. 2003. *Baetica Felix: People and Prosperity in Southern Spain from Caesar to Septimius Severus*. Austin.

Hallof, K. 1994. Die Inschrift von Skaptopara. Neue Dokumente und neue Lesungen. *Chiron* 24: 405–41.

Hamza, G. 1999. Zum Verhältinis zwischen *usucapio* und *longi temporis praescriptio* im klassischen römischen Recht. In *Mélanges Fritz Sturm*, ed. J.-F. Gerkens, H. Peter, P. Trenk-Hinterberger, and R. Vigneron, vol. I, 189–203. Liège.

Harries, J. 1999. *Law and Empire in Late Antiquity*. Cambridge.

Harris, R. 2003. The Encounters of Economic History and Legal History. *Law and History Review* 21: 297–346.

Harris, W. V. 1993. Between Archaic and Modern: Some Current Problems in the History of the Roman Economy. In *The Inscribed Economy: Production and Distribution in the Roman Empire in the Light of Instrumentum Domesticum*, ed. W. V. Harris, 11–29. *JRA* Suppl. 6. Ann Arbor.

Hauken, T. 1998. *Petition and Response: An Epigraphic Study of Petitions to Roman Emperors 181–249*. Monographs from the Norwegian Institute at Athens 2. Bergen.

Hendy, M. F. 1985. *Studies in the Byzantine Monetary Economy c. 300–1450*. Cambridge.

Herrmann, J. 1958. *Studien zur Bodenpacht im Recht der graeco-aegyptischen Papyri*. Münch. Beitr. 41. Munich.

Hickey, T. M. 2001. A Public "House" but Closed: "Fiscal Participation" and Economic Decision Making on the Oxyrhynchite Estate of the Flavii Apiones. Diss. Univ. of Chicago.

Hitchner, R. B. 1993. Olive Production and the Roman Economy: The Case for Intensive Growth in the Roman Empire. In Amouretti and Brun 1993, 499–508.

———. 2005. "The Advantages of Wealth and Luxury": The Case for Economic Growth in the Roman Empire. In Manning and Morris 2005, 207–22.

Hobson, D. W. 1993. The Impact of Law on Village Life in Roman Egypt. In *Law, Politics and Society in the Ancient Mediterranean World*, ed. B. Halpern and D. W. Hobson, 193–219. Sheffield.

Hodgson, G. M. 1993. Transaction Costs and the Evolution of the Firm. In *Transaction Costs, Markets and Hierarchies: Critical Assessments*, ed. C. Pitelis, 77–100. Oxford. Revised and reprinted in Hodgson 1999, 199–219.

———. 1999. *Evolution and Institutions: On Evolutionary Economics and the Evolution of Economics*. Cheltenham, UK, and Northampton.

Honoré, T. 1994. *Emperors and Lawyers*. 2d ed. Oxford.

———. 1998. *Law and the Crisis of Empire 379–455 AD*. Oxford.

Hopkins, K. 1995/1996. Rome, Taxes, Rents and Trade. *Kodai* 6/7: 41–75. Reprinted in Scheidel and von Reden 2002, 190–230.

Horden, P., and N. Purcell. 2000. *The Corrupting Sea: A Study of Mediterranean History*. Oxford and Malden, MA.

Horstkotte, H. 1988. *Die "Steuerhaftung" im spätrömischen "Zwangsstaat."* 2d ed. Beiträge zur klassischen Philologie 185. Frankfurt am Main.

Howgego, C. 1992. The Supply and Use of Money in the Roman World, 200 B.C. to A.D. 300. *JRS* 82 (1992): 1–31.

Hviid, M. 2000. Long-Term Contracts and Relational Contracts. In Bouckaert and De Geest 2000, III: 46–72.

Iannatou, M. 2004. Le code de l'honneur des paiements: Créanciers et débiteurs à la fin de la République romaine. In Andreau, France, and Pittia 2004, 87–107.

Johne, K.-P., J. Köhn, and V. Weber. 1983. *Die Kolonen in Italien und den westlichen Provinzen des Römischen Reiches: Eine Untersuchung der literarischen, juristischen und epigraphischen Quellen vom 2. Jahrhundert v.u.Z. bis zu den Severern*. Berlin.

Jolls, C. 1997. Contracts as Bilateral Commitments: A New Perspective on Contract Modification. *Journal of Legal Studies* 26 (1): 203–37.

Jones, A. H. M. 1964. *The Later Roman Empire, 284–602*. 2 vols. Norman. Repr., Baltimore, 1992.

Jones, C. P. 1984. The Sacrae Litterae of 204: Two Colonial Copies. *Chiron* 14: 93–99.

Jones, E. L. 1988. *Growth Recurring: Economic Change in World History*. Oxford. Repr., 2000.

Jongman, W. 1988. *The Economy and Society of Pompeii*. Dutch Monographs on Ancient History and Archaeology 4. Amsterdam.

Jördens, A. 1990. *Vertragliche Regelungen von Arbeiten im späten griechischsprachigen Ägypten (P.Heid. V)*. Heidelberg.

Kaplow, L., and S. Shavell. 1996. Property Rules versus Liability Rules: An Economic Analysis. *Harvard Law Review* 109 (4): 713–90.

Kaser, M. 1967. Vulgarrecht. *RE* 9.A.2: 1283–1304.

———. 1971. *Das römische Privatrecht*. Erster Abschnitt, *Das altrömische, das vorklassische und klassische Recht*. Handbuch der Altertumswissenschaft, 10.3.3.1. 2d ed. Munich.

———. 1975. *Das römische Privatrecht*. Zweiter Abschnitt, *Die nachklassische Entwicklungen*. Handbuch der Altertumswissenschaft, 10.3.3.2. 2d ed. Munich.

Kaser, M., and K. Hackl. 1996. *Das römische Zivilprozeßrecht*. Handbuch der Altertumswissenschaft, 10.3.4. Munich.

Katz, A. W. 1990. The Strategic Structure of Offer and Acceptance: Game Theory and the Law of Contract Formation. *Michigan Law Review* 89 (2): 215–95. Excerpted in Katz 1998, 189–97.

———, ed. 1998. *Foundations of the Economic Approach to Law*. New York.

Keenan, J. G. 2000. Egypt. In Cameron, Ward-Perkins, and Whitby 2000, 612–37.

Kehoe, D. P. 1984. Private and Imperial Management of Estates in North Africa. *Law and History Review* 2 (2): 241–63.

———. 1988a. *The Economics of Agriculture on Roman Imperial Estates in North Africa*. Hypomnemata 89. Göttingen.

———. 1988b. Allocation of Risk and Investment on the Estates of Pliny the Younger. *Chiron* 18: 15–42.

———. 1992. *Management and Investment on Estates in Roman Egypt during the Early Empire*. PTA 40. Bonn.

———. 1995. Legal Institutions and the Bargaining Power of the Tenant in Roman Egypt. *APF* 41 (2): 232–62.

———. 1996. The Sources for Roman Farm Tenancy. *JRA* 9: 388–94.

———. 1997. *Investment, Profit, and Tenancy: The Jurists and the Roman Agrarian Economy*. Ann Arbor.

———. 1999. Tenancy and Oasis Agriculture on an Egyptian Estate of the 4th c. A.D. *JRA* 12: 745–51.

———. 2003. Aristocratic Dominance in the Late Roman Agrarian Economy and the Question of Economic Growth. *JRA* 16: 711–21.

Kelly, C. 2004. *Ruling the Later Roman Empire*. Cambridge, MA.

Kelly, J. M. 1966. *Roman Litigation*. Oxford.

King, C. E., ed. 1980. *Imperial Revenue, Expenditure and Monetary Policy in the Fourth Century A.D.* BAR International Series 76. Oxford.

Klein, B. 1992. Contracts and Incentives: The Role of Contract Terms in Assuring Performance. In Werin and Wijkander 1992, 149–72.

Klein, B., R. G. Crawford, and A. A. Alchian. 1978. Vertical Integration, Appropriable Rents, and the Competitive Contracting Process. *Journal of Law and Economics* 21: 297–326.

Klein, P. G. 2000. New Institutional Economics. In Bouckaert and De Geest 2000, I: 456–89.

Knoeber, C. R. 2000. Land and Livestock Contracting in Agriculture: A Principal-Agent Perspective. In Bouckaert and De Geest 2000, III: 1133–53.

Köhn, J. 1983. Die Kolonen in den Rechtsbestimmungen. In Johne, Köhn, and Weber 1983, 167–257.

Kolb, A. 2000. *Transport und Nachrichtentransfer im Römischen Reich*. Klio Beiträge zur Alten Geschichte Beihefte, Neue Folge Band 2. Berlin.

Kolendo, J. 1991. *Le colonat en Afrique sous le haut-empire*. 2d ed. Paris.

Kramer, B., W. Luppe, H. Maehler, and G. Poethke, eds. 1997. *Akten des 21. internationalen Papyrologenkongresses Berlin*. 13.-19.8.1995. APF Beiheft 3. 2 vols. Leipzig.

Krause, J.-U. 1987. *Spätantike Patronatsformen im Westen des Römischen Reiches*. Vestigia, Beiträge zur Aten Geschichte 38. Munich.

———. 1995. *Witwen und Waisen im römischen Reich*. Vol. III, *Rechtliche und soziale Stellung von Waisen*. Heidelberger Althistorische Beiträge und Epigraphische Studien 18. Stuttgart.

———. 1996. *Gefängnisse im römischen Reich*. Heidelberger Althistorische Beiträge und Epigraphische Studien 23. Stuttgart.

Kunkel, W. 1974. Der Prozeß der Gohariener vor Caracalla. *Kleine Schiften*, 254–66. Weimar. First published in *Festschrift Hans Lewald*. Basel, 1953, 81–91.

Lendon, J. E. 1997. *Empire of Honour: The Art of Government in the Roman World*. Oxford.

Lenski, N. 2002. *Failure of Empire: Valens and the Roman State in the Fourth Century A.D.* Berkeley, Los Angeles, and London.

Leppeley, C. 1989. Trois documents méconnus sur l'histoire sociale et religieuse de l'Afrique romaine tardive, retrouvés parmi les *spuria* de Sulpice Sévère. *AntAfr* 25: 235–62.

Levi, M. 1988. *Of Rule and Revenue*. Berkeley.

Levy, E. 1951. *West Roman Vulgar Law: The Law of Property*. Memoirs of the American Philosophical Society 29. Philadelphia.

———. 1956. *Weströmisches Vulgarrecht: Das Obligationenrecht*. Weimar.

Liebeschuetz, J. H. W. G. 1972. *Antioch: City and Imperial Administration in the Later Roman Empire*. Oxford.

Liebowitz, S. J., and S. E. Margolis. 2000. Path Dependence. In Bouckaert and De Geest 2000, I: 981–98.

Lipsius, J. H. 1966. *Das attische Recht und Rechtsverfahren*. Darmstadt. Reprint of 1905–15 edition in 3 vols.
Lo Cascio, E. 1991a. Forme dell'economia imperiale. In *Storia di Roma,* ed. A. Schiavone, vol. II, pt. 2, 313–65. Turin.
———. 1991b. Fra equlibrio e crisi. In *Storia di Roma,* ed. A. Schiavone, vol. II, pt. 2, 701–31. Turin.
———. 1993. Considerazioni sulla struttura e sulla dinamica dell'affitto agraria in età imperiale. In Sancisi-Weerdenburg et al. 1993, 296–316.
———, ed. 1997a. *Terre, proprietari e contadini dell'impero romano: Dall'affitto agrario al colonato tardoantico*. Rome, 1997.
———. 1997b. Introduzione, Dall'affitto agrario al colonato tardoantico: continuità o frattura? In Lo Cascio 1997a, 15–25.
———. 2000. The Roman Principate: The Impact of the Organization of the Empire on Production. In Lo Cascio and Rathbone 2000, 77–85.
Lo Cascio, E., and D. W. Rathbone, eds. 2000. *Production and Public Powers in Classical Antiquity*. Cambridge Philological Society, Suppl. vol. 26. Cambridge.
MacMullen, R. 1964. Social Mobility and the Theodosian Code. *JRS* 54: 49–53.
———. 1974. *Roman Social Relations 50 B.C. to A.D. 284*. New Haven and London.
———. 1987. Tax-Pressure in the Roman Empire. *Latomus* 46: 737–54.
———. 1988. *Corruption and the Decline of Rome*. New Haven and London.
Macneil, I. R. 1974. The Many Futures of Contracts. *Southern California Law Review* 47 (3): 691–816.
———. 1978. Contracts: Adjustment of Long-Term Economic Relations under Classical, Neoclassical, and Relational Contract Law. *Northwestern University Law Review* 72 (6): 854–905.
———. 1983. Values in Contract: Internal and External. *Northwestern Law Review* 78 (2): 340–418.
Manning, J. G., and I. Morris, eds. 2005. *The Ancient Economy: Evidence and Models*. Stanford.
Marcone, A. 1993. Il lavoro nelle campagne. In *Storia di Roma,* ed. A. Schiavone, vol. III, pt. 1, 823–43. Turin.
———. 1997. Il colonato tardoantico: i problemi aperti. In Lo Cascio 1997a, 225–39.
Martin, S. D. 1989. *The Roman Jurists and the Organization of Private Building in the Late Republic and Early Empire*. Collection Latomus 204. Brussels.
———. 2002. Roman Law and the Study of Land Transportation. In *Speculum Iuris: Roman Law as a Reflection of Social and Economic Life in Antiquity,* ed. J.-J. Aubert and B. Sirks, 151–68. Ann Arbor.
Masten, S. E. 2000. Contractual Choice. In Bouckaert and De Geest 2000, III: 25–45.
Matthews, J. F. 2000. *Laying Down the Law: A Study of the Theodosian* Code. New Haven and London.
Mattingly, D. J. 1988a. Oil for Export? A Comparison of Libyan, Spanish and Tunisian Olive Oil Production in the Roman Empire. *JRA* 1: 33–56.
———. 1988b. Olea Mediterranea? *JRA* 1: 153–61.
———. 1988c. The Olive Boom. Oil Surpluses, Wealth and Power in Roman Tripolitantia. *Libyan Studies* 19: 21–41.
———. 1989. Olive Cultivation and the Albertini Tablets. In *L'Africa romana,* Atti del VI convengno di studio, Sassari, 16–18 dicembre 1988. Sassari, 403–15.

———. 1993. Maximum Figures and Maximizing Strategies of Oil Production? Further Thoughts on the Processing Capacity of Roman Olive Presses. In Amouretti and Brun 1993, 483–98.

———. 1994. *Tripolitania*. Ann Arbor.

Mattingly, D. J., and R. B. Hitchner. 1993. Technical Specifications for Some North African Olive Presses of Roman Date. In Amouretti and Brun 1993, 439–62.

———. 1995. Roman Africa: An Archaeological Review. *JRS* 85: 165–213.

Mayer-Maly, T. 1956. *Locatio Conductio: Eine Untersuchung zum klassischen römischen Recht*. Wiener rechtgeschichtliche Arbeiten 4. Vienna.

McGinn, T. A. J. 1998. *Prostitution, Sexuality, and the Law in Ancient Rome*. Oxford.

Meckling, W. H. 1992. Comments. In Werin and Wijkander 1992, 173–75.

Medema, S. G., N. Mercuro, and W. J. Samuels. 2000. Institutional Law and Economics. In Bouckaert and De Geest 2000, I: 418–55.

Medema, S. G., and R. O. Zerbe, Jr. 2000. The Coase Theorem. In Bouckaert and De Geest, I: 836–92.

Mercuro, N., and S. G. Medema. 1997. *Economics and the Law: From Posner to Post-Modernism*. Princeton.

Metzger, E. 1997. *A New Outline of the Roman Civil Trial*. Oxford.

Meyer, E. A. 2004. *Legitimacy and Law in the Roman World: Tabulae in Roman Belief and Practice*. Cambridge.

Millar, F. 1963. The Fiscus in the First Two Centuries. *JRS* 53: 29–42.

———. 1977. *The Emperor in the Roman World*. Ithaca. 2d ed., 1991.

———. 1981. The World of the *Golden Ass*. *JRS* 71: 63–75.

———. 1993. *The Roman Near East 31 BC–AD 337*. Cambridge, MA.

Millett, P. 2001. Productive to Some Purpose? The Problem of Ancient Economic Growth. In *Economics beyond Agriculture in the Classical World*, ed. D. J. Mattingly and J. Salmon, 17–48. London and New York.

Minaud, G. 2005. Rationalité modulable des comptabilités. *Topoi Orient-Occident* 12–13: 271–81.

Mirković, M. 1997. *The Later Roman Colonate and Freedom*. Transactions of the American Philosophical Society, vol. LXXXVII, pt. 2. Philadelphia.

Mitchell, S. 1976. Requisitioned Transport in the Roman Empire: A New Inscription from Pisidia. *JRS* 66: 106–31.

———. 1993. *Anatolia: Land, Men, and Gods in Asia Minor*. Vol. I, *The Celts in Anatolia and the Impact of Roman Rule*. Oxford.

Mnookin, R. H., and L. Kornhauser. 1979. Bargaining in the Shadow of the Law: The Case of Divorce. *Yale Law Journal* 88: 950–97.

Moore, J. 1992. Comments. In Werin and Wijkander 1992, 176–80.

Morley, N. 1996. *Metropolis and Hinterland: The City of Rome and the Italian Economy 200 B.C.–A.D. 200*. Cambridge.

Morris, I., R. P. Saller, and W. Scheidel, eds. Forthcoming. *The Cambridge Economic History of the Greco-Roman World*. Cambridge.

Müller, C. H. 2002. *Gefahrtragung bei der locatio conductio: Miete, Pacht, Dienst- und Werkvertrag im Kommentar römischer Juristen*. Rechts- und Staatswissenschaftliche Veröffentlichungen der Görres-Gesellschaft, Neue Folge, Band 99. Paderborn, Munich, Vienna, and Zurich.

Neesen, L. 1980. *Untersuchungen zu den direkten Staatsabgaben der römischen Kaiserzeit (27 v.Chr.–284 n.Chr.)*. Antiquitas Reihe 1, Abhandlungen zur alten Geschichte. Bonn.

Newman, P. ed. 1998. *The New Palgrave Dictionary of Economics and the Law*. London.

Nicholas, B. 1962. *Introduction to Roman Law*. Oxford.

Noordraven, B. 1999. *Die Fiduzia im römischen Recht*. Studia Amstelodamensia, Studies in Ancient Law and Society 37. Amsterdam.

Nörr, D. 1969. *Die Entstehung der longi temporis praescriptio: Studien zum Einfluß der Zeit im Recht und zur Rechtspolitik in der Kaiserzeit*. Arbeitsgemeinschaft für Forschung des Landes Nordrhein-Westfalen, Geisteswissenschaften, Heft 156. Köln—Opladen.

———. 1981. Zur Reskriptenpraxis in der hohen Prinzipatszeit. *ZRG* 98: 1–46.

———. 1998. Römisches Zivilprozeßrecht nach Max Kaser: Prozeßrecht und Prozeßpraxis in der Provinz Arabia. *ZRG* 115: 80–98.

North, D. C. 1981. *Structure and Change in Economic History*. New York.

———. 1990. *Institutions, Institutional Change and Economic Performance*. Cambridge. Repr., 2002.

———. 2005. *Understanding the Process of Economic Change*. Princeton.

North, D. C., and R. P. Thomas. 1973. *The Rise of the Western World: A New Economic History*. Cambridge.

Oliver, J. H. 1989. *Greek Constitutions of Early Roman Empire from Inscriptions and Papyri*. Memoirs of the American Philosophical Society 178. Philadelphia.

Osborne, R. 1988. Social and Economic Implications of the Leasing of Land and Property in Classical and Hellenistic Greece. *Chiron* 18: 279–323.

Panitschek, P. 1990. Der spätantike Kolonat: Ein Substitut für die "Halbfreiheit" peregriner Rechtssetzungen? *ZRG* 107: 137–54.

Panther, S. 2000. Non-legal Sanctions. In Bouckaert and De Geest 2000, I: 999–1028.

Parássoglou, G. M. 1978. *Imperial Estates in Roman Egypt*. Am. Stud. Pap. XVIII. Amsterdam.

Parisi, F. 2000. Spontaneous Emergence of Law Customary Law. In Bouckaert and De Geest 2000, V: 603–30.

Patlagean, E. 1977. *Pauvreté économique et pauvreté sociale à Byzance 4e–7e siècles*. Mouton, Paris, and La Haye.

Peachin, M. 1996. *Iudex vice Caesaris: Deputy Emperors and the Administration of Justice during the Principate*. Heidelberger Althistorische und Epigraphische Beiträge 21. Stuttgart.

Pleket, H. W. 1984. Urban Elites and the Economy in the Greek Cities of the Roman Empire. *MBAH* 3 (1): 3–35.

———. 1990. Wirtschaft. In *Europäische Wirtschafts- und Sozialgeschichte in der Kaiserzeit*, 25–160. Vol. I of *Handbuch der Europäischen Wirtschafts- und Sozialgeschichte*, ed. F. Vittinghoff, Stuttgart.

———. 1993. Agriculture in the Roman Empire in Comparative Perspective. In Sancisi-Weerdenburg et al. 1993, 317–43.

Poblome, J. 2004. Comparing Ordinary Craft Production: Textile and Pottery Production in Roman Asia Minor. *JESHO* 47 (4): 491–506.

Pollard, N. 2000. *Soldiers, Cities, and Civilians in Roman Syria*. Ann Arbor.

Posner, R. A., and A. M. Rosenfield. 1977. Impossibility and Related Doctrines in Contract Law: An Economic Analysis. *Journal of Legal Studies* 6: 83–118. Excerpted in Katz 1998, 227–36.

Rathbone, D. 1991. *Economic Rationalism and Rural Society in Third-Century A.D. Egypt: The Heroninos Archive and the Appianus Estate*. Cambridge.

———. 1994. More (or Less?) Economic Rationalism in Roman Agriculture. *JRA* 7: 432–36.

———. 2005. Economic Rationalism and the Heroninos Archive. *Topoi Orient-Occident* 12–13: 261–69.

Rickman, G. 1980. *The Corn Supply of Ancient Rome*. Oxford.

Rosafio, P. 1993. Rural Labour Organization in Pliny the Younger. *ARID* 21: 67–79.

———. 2002. *Studi sul colonato*. Dipartimento di Scienze dell'antichità dell'Università di Bari, Sezione storica, Documenti e studi 32. Bari.

Rowlandson, J. 1994. Crop Rotation and Rent Payment in Oxyrhynchite Land Leases: Social and Economic Interpretations. In *Proceedings of the 20th International Congress of Papyrologists*, ed. A. Bülow-Jacobsen, 495–99. Copenhagen.

———. 1996. *Landowners and Tenants in Roman Egypt: The Social Relations of Agriculture in the Oxyrhynchite Nome*. Oxford Classical Monographs. Oxford.

———. 1999. Agricultural Tenancy and Village Society in Roman Egypt. In Bowman and Rogan 1999, 139–58.

Ruggini, L. 1995. *Economia e società nell' "Italia annonaria": Rapporti fra agricoltura e commercio dal IV al VI secolo d.C.* 2d ed. Studi storici sulla Tarda Antichità. Bari. First published Milan, 1961.

Rupprecht, H.-A. 1994. *Kleine Einführung in die Papyruskunde*. Darmstadt.

Rutherford, M. 1994. *Institutions in Economics: The Old and the New Institutionalism*. Historical Perspectives on Modern Economics. Cambridge.

Sachers, E. 1948. Tutela. *RE* 7: 1497–1599.

Safrai, Z. 1994. *The Economy of Roman Palestine*. London.

Saller, R. P. 1982. *Personal Patronage in the Roman Empire*. Cambridge.

———. 1994. *Patriarchy, Property and Death in the Roman Family*. Cambridge.

———. 2002. Framing the Debate over Growth in the Ancient Economy. In Scheidel and von Reden 2002, 251–69. Reprinted in Manning and Morris 2005, 223–38.

Sancisi-Weerdenburg, H. R. J. van der Spek, H. C. Teitler, and H. T. Wallinga, eds. 1993. *De Agricultura: In Memoriam Pieter Willem de Neeve*. Dutch Monographs on Ancient History and Archaeology 10. Amsterdam.

Scheidel, W. 1994. *Grundpacht und Lohnarbeit in der Landwirtschaft des römischen Italien*. Frankfurt.

———. 2000. Slaves of the Soil. *JRA* 13: 727–32.

———. 2001. *Death on the Nile: Disease and Demography of Roman Egypt*. Leiden.

———. 2002. A Model of Demographic and Economic Change in Roman Egypt after the Antonine Plague. *JRA* 15: 97–114.

———. 2004. Human Mobility in Roman Italy, 1: The Free Population. *JRS* 94: 1–26.

———. Forthcoming. Demography. In Morris, Saller, and Scheidel, forthcoming.

Scheidel, W., and S. von Reden, eds. 2002. *The Roman Economy*. New York.

Schubert, P. 2001. *A Yale Papyrus (P Yale III 137) in the Beinecke Rare Book Room and Manuscript Library III*. American Studies in Papyrology 41. Oakville, CT.

Schultheß, O. 1932. Misthosis. *RE* 15.2: 2095–2129.
Schulz, F. 1951. *Classical Roman Law*. Oxford 1951. Repr., 1992.
Schwartz, A. 1992a. Relational Contracts in the Courts: An Analysis of Incomplete Agreements and Judicial Strategies. *Journal of Legal Studies* 21: 271–318.
———. 1992b. Legal Contract Theories and Incomplete Contracts. In Werin and Wijkander 1992, 76–108.
———. 1998. Incomplete Contracts. In Newman 1998, II: 277–83.
Scott, R. E. 1990. A Relational Theory of Default Rules for Commercial Contracts. *Journal of Legal Studies* 19: 597–616.
Seeck, O. 1919. *Regesten der Kaiser und Päpste für die Jahre 311 bis 476 n. Chr.: Vorarbeit zu einer Prosopographie der christlichen Kaiserzeit*. Stuttgart. Repr., Frankfurt am Main, 1964.
Sharp, M. 1999. The Village of Theadelphia in the Fayyum: Land and Population in the Second Century. In Bowman and Rogan 1999, 159–92.
Shavell, S. 2004. *Foundations of Economic Analysis of Law*. Cambridge, MA.
Shaw, B. D. 1981. Rural Markets in North Africa and the Political Economy of the Roman Empire. *AntAfr* 17: 37–83.
———. 1982. Lamasba: An Ancient Irrigation Community. *AntAfr* 18: 61–103.
Simon, H. 1983. *Reason in Human Affairs*. Stanford.
———. 1986. Rationality in Psychology and Economics. *Journal of Business* 59: 209–24. Excerpted in Katz 1998, 288–303.
Sirks, B. 1991. *Food for Rome: The Legal Structure of the Transportation and Processing of Supplies for the Imperial Distributions in Rome and Constantinople*. Amsterdam.
———. 1993. Reconsidering the Roman Colonate. *ZRG* 110: 331–69.
———. 1995. Laesio enormis und die Auflösung fiskalischer Verkaüfe. *ZRG* 112: 411–22.
———. 1997. Continuità nel colonato? In Lo Cascio 1997a, 163–84.
Sitzia, F. 1978. Considerazioni in tema di *periculum locatoris* e di *remissio mercedis*. *Studi storico-giuridici*, 331–61. Vol. I of *Studi in memoria di Giuliana D'Amelio*. Milan.
Steinwenter, A. 1954. Precarium. *RE* 22.2: 1814–27.
Tchalenko, G. 1953. *Villages antiques de la Syrie du nord: le massif du Bélus à l'époque romaine*. Paris.
Tchernia, A. 2005. Quelle rationalité? *Topoi Orient-Occident* 12–13: 283–91.
Temin, P. 2004. Financial Intermediation in the Early Roman Empire. *Journal of Economic History* 64 (3): 705–33.
Thomas, J. D. 2004. Notes on Papyri Relating to Claudia Isidora Also Called Apia. *BASP* 41: 139–53.
Todd, S. C. 1993. *The Shape of Athenian Law*. Oxford.
Tollison, R. D. 1998. Rent Seeking. In Newman 1998, III: 15–22.
Turpin, W. 1991. Imperial Subscriptions and the Administration of Justice. *JRS* 81: 101–18.
Ulen, T. S. 2000. Rational Choice Theory in Law and Economics. In Bouckaert and De Geest 2000, I: 790–818.
Vera, D. 1986. Enfiteusi, colonato e trasformazioni agrarie nell'Africa Proconsolare del tardo impero. *L'Africa Romana* 4: 268–93.
———. 1988. Terra e lavoro nell'Africa romana. *Studi Storici* 4: 967–92.

———. 1992–93. Schiavitù rurale e colonato nell'Italia imperiale. *Scienze dell'antichità, Storia, Archeologia, Antropologia* 6–7: 291–339.

———. 1995a. Dalla "villa perfecta" alla villa di Palladio: Sulle trasformazioni del sistema agrario in Italia fra principato e dominato. Pt. 1. *Athenaeum* 83 (1): 189–211.

———. 1995b. Dalla "villa perfecta" alla villa di Palladio: Sulle trasformazioni del sistema agrario in Italia fra principato e dominato. Pt. 2. *Athenaeum* 83 (2): 331–56.

———. 1997. Padroni, contadini, contratti: *realia* del colonato tardoantico. In Lo Cascio 1997a, 185–224.

Verboven, K. 2002. *The Economy of Friends: Economic Aspects of Amicitia and Patronage in the Late Republic*. Collection Latomus 269. Brussels.

Veyne, P. 1979. Mythe et réalité de l'autarcie à Rome. *REA* 81: 261–80.

Wacke, A. 1980. Die *potentiores* in den Rechtsquellen: Einfluß und Abwehr gesellschaftlicher Übermacht in der Rechtspflege der Römer. *ANRW* II, 13: 562–607.

———. 1998. Max Kasers Lehren zum Ursprung und Wesen des römsichen Pfandrechts. *ZRG* 115: 168–202.

Wallace, S. L. 1938. *Taxation in Egypt from Augustus to Diocletian*. Princeton.

Ward-Perkins, B. 2000a. Land, Labour and Settlement. In Cameron, Ward-Perkins, and Whitby 2000, 315–45.

———. 2000b. Specialized Production and Exchange. In Cameron, Ward-Perkins, and Whitby 2000, 346–91.

Watson, A. 1995. *The Spirit of Roman Law*. Athens, GA.

Weber, V. 1983. Die Kolonen in Italien und den westlichen Provinzen des Römsichen Reiches nach den Inschriften. In Johne, Köhn, and Weber 1983, 258–414.

Werin, L., and H. Wijkander, eds. 1992. *Contract Economics*. Oxford and Cambridge, MA.

Weßel, H. 2003. *Das Recht der Tablettes Albertini*. Berlin.

Whitehead, D. 1986. *The Demes of Attica ca. 508/7–ca. 250 BC: A Political and Social Study*. Princeton.

Whittaker, C. R. 1976. Agri Deserti. In Finley 1976a, 137–65. Reprinted in Whittaker 1993.

———. 1980a. Inflation and the Economy in the Fourth Century A.D. In King 1980, 1–22.

———. 1980b. Rural Labour in Three Roman Provinces. In Garnsey 1980a, 73–99. Reprinted in Whittaker 1993.

———. 1982. Labour Supply in the Later Roman Empire. *Opus* 1: 171–79. Reprinted in Whittaker 1993.

———. 1987. Circe's Pigs: From Slavery to Serfdom in the Later Roman World. In *Classical Slavery*, ed. M. I. Finley, 88–120. London. Reprinted in Whittaker 1993.

———. 1990. The Consumer City Revisited: The Vicus and the City. *JRA* 3: 110–18. Reprinted in Whittaker 1993.

———. 1993. *Land, City and Trade in the Roman Empire*. Aldershot.

———. 1996. Roman Africa: Augustus to Vespasian. In *The Cambridge Ancient History*, 2d ed., ed. A. K. Bowman, E. Champlin, and A. Lintot, vol. X, 586–618. Cambridge.

———. 1997. Agostino e il colonato. In Lo Cascio 1997a, 295–309.

———. 2000. Africa. In Bowman, Garnsey, and Rathbone 2000, 514–46.

Whittaker, C. R., and P. Garnsey. 1998. Rural Life in the Later Roman. In *The Late Empire, A.D. 337–425*, ed. A. Cameron and P. Garnsey, 277–311. Vol. XIII of *The Cambridge Ancient History*. 2d ed. Cambridge.

Wilhelm, A. 1935. Attische Pachturkunden. *APF* 11: 189–217.

Williams, W. 1974. Caracalla and the Rethoricians [*sic*]. *Latomus* 33: 663–67.

Williamson, O. E. 1979. Transaction-Cost Economics: The Governance of Contractual Relations. *Journal of Law and Economics* 22: 233–61.

———. 1985. *The Economic Institutions of Capitalism: Firms, Markets, Relational Contracting*. New York.

———. 1996. *The Mechanisms of Governance*. New York and Oxford.

Wilson, A. 2002. Machines, Power and the Ancient Economy. *JRS* 92: 1–32.

Woolf, G. 1998. *Becoming Roman: The Origins of Provincial Civilization in Gaul*. Cambridge.

Worp, K. A. 1991. *Die Archive der Aurelii Adelphios und Asklepiades*. *Corpus Papyrorum Raineri*. Band XVIIA, Griechische Texte XIIA (*CPR* XVIIA). Vienna.

Zelener, Y. 2003. Smallpox and the Disintegration of the Roman Economy after 165 AD. Diss. Columbia University.

Zimmermann, R. 1990. *The Law of Obligations: Roman Foundations of the Civilian Tradition*. Cape Town.

General Index

Index of Ancient Sources

LITERARY SOURCES